Birnbaum's

Paris

A BIRNBAUM TRAVEL GUIDE

Alexandra Mayes Birnbaum
EDITORIAL CONSULTANT

Lois Spritzer
Editorial Director

Laura L. Brengelman
Managing Editor

Mary Callahan
Senior Editor

David Appell
Patricia Canole
Gene Gold
Jill Kadetsky
Susan McClung
Associate Editors

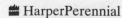 **HarperPerennial**
A Division of HarperCollins*Publishers*

To Stephen, who merely made all this possible.

FIRST EDITION

ISSN 0749-2561 (Birnbaum Travel Guides)
ISSN 0749-2553 (France)
ISBN 0-06-278190-1 (pbk.)

95 96 97 98 ❖/RRD 5 4 3 2

Cover design © Drenttel Doyle Partners
Cover photograph © Tom Benoit/AllStock
Artist in Latin Quarter overlooking Seine, Paris

BIRNBAUM TRAVEL GUIDES

Bahamas, and Turks & Caicos
Berlin
Bermuda
Boston
Canada
Cancun, Cozumel & Isla Mujeres
Caribbean
Chicago
Country Inns and Back Roads
Disneyland
Eastern Europe
Europe
Europe for Business Travelers
France
Germany
Great Britain
Hawaii
Ireland
Italy
London
Los Angeles
Mexico
Miami & Ft. Lauderdale
Montreal & Quebec City
New Orleans
New York
Paris
Portugal
Rome
San Francisco
Santa Fe & Taos
South America
Spain
United States
USA for Business Travelers
Walt Disney World
Walt Disney World for Kids, By Kids
Washington, DC

Contributing Editors

Stephanie Curtis
Emily Emerson
Joan Gannij
Susan Kelly

Maps

B. Andrew Mudryk

Contents

Getting Ready to Go

Practical information for planning your trip.

The City

*Thorough, qualitative guide to Paris,
highlighting the city's attractions, services,
hotels, and restaurants.*

Diversions

A selective guide to a variety of unexpected pleasures, pinpointing the best places to pursue them.

Directions

Seven of the most delightful walks through Paris.

Glossary

Foreword

My first trip to the City of Light coincided with Bastille Day. I was 15 years old, and I will never forget watching the Algerian troops (remember, Algeria was French back then) on camelback clomping down the Champs-Elysées as part of the celebrations; nor my first evening in Paris when I was taken to the Lido—no easy entertainment for a naive 1950s American teen.

To say that my first look at l'Etoile and Les Invalides forever made a difference is to understate the impact. On many a subsequent foray with my husband, Steve Birnbaum—whether staying in an intimate pension on the left bank or luxuriating at the *Ritz*—we agreed that it wouldn't be the worst thing if we spent a significant portion of the rest of our lives learning what all was out there. Even after dozens of visits to Paris, we never failed to find something we missed last time through.

That's why we've tried to create a guide to Paris that's specifically organized, written, and edited for today's demanding traveler, one for whom qualitative information is infinitely more desirable than mere quantities of unappraised data. We realize it's impossible for any single travel writer to visit thousands of restaurants (and nearly as many hotels) in any given year and provide accurate appraisals of each. And even if it were physically possible for one human being to survive such an itinerary, it would of necessity have to be done at a dead sprint, and the perceptions derived therefrom would probably be less valid than those of any other intelligent individual visiting the same establishments. It is, therefore, both impractical and undesirable (especially in a large, annually revised and updated guidebook *series* such as we offer) to have only one person provide all the data on the entire world. Instead, we have chosen what we like to describe as the "thee and me" approach to restaurant and hotel evaluation and, to a somewhat more limited degree, to the sites and sights we have included in the other sections of our text. What this really reflects is a personal sampling tempered by intelligent counsel from informed local sources.

This guidebook is directed to the "visitor," and such elements as restaurants have been specifically picked to provide the visitor with a representative, enlightening, and, above all, pleasant experience. Since so many extraneous considerations can affect the reception and service accorded a regular restaurant patron, our choices can in no way be construed as an exhaustive guide to resident dining. We think we've listed all the best places, in various price ranges, but they were chosen with a visitor's enjoyment in mind.

Other evidence of how we've tried to tailor our text to reflect modern travel habits is apparent in the section we call DIVERSIONS. Where once it was common for travelers to spend an urban visit seeing only the obvious sights, today's traveler is more likely to want to pursue a special interest or to venture off the beaten path. In response to this trend, we have collected a series of special experiences so that it is no longer necessary to wade through a pound or two of superfluous prose just to find exceptional pleasures and treasures.

Finally, I also should point out that every good travel guide is a living enterprise; that is, no part of this text is carved in stone. In our annual revisions, we refine, expand, and further hone all our material to serve your travel needs better. To this end, no contribution is of greater value to us than your personal reaction to what we have written, as well as information reflecting your own experiences while using the book. Please write to us at 10 E. 53rd St., New York, NY 10022.

We sincerely hope to hear from you.

Alexandra Mayes Birnbaum

ALEXANDRA MAYES BIRNBAUM, editorial consultant to the *Birnbaum Travel Guides*, worked with her late husband, Stephen Birnbaum, as co-editor of the series. She has been a world traveler since childhood and is known for her travel reports on radio on what's hot and what's not.

Paris

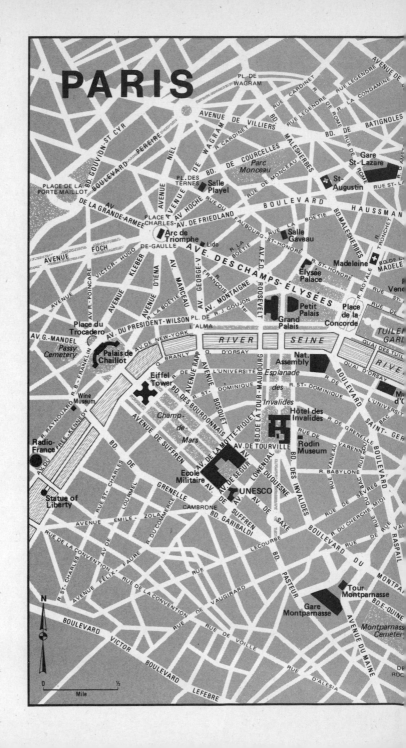

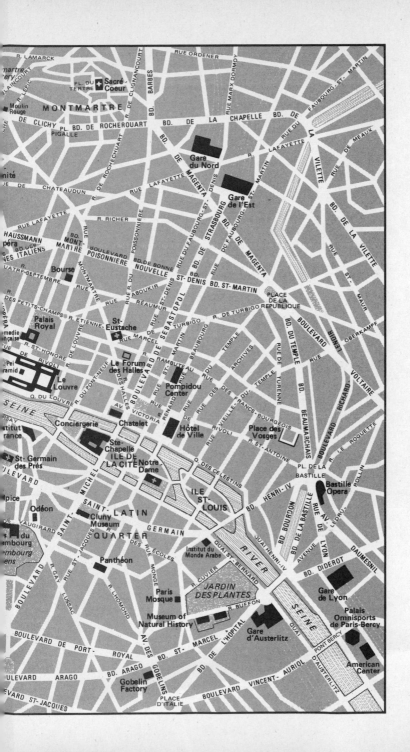

How to Use This Guide

A great deal of care has gone into the special organization of this guide-book, and we believe it represents a real breakthrough in the presentation of travel material.

Our text is divided into five basic sections in order to present information in the best way on every possible aspect of a Paris vacation. Our aim is to highlight what's where and to provide basic information—how, when, where, how much, and what's best—to assist you in making the most intelligent choices possible.

Here is a brief summary of what you can expect to find in each section. We believe that you will find both your travel planning and en route enjoyment enhanced by having this book at your side.

GETTING READY TO GO

A mini-encyclopedia of practical travel facts with all the precise data necessary to create a successful trip to Paris. Here you will find how to get where you're going, currency information and exchange rates, plus selected resources—including useful publications, and companies and organizations specializing in discount and special-interest travel—providing a wealth of information and assistance useful both before and during your trip.

THE CITY

The individual report on Paris offers a short-stay guide, including an essay introducing the city as a historic entity and a contemporary place to visit; an *At-a-Glance* section that's a site-by-site survey of the most important, interesting, and unique sights to see and things to do; *Sources and Resources,* a concise listing of pertinent tourism information, such as the address of the local tourist office, which sightseeing tours to take, where to find the best nightspot or hail a taxi, which shops have the finest merchandise and/or the most irresistible bargains, and where the best museums and theaters are to be found; and *Best in Town,* which lists our choices of the best places to eat and sleep on a variety of budgets.

DIVERSIONS

This section is designed to help travelers find the best places in which to engage in a variety of exceptional experiences, without having to wade through endless pages of unrelated text. In every case, our particular suggestions are intended to guide you to that special place where the quality of experience is likely to be highest.

DIRECTIONS

Here are seven walks that cover Paris, its main thoroughfares and side streets, its most spectacular landmarks and magnificent parks.

GLOSSARY

This compendium of helpful travel information includes a weights and measures table and *Useful Words and Phrases,* a brief introduction to the French language that will help you to make a hotel or dinner reservation, order a meal, mail a letter, and even buy toothpaste in France.

To use this book to full advantage, take a few minutes to read the table of contents and random entries in each section to get a firsthand feel for how it all fits together. You will find that the sections of this book are building blocks designed to help you put together the best possible trip. Use them selectively as a tool, a source of ideas, a reference work for accurate facts, and a guidebook to the best buys, the most exciting sights, the most pleasant accommodations, and the tastiest foods—the *best travel experience* that you can possibly have.

Getting
Ready to Go

Getting Ready to Go

When to Go

Paris has a temperate climate. Summer temperatures rarely rise above 80F and winter temperatures usually do not fall much below freezing. It rains fairly often year-round.

The peak travel period generally is from mid-May to mid-September. Travel during the off-season (roughly November to *Easter*) and shoulder seasons (the months immediately before and after the peak months) also offers relatively fair weather and smaller crowds. During these periods, travel can be less expensive.

If you have a touch-tone phone, you can call *The Weather Channel Connection* (phone: 900-WEATHER) for current worldwide weather forecasts. This service, available from *The Weather Channel* (2600 Cumberland Pkwy., Atlanta, GA 30339; phone: 404-434-6800), costs 95¢ per minute; the charge will appear on your phone bill.

Traveling by Plane

SCHEDULED FLIGHTS

Leading airlines offering flights between the US and Paris include *Aer Lingus, Air France, American, British Airways, Continental, Delta, IcelandAir, Northwest, Sabena, Tower Air, TWA, United,* and *USAir.*

FARES The great variety of airfares can be reduced to the following basic categories: first class, business class, coach (also called economy or tourist class), excursion or discount, and standby, as well as various promotional fares. For information on applicable fares and restrictions, contact the airlines listed above or ask your travel agent. Most airfares are offered for a limited time. Once you've found the lowest fare for which you can qualify, purchase your ticket as soon as possible.

RESERVATIONS Reconfirmation is strongly recommended for all international flights. It is essential that you confirm your round-trip reservations—*especially the return leg*—as well as any flights within Europe.

SEATING Airline seats usually are assigned on a first-come, first-served basis at check-in, although you may be able to reserve a seat when purchasing your ticket. Seating charts sometimes are available from airlines and also are included in the *Airline Seating Guide* (Carlson Publishing Co., 11132 Los Alamitos Blvd., Los Alamitos, CA 90720; phone: 310-493-4877).

SMOKING US law prohibits smoking on flights scheduled for six hours or less within the US and its territories on both domestic and international carriers. These restrictions do not apply to nonstop flights between the US and international destinations, and, at press time, major carriers permitted smoking on all flights to France. If the flight includes European connections, however, smoking may not be permitted on the intra-European leg of the trip. A free wallet-size guide that describes the rights of nonsmokers under current regulations is available from *ASH* (*Action on Smoking and Health;* DOT Card, 2013 H St. NW, Washington, DC 20006; phone: 202-659-4310).

SPECIAL MEALS When making your reservation, you can request one of the airline's alternate menu choices for no additional charge. Though not always required, it's a good idea to reconfirm your request the day before departure.

BAGGAGE On major international airlines, passengers usually are allowed to carry on board one bag that will fit under a seat or in an overhead bin and to check two bags in the cargo hold. Specific regulations regarding dimensions and weight restrictions vary among airlines, but a checked bag usually cannot exceed 62 inches in combined dimensions (length, width, and depth), or weigh more than 70 pounds. There may be charges for additional, oversize, or overweight luggage, and for special equipment or sporting gear. Note that baggage allowances may be more limited on intra-European flights. Check that the tags the airline attaches are correctly coded for your destination.

CHARTER FLIGHTS

By booking a block of seats on a specially arranged flight, charter operators frequently can offer travelers bargain airfares. If you do fly on a charter, however, read the contract's fine print carefully. Federal regulations permit charter operators to cancel a flight or assess surcharges of as much as 10% of the airfare up to 10 days before departure. You usually must book in advance, and once booked, no changes are permitted, so buy trip cancellation insurance. Also, make your check out to the company's escrow account, which provides some protection for your investment in the event that the charter operator fails. For further information, consult the publication *Jax Fax* (397 Post Rd., Darien, CT 06820; phone: 203-655-8746; fax: 203-655-6257).

DISCOUNTS ON SCHEDULED FLIGHTS

COURIER TRAVEL In return for arranging to accompany some kind of freight, a traveler pays only a portion of the total airfare (and sometimes a small registration fee). One agency that matches up would-be couriers with courier companies is *Now Voyager* (74 Varick St., Suite 307, New York, NY 10013; phone: 212-431-1616; fax: 212-334-5243).

Courier Companies

Discount Travel International (169 W. 81st St., New York, NY 10024; phone: 212-362-3636; fax: 212-362-3236; and 801 Alton Rd., Suite 1, Miami Beach, FL 33139; phone: 305-538-1616; fax: 305-673-9376).

F.B. On Board Courier Club (10225 Ryan Ave., Suite 103, Dorval, Quebec H9P 1A2, Canada; phone: 514-633-0740; fax: 514-633-0735).

Halbart Express (147-05 176th St., Jamaica, NY 11434; phone: 718-656-8279; fax: 718-244-0559).

Midnite Express (925 W. Hyde Park Blvd., Inglewood, CA 90302; phone: 310-672-1100; fax: 310-671-0107).

Way to Go Travel (6679 Sunset Blvd., Hollywood, CA 90028; phone: 213-466-1126; fax: 213-466-8994).

Publications

Insiders Guide to Air Courier Bargains, by Kelly Monaghan (The Intrepid Traveler, PO Box 438, New York, NY 10034; phone: 212-569-1081 for information; 800-356-9315 for orders; fax: 212-942-6687).

Travel Unlimited (PO Box 1058, Allston, MA 02134-1058; no phone).

CONSOLIDATORS AND BUCKET SHOPS These companies buy blocks of tickets from airlines and sell them at a discount to travel agents or directly to consumers. Since many bucket shops operate on a thin margin, be sure to check a company's record with the *Better Business Bureau*—before parting with any money.

Council Charter (205 E. 42nd St., New York, NY 10017; phone: 800-800-8222 or 212-661-0311; fax: 212-972-0194).

International Adventures (60 E. 42nd St., Room 763, New York, NY 10165; phone: 212-599-0577; fax: 212-599-3288).

Travac Tours and Charters (989 Ave. of the Americas, New York, NY 10018; phone: 800-872-8800 or 212-563-3303; fax: 212-563-3631).

Unitravel (1177 N. Warson Rd., St. Louis, MO 63132; phone: 800-325-2222 or 314-569-0900; fax: 314-569-2503).

LAST-MINUTE TRAVEL CLUBS Members of such clubs receive information on imminent trips and other bargain travel opportunities. There usually is an annual fee, although a few clubs offer free membership. Despite the names of some of the clubs listed below, you don't have to wait until literally the last minute to make travel plans.

Discount Travel International (114 Forrest Ave., Suite 203, Narberth, PA 19072; phone: 215-668-7184; fax: 215-668-9182).

FLY ASAP (PO Box 9808, Scottsdale, AZ 85252-3808; phone: 800-FLY-ASAP or 602-956-1987; fax: 602-956-6414).

Last Minute Travel (1249 Boylston St., Boston, MA 02215; phone: 800-LAST-MIN or 617-267-9800; fax: 617-424-1943).

Moment's Notice (425 Madison Ave., New York, NY 10017; phone: 212-486-0500/1/2/3; fax: 212-486-0783).

Spur of the Moment Cruises (411 N. Harbor Blvd., Suite 302, San Pedro, CA 90731; phone: 800-4-CRUISES or 310-521-1070 in California; 800-343-1991 elsewhere in the US; 24-hour hotline: 310-521-1060; fax: 310-521-1061).

Traveler's Advantage (3033 S. Parker Rd., Suite 900, Aurora, CO 80014; phone: 800-548-1116 or 800-835-8747; fax: 303-368-3985).

Vacations to Go (1502 Augusta Dr., Suite 415, Houston, TX 77057; phone: 713-974-2121 in Texas; 800-338-4962 elsewhere in the US; fax: 713-974-0445).

Worldwide Discount Travel Club (1674 Meridian Ave., Miami Beach, FL 33139; phone: 305-534-2082; fax: 305-534-2070).

GENERIC AIR TRAVEL These organizations operate much like an ordinary airline standby service, except that they offer seats on not one but several scheduled and charter airlines. One pioneer of generic flights is *Airhitch* (2790 Broadway, Suite 100, New York, NY 10025; phone: 212-864-2000).

BARTERED TRAVEL SOURCES Barter—the exchange of commodities or services in lieu of cash payment—is a common practice among travel suppliers. Companies that have obtained travel services through barter may sell these services at substantial discounts to travel clubs, who pass along the savings to members. One organization offering bartered travel opportunities is *Travel World Leisure Club* (225 W. 34th St., Suite 909, New York, NY 10122; phone: 800-444-TWLC or 212-239-4855; fax: 212-564-5158).

CONSUMER PROTECTION

Passengers whose complaints have not been satisfactorily addressed by the airline can contact the *US Department of Transportation* (*DOT;* Consumer Affairs Division, 400 Seventh St. SW, Room 10405, Washington, DC 20590; phone: 202-366-2220). Also see *Fly Rights* (Publication #050-000-00513-5; *US Government Printing Office,* PO Box 371954, Pittsburgh, PA 15250-7954; phone: 202-783-3238; fax: 202-512-2250). If you have safety-related questions or concerns, write to the *Federal Aviation Administration* (*FAA;* 800 Independence Ave. SW, Washington, DC 20591) or call the *FAA Consumer Hotline* (phone: 800-322-7873). If you have a complaint against a local travel service in France, contact the French tourist authorities or *La Partie Administrative du Tourisme* (2 Rue Linois, Paris 75015, France; phone: 33-1-44-37-36-00).

On Arrival

FROM THE AIRPORT TO THE CITY

Paris has two airports: *Charles de Gaulle* airport is located 14 miles (23 km) northeast of the center of Paris; *Orly* is 9 miles (14 km) south of the city center. The trip from either airport to central Paris takes between 30 and 45 minutes by taxi. The fare is about 150F to 250F (about $26 to $43 at press time), with an extra charge of about 5F (90¢) for each bag.

The *RER* suburban train runs between the city and both airports. *Roissy-Rail,* part of the *RER B* line, runs between *Charles de Gaulle* airport (there is a shuttle bus to the *Roissy* station) and the Gare du Nord; you can buy a ticket for 35F (about $6) at the airport. The *Roissybus* (city bus No. 352), operated by the *Régie de Transports Parisiens* (*RATP;* phone: 33-1-48-43-46-14-14), runs between the airport and the *Opera/Palais Garnier;* the trip takes about 45 minutes and costs 30F (about $5.15).

From *Orly,* there is shuttle bus to the *RER C* line (sometimes called *Orly-Rail*), which stops at Luxembourg, St-Michel, Invalides, and other points in the city. Depending on where you get off, the combined shuttle-bus/train trip takes from about 35 to 50 minutes. *Orly* also is connected to the *RER C* line by the *Orlyval* monorail service; the combined monorail/train trip takes about 30 to 45 minutes (again depending on the stop), and costs 45F (about $7.80). *RATP*'s *Orlybus* (city bus No. 215) links the airport to Place Denfert-Rochereau in the southern part of the city; the 30-minute trip costs 27F (about $4.65).

From either airport (or for transportation between the two airports), you also can take the *Air France* bus. From *Charles de Gaulle,* there are two routes to the city—one goes to *Le Palais de Congrès* (*Métro;* Porte Maillot) and the *Arc de Triomphe* (*Métro;* Charles de Gaulee-Etoile), and takes about 40 minutes; the other goes to the Gare Montparnasse on the Rive Gauche and takes about 45 minutes. From *Orly,* the *Air France* bus goes to a terminus on the Esplanade des Invalides; the trip takes about 40 minutes. Additional information is available from *Air France*; you can call their offices at *Charles de Gaulle* (phone: 33-42-99-20-18 or 33-49-38-57-57) or *Orly* (phone: 33-43-23-97-10 or 33-49-38-57-57).

CAR RENTAL

Although useful for day trips outside Paris, cars usually are more trouble than they are worth for touring within the city. You can rent a car through a travel agent or international rental firm before leaving home, or from a regional or local company once in Paris. Reserve in advance.

Most car rental companies require a credit card, although some will accept a substantial cash deposit. The minimum age to rent a car is set by the company; some also may impose special conditions on drivers above a certain age. Electing to pay for collision damage waiver (CDW) protection will add to the cost of renting a car, but releases you from financial liability for the vehicle. Additional costs include drop-off charges or one-way service fees.

Car Rental Companies

Auto Europe (phone: 800-223-5555).

Avis (phone: 800-331-1084).

Budget (phone: 800-472-3325).

Dergi Location (phone: 33-1-45-87-27-04).

Dollar Rent A Car (known in Europe as *EuroDollar Rent A Car;* phone: 800-800-6000).

Europe by Car (phone: 212-581-3040 in New York State; 800-223-1516 elsewhere in the US).

European Car Reservations (phone: 800-535-3303).

Foremost Euro-Car (phone: 800-272-3299).

Hertz (phone: 800-654-3001).

Kemwel Group (phone: 800-678-0678).

Meier's International (phone: 800-937-0700).

National (known in Europe as *Europcar;* phone: 800-CAR-EUROPE).

Town and Country/ITS (phone: 800-248-4350 in Florida; 800-521-0643 elsewhere in the US).

Package Tours

A package is a collection of travel services that can be purchased in a single transaction. Its principal advantages are convenience and economy— the cost usually is lower than that of the same services purchased separately. Tour programs generally can be divided into two categories: escorted or locally hosted (with a set itinerary) and independent (usually more flexible).

When considering a package tour, read the brochure *carefully* to determine exactly what is included and any conditions that may apply, and check the company's record with the *Better Business Bureau.* The *United States Tour Operators Association* (*USTOA;* 211 E. 51st St., Suite 12B, New York, NY 10022; phone: 212-750-7371; fax: 212-421-1285) also can be helpful in determining a package tour operator's reliability. As with charter flights, to safeguard your funds, always make your check out to the company's escrow account.

Many tour operators offer packages focused on special interests such as the arts, local history, food and wine, sports, and other recreations. *All Adventure Travel* (5589 Arapahoe St., Suite 208, Boulder, CO 80303; phone: 800-537-4025 or 303-440-7924; fax: 303-440-4160) represents such specialized packagers. Many also are listed in the *Specialty Travel Index* (305 San

Anselmo Ave., Suite 313, San Anselmo, CA 94960; phone: 415-459-4900 in California; 800-442-4922 elsewhere in the US; fax: 415-459-4974).

Package Tour Operators

AHI International (701 Lee St., Des Plaines, IL 60016; phone: 800-323-7373 or 312-694-9330; fax: 708-699-7108).

American Airlines FlyAAway Vacations (offices throughout the US; phone: 800-321-2121).

American Express Vacations (offices throughout the US; phone: 800-YES-AMEX).

American Museum of Natural History Discovery Tours (Central Park W. at 79th St., New York, NY 10024; phone: 212-769-5700).

Bacchants' Pilgrimages (475 Sansome St., Suite 840, San Francisco, CA 94111; phone: 800-952-0226 or 415-981-8518; fax: 415-291-9419).

Blue Marble Travel (2 Rue Dussoubs, Paris 75002, France; phone: 33-1-42-36-02-34; fax: 33-1-42-21-14-77; in the US, contact *Odyssey Adventures,* 305 Commercial St., Suite 505, Portland, ME 04101; phone: 800-544-3216 or 207-773-0905; fax: 207-773-0943).

Brendan Tours (15137 Califa St., Van Nuys, CA 91411; phone: 800-421-8446 or 818-785-9696; fax: 818-902-9876).

British Airways Holidays (75-20 Astoria Blvd., Jackson Heights, NY 11370; phone: 800-AIRWAYS).

Caravan Tours (401 N. Michigan Ave., Chicago, IL 60611; phone: 800-CARAVAN or 312-321-9800; fax: 312-321-9810).

Catholic Travel (10018 Cedar Lane, Kensington, MD 20895; phone: 301-530-8963 or 301-530-7682; fax: 301-530-6614).

Certified Vacations (110 E. Broward Blvd., Ft. Lauderdale, FL 33302; phone: 800-233-7260 or 305-522-1440; fax: 305-468-4781).

Collette Tours (162 Middle St., Pawtucket, RI 02860; phone: 800-752-2655 in New England; 800-832-4656 elsewhere in the US; fax: 401-727-4745).

Contiki Holidays (300 Plaza Alicante, Suite 900, Garden Grove, CA 92640; phone: 800-266-8454 or 714-740-0808; fax: 714-740-0818).

Continental Grand Destinations (offices throughout the US; phone: 800-634-5555).

Delta's Dream Vacations (PO Box 1525, Ft. Lauderdale, FL 33302; phone: 800-872-7786).

DER Tours (11933 Wilshire Blvd., Los Angeles, CA 90025; phone: 800-782-2424 or 310-479-4411; fax: 310-479-2239; and 9501 W. Devon Ave., Rosemont, IL 60018; phone: 800-782-2424 or 708-692-6300; fax: 708-692-4506).

DMI Tours (11757 Katy Fwy., Suite 250, Houston, TX 77079; phone: 800-553-5090 or 713-497-5666; fax: 713-497-8694).

Educational Adventures (815 North Rd., Westfield, MA 01085; phone: 800-628-9655 or 413-568-2855; fax: 413-562-3621).

Edwards & Edwards (1 Times Square Plaza, 12th Floor, New York, NY 10036-6585; phone: 212-944-0290 in New York State; 800-223-6108 elsewhere in the US; fax: 212-944-7497).

EuroConnection (2004 196th St. SW, Suite 4, Lynnwood, WA 98036; phone: 800-645-3876 or 206-670-1140; fax: 206-775-7561).

Europe Through the Back Door (PO Box 2009, Edmonds, WA 98020; phone: 206-771-8303; fax: 206-771-0833).

Extra Value Travel (683 S. Collier Blvd., Marco Island, FL 33937; phone: 813-394-3384; fax: 813-394-4848).

Five Star Touring (60 E. 42nd St., Suite 612, New York, NY 10165; phone: 212-818-9140 in New York City; 800-792-7827 elsewhere in the US; fax: 212-818-9142).

4th Dimension Tours (1150 NW 72nd Ave., Suite 333, Miami, FL 33126; phone: 800-343-0020 or 305-477-1525; fax: 305-477-0731).

Frames Rickards (11 Herbrand St., London WC1N 1EX, England; phone: 44-171-837-3111; fax: 44-171-833-3752; in the US, contact *Trophy Tours,* 1850 Greenville Ave., Suite 146, Richardson, TX 75081; phone: 800-527-2473 or 214-690-3875; or *California Parlor Car Tours,* 1101 Van Ness Ave., San Francisco, CA 94109; phone: 800-331-9259 or 415-474-7500; fax: 415-673-1539).

The French Experience (370 Lexington Ave., New York, NY 10017; phone: 212-986-1115; fax: 212-986-3808).

Funway Holidays Funjet (PO Box 1460, Milwaukee, WI 53201-1460; phone: 800-558-3050 for reservations; 800-558-3060 for customer service).

Gadabout Tours (700 E. Tahquitz Canyon Way, Palm Springs, CA 92262-6767; phone: 800-952-5068 or 619-325-5556; fax: 619-325-5127).

Globus/Cosmos (5301 S. Federal Circle, Littleton, CO 80123; phone: 800-221-0090, 800-556-5454, or 303-797-2800; fax: 303-347-2080).

GOGO Tours (69 Spring St., Ramsey, NJ 07446-0507; phone: 201-934-3759).

Golf International (275 Madison Ave., New York, NY 10016; phone: 800-833-1389 or 212-986-9176; fax: 212-986-3720).

Grand Slam Tennis Tours (222 Milwaukee St., Suite 407, Denver, CO 80206; phone: 800-289-3333 or 303-321-1760; fax: 303-321-1771).

HSA Voyages (160 E. 26th St., Suite 5H, New York, NY 10010; phone: 800-927-4765 or 212-689-5400; fax: 212-689-5435).

In Quest of the Classics (PO Box 890745, Temecula, CA 92589-0745; phone: 800-227-1393 or 909-694-5866 in California; 800-221-5246 elsewhere in the US; fax: 909-694-5873).

Insight International Tours (745 Atlantic Ave., Suite 720, Boston, MA 02111; phone: 800-582-8380 or 617-482-2000; fax: 617-482-2425).

INTRAV (7711 Bonhomme Ave., St. Louis, MO 63105-1961; phone: 800-456-8100; fax: 314-727-6198).

Jet Vacations (1775 Broadway, New York, NY 10019; phone: 800-JET-0999 or 212-247-0999; fax: 212-586-2069).

KLM/Northwest Vacations Europe (c/o *MLT,* 5130 Hwy. 101, Minnetonka, MN 55345; phone: 800-727-1111; fax: 800-655-7890).

Liberty Travel (for the nearest location, contact the central office: 69 Spring St., Ramsey, NJ 07446; phone: 201-934-3500; fax: 201-934-3888).

Marathon Tours (108 Main St., Charlestown, MA 02129; phone: 800-444-4097 or 617-242-7845; fax: 617-242-7686).

Matterhorn Travel Service (2450 Riva Rd., Annapolis, MD 21401; phone: 410-224-2230 in Maryland; 800-638-9150 elsewhere in the US; fax: 410-266-3868).

Maupintour (PO Box 807, Lawrence, KS 66044; phone: 800-255-4266 or 913-843-1211; fax: 913-843-8351).

Mercator Travel (122 E. 42nd St., New York, NY 10168; phone: 800-514-9880 or 212-682-6979; fax: 212-682-7379).

Odyssey Adventures (305 Commercial St., Suite 505, Portland, ME 04101; phone: 800-544-3216 or 207-773-1156; fax: 207-773-0943).

Olson Travelworld (970 W. 190th St., Suite 425, Torrance, CA 90502; phone: 800-421-2255 or 310-354-2600; fax: 310-768-0050).

Past Times Tours (800 Larch La., Sacramento, CA 95864-5042; phone: 916-485-8140; fax: 916-488-4804).

Petrabax Tours (97-45 Queens Blvd., Suite 600, Rego Park, NY 11374; phone: 800-367-6611 or 718-897-7272; fax: 718-275-3943).

Pleasure Break (3701 Algonquin Rd., Suite 900, Rolling Meadows, IL 60008; phone: 708-670-6300 in Illinois; 800-777-1885 elsewhere in the US; fax: 708-670-7689).

Regina Tours (401 South St., Room 4B, Chardon, OH 44024; phone: 800-228-4654 or 216-286-9166; fax: 216-286-4231).

Select Travel Service (main office: Bridgefoot House, 159 High St., Huntington, Cambridgeshire PE18 7TF, England; phone: 44-181-480-433783; fax: 44-181-480-433514; US office: 795 Franklin Ave., Franklin Lakes, NJ 07417; phone: 800-752-6787 or 201-891-4143; fax: 201-847-0053).

Smithsonian Study Tours and Seminars (1100 Jefferson Dr. SW, Room 3045, Washington, DC 20560; phone: 202-357-4700; fax: 202-786-2315).

Steve Lohr's Holidays (206 Central Ave., Jersey City, NJ, 07307; phone: 201-798-3900 in New Jersey; 800-929-5647 elsewhere in the US; fax: 201-693-0966).

Take-A-Guide (main office: 11 Uxbridge St., London W8 7TQ, England; phone: 44-181-960-0459; fax: 44-181-964-0990; US office: 954

Lexington Ave., New York, NY 10021; phone: 800-825-4946; fax: 800-635-7177).

Thomas Cook (headquarters: 45 Berkeley St., Piccadilly, London W1A 1EB, England; phone: 44-171-499-4000; fax: 44-171-408-4299; main US office: 100 Cambridge Park Dr., Cambridge, MA 02140; phone: 800-846-6272; fax: 617-349-1094).

Trafalgar Tours (11 E. 26th St., Suite 1300, New York, NY 10010-1402; phone: 800-854-0103 or 212-689-8977; fax: 212-725-7776).

TRAVCOA (PO Box 2630, Newport Beach, CA 92658; phone: 800-992-2004 or 714-476-2800 in California; 800-992-2003 elsewhere in the US; fax: 714-476-2538).

Travel Bound (599 Broadway, Penthouse, New York, NY 10012; phone: 212-334-1350 in New York State; 800-456-8656 elsewhere in the US; fax: 800-208-7080).

TWA Getaway Vacations (Getaway Vacation Center, 10 E. Stow Rd., Marlton, NJ 08053; phone: 800-GETAWAY; fax: 609-985-4125).

United Airlines Vacations (PO Box 24580, Milwaukee, WI 53224-0580; phone: 800-328-6877).

Value Holidays (10224 N. Port Washington Rd., Mequon, WI 53092; phone: 800-558-6850 or 414-241-6373; fax: 414-241-6379).

X.O. Travel Consultants (38 W. 32nd St., Suite 1009, New York, NY 10001; phone: 212-947-5530 in New York State; 800-262-9682 elsewhere in the US; fax: 212-971-0924).

Insurance

The first person with whom you should discuss travel insurance is your own insurance broker. You may discover that the insurance you already carry protects you adequately while traveling and that you need little additional coverage. If you charge travel services, the credit card company also may provide some insurance coverage (and other safeguards).

Types of Travel Insurance

Automobile insurance: Provides collision, theft, property damage, and personal liability protection while driving.

Baggage and personal effects insurance: Protects your bags and their contents in case of damage or theft at any point during your travels.

Default and/or bankruptcy insurance: Provides coverage in the event of default and/or bankruptcy on the part of the tour operator, airline, or other travel supplier.

Flight insurance: Covers accidental injury or death while flying.

Personal accident and sickness insurance: Covers cases of illness, injury, or death in an accident while traveling.

Trip cancellation and interruption insurance: Guarantees a refund if you must cancel a trip; may reimburse you for additional travel costs incurred in catching up with a tour or traveling home early.
Combination policies: Include any or all of the above.

Disabled Travelers

Make travel arrangements well in advance. Specify to all services involved the nature of your disability to determine if there are accommodations and facilities that meet your needs. Information about accessibility and transportation for the disabled in Paris is provided by the *Comité National Français de Liaison pour la Réadaptation des Handicapés* (38 Bd. Raspail, Paris 75007, France; phone: 33-1-45-48-90-13; fax: 33-1-45-48-99-21). For information on the accessibility of Paris's airports, contact the US representative of the *Paris Airport Authority, Marketing Challenges International* (10 E. 21st St., Suite 600, New York, NY 10010; phone: 212-529-8484; fax: 212-460-8287).

The *French Government Tourist Office* in the US distributes the *Paris Hotel Guide* and *Paris Guide to Monuments and Museums;* both list wheelchair accessibility. Hotel and restaurant guides, such as the *Michelin Red Guide to France* (*Michelin Travel Publications,* PO Box 19008, Greenville, SC 29602-9008; phone: 803-458-5000 in South Carolina; 800-423-0485 elsewhere in the US; fax: 803-458-5665), use the standard symbol of access (person in a wheelchair) to point out accommodations suitable for wheelchair-bound guests.

Organizations

ACCENT on Living (PO Box 700, Bloomington, IL 61702; phone: 800-787-8444 or 309-378-2961; fax: 309-378-4420).

Access: The Foundation for Accessibility by the Disabled (PO Box 356, Malverne, NY 11565; phone/fax: 516-887-5798).

American Foundation for the Blind (15 W. 16th St., New York, NY 10011; phone: 800-232-5463 or 212-620-2147; fax: 212-727-7418).

Holiday Care Service (2 Old Bank Chambers, Station Rd., Horley, Surrey RH6 9HW, England; phone: 44-1293-774535; fax: 44-1293-784647).

I.CARE (69-73 Av. du Général Leclerc, Boîte Postal 113, Boulogne 92106, France; phone: 33-1-46-09-91-96; fax: 33-1-46-21-50-80).

Information Center for Individuals with Disabilities (Ft. Point Pl., 27-43 Wormwood St., Boston, MA 02210; phone: 800-462-5015 in Massachusetts; 617-727-5540 elsewhere in the US; TDD: 617-345-9743; fax: 617-345-5318).

International Help for the Disabled (*IHD;* Boîte Postale 62, Puget-sur-Argens 83480, France; phone: 33-94-81-61-51; fax: 33-94-81-61-43).

Mobility International (main office: 228 Borough High St., London SE1 1JX, England; phone: 44-171-403-5688; fax: 44-171-378-1292; US office: *MIUSA,* PO Box 10767, Eugene, OR 97440; phone/TDD: 503-343-1284; fax: 503-343-6812).

Moss Rehabilitation Hospital Travel Information Service (telephone referrals only; phone: 215-456-9600; TDD: 215-456-9602).

National Rehabilitation Information Center (8455 Colesville Rd., Suite 935, Silver Spring, MD 20910; phone: 301-588-9284; fax: 301-587-1967).

Paralyzed Veterans of America (*PVA;* PVA/ATTS Program, 801 18th St. NW, Washington, DC 20006; phone: 202-872-1300 in Washington, DC; 800-424-8200 elsewhere in the US; fax: 202-785-4452).

Royal Association for Disability and Rehabilitation (*RADAR;* 12 City Forum, 250 City Rd., London EC1V 8AF, England; phone: 44-171-250-3222; fax: 44-171-250-0212).

Society for the Advancement of Travel for the Handicapped (*SATH;* 347 Fifth Ave., Suite 610, New York, NY 10016; phone: 212-447-7284; fax: 212-725-8253).

Travel Industry and Disabled Exchange (*TIDE;* 5435 Donna Ave., Tarzana, CA 91356; phone: 818-368-5648).

Tripscope (The Courtyard, Evelyn Rd., London W4 5JL, England; phone: 44-181-994-9294; fax: 44-181-994-3618).

Publications

Access Travel: A Guide to the Accessibility of Airport Terminals (Consumer Information Center, Dept. 578Z, Pueblo, CO 81009; phone: 719-948-3334).

Air Transportation of Handicapped Persons (Publication #AC-120-32; *US Department of Transportation,* Distribution Unit, Publications Section, M-443-2, 400 Seventh St. SW, Washington, DC 20590; phone: 202-366-0039).

The Diabetic Traveler (PO Box 8223 RW, Stamford, CT 06905; phone: 203-327-5832; fax: 203-975-1748).

Directory of Travel Agencies for the Disabled and Travel for the Disabled, both by Helen Hecker (Twin Peaks Press, PO Box 129, Vancouver, WA 98666; phone: 800-637-CALM or 206-694-2462; fax: 206-696-3210).

Guide to Traveling with Arthritis (Upjohn Company, PO Box 989, Dearborn, MI 48121; phone: 800-253-9860).

The Handicapped Driver's Mobility Guide (*American Automobile Association,* 1000 AAA Dr., Heathrow, FL 32746-5080; phone: 407-444-7000; fax: 407-444-7380).

Handicapped Travel Newsletter (PO Box 269, Athens, TX 75751; phone/fax: 903-677-1260).

Handi-Travel: A Resource Book for Disabled and Elderly Travellers, by Cinnie Noble (*Canadian Rehabilitation Council for the Disabled,* 45

Sheppard Ave. E., Suite 801, Toronto, Ontario M2N 5W9, Canada; phone/TDD: 416-250-7490; fax: 416-229-1371).

Holidays and Travel Abroad, edited by John Stanford *(Royal Association for Disability and Rehabilitation,* address above).

Incapacitated Passengers Air Travel Guide (International Air Transport Association, Publications Sales Department, 2000 Peel St., Montreal, Quebec H3A 2R4, Canada; phone: 514-844-6311; fax: 514-844-5286).

Ticket to Safe Travel (American Diabetes Association, 1660 Duke St., Alexandria, VA 22314; phone: 800-232-3472 or 703-549-1500; fax: 703-836-7439).

Travel for the Patient with Chronic Obstructive Pulmonary Disease (Dr. Harold Silver, 1601 18th St. NW, Washington, DC 20009; phone: 202-667-0134; fax: 202-667-0148).

Travel Tips for Hearing-Impaired People (American Academy of Otolaryngology, 1 Prince St., Alexandria, VA 22314; phone: 703-836-4444; fax: 703-683-5100).

Travel Tips for People with Arthritis (Arthritis Foundation, 1314 Spring St. NW, Atlanta, GA 30309; phone: 800-283-7800 or 404-872-7100; fax: 404-872-0457).

Traveling Like Everybody Else: A Practical Guide for Disabled Travelers, by Jacqueline Freedman and Susan Gersten (Modan Publishing, PO Box 1202, Bellmore, NY 11710; phone: 516-679-1380; fax: 516-679-1448).

Package Tour Operators

Accessible Journeys (35 W. Sellers Ave., Ridley Park, PA 19078; phone: 800-846-4537 or 215-521-0339; fax: 215-521-6959).

Accessible Tours/Directions Unlimited (Attn.: Lois Bonnani, 720 N. Bedford Rd., Bedford Hills, NY 10507; phone: 800-533-5343 or 914-241-1700; fax: 914-241-0243).

Beehive Business and Leisure Travel (1130 W. Center St., N. Salt Lake, UT 84054; phone: 800-777-5727 or 801-292-4445; fax: 801-298-9460).

Classic Travel Service (8 W. 40th St., New York, NY 10018; phone: 212-869-2560 in New York State; 800-247-0909 elsewhere in the US; fax: 212-944-4493).

Croisières Handy (Port Minervois, Homps 11200, France; phone: 33-68-91-16-48; fax: 33-94-81-61-43).

Evergreen Travel Service (4114 198th St. SW, Suite 13, Lynnwood, WA 98036-6742; phone: 800-435-2288 or 206-776-1184; fax: 206-775-0728).

Flying Wheels Travel (143 W. Bridge St., PO Box 382, Owatonna, MN 55060; phone: 800-535-6790 or 507-451-5005; fax: 507-451-1685).

Good Neighbor Travel Service (124 S. Main St., Viroqua, WI 54665; phone: 800-338-3245 or 608-637-2128; fax: 608-637-3030).

The Guided Tour (7900 Old York Rd., Suite 114B, Elkins Park, PA 19117-2339; phone: 800-783-5841 or 215-782-1370; fax: 215-635-2637).

Hinsdale Travel (201 E. Ogden Ave., Hinsdale, IL 60521; phone: 708-325-1335 or 708-469-7349; fax: 708-325-1342).

MedEscort International (*ABE International Airport,* PO Box 8766, Allentown, PA 18105-8766; phone: 800-255-7182 or 215-791-3111; fax: 215-791-9189).

Prestige World Travel (5710-X High Point Rd., Greensboro, NC 27407; phone: 800-476-7737 or 910-292-6690; fax: 910-632-9404).

Sprout (893 Amsterdam Ave., New York, NY 10025; phone: 212-222-9575; fax: 212-222-9768).

Weston Travel Agency (134 N. Cass Ave., Westmont, IL 60559; phone: 708-968-2513 in Illinois; 800-633-3725 elsewhere in the US; fax: 708-968-2539).

Single Travelers

The travel industry is not very fair to people who vacation by themselves—they often end up paying more than those traveling in pairs. There are services catering to single travelers, however, that match travel companions, offer travel arrangements with shared accommodations, and provide information and discounts. Useful publications include *Going Solo* (Doerfer Communications, PO Box 123, Apalachicola, FL 32329; phone/fax: 904-653-8848) and *Traveling on Your Own,* by Eleanor Berman (Random House, Order Dept., 400 Hahn Rd., Westminster, MD 21157; phone: 800-733-3000; fax: 800-659-2436).

Organizations and Companies

Club Europa (802 W. Oregon St., Urbana, IL 61801; phone: 800-331-1882 or 217-344-5863; fax: 217-344-4072).

Contiki Holidays (300 Plaza Alicante, Suite 900, Garden Grove, CA 92640; phone: 800-466-0610 or 714-740-0808; fax: 714-740-0818).

Gallivanting (515 E. 79th St., Suite 20F, New York, NY 10021; phone: 800-933-9699 or 212-988-0617; fax: 212-988-0144).

Globus/Cosmos (5301 S. Federal Circle, Littleton, CO 80123; phone: 800-221-0090, 800-556-5454, or 303-797-2800; fax: 303-347-2080).

Insight International Tours (745 Atlantic Ave., Boston, MA 02111; phone: 800-582-8380 or 617-482-2000; fax: 617-482-2425).

Jane's International and Sophisticated Women Travelers (2603 Bath Ave., Brooklyn, NY 11214; phone: 718-266-2045; fax: 718-266-4062).

Marion Smith Singles (611 Prescott Pl., N. Woodmere, NY 11581; phone: 516-791-4852, 516-791-4865, or 212-944-2112; fax: 516-791-4879).

Partners-in-Travel (11660 Chenault St., Suite 119, Los Angeles, CA 90049; phone: 310-476-4869).

Singles in Motion (545 W. 236th St., Riverdale, NY 10463; phone/fax: 718-884-4464).

Singleworld (401 Theodore Fremd Ave., Rye, NY 10580; phone: 800-223-6490 or 914-967-3334; fax: 914-967-7395).

Solo Flights (63 High Noon Rd., Weston, CT 06883; phone: 800-266-1566 or 203-226-9993).

Suddenly Singles Tours (161 Dreiser Loop, Bronx, NY 10475; phone: 718-379-8800 in New York City; 800-859-8396 elsewhere in the US; fax: 718-379-8858).

Travel Companion Exchange (PO Box 833, Amityville, NY 11701; phone: 516-454-0880; fax: 516-454-0170).

Travel Companions (Atrium Financial Center, 1515 N. Federal Hwy., Suite 300, Boca Raton, FL 33432; phone: 800-383-7211 or 407-393-6448; fax: 407 451-8560).

Travel in Two's (239 N. Broadway, Suite 3, N. Tarrytown, NY 10591; phone: 914-631-8301 in New York State; 800-692-5252 elsewhere in the US).

Umbrella Singles (PO Box 157, Woodbourne, NY 12788; phone: 800-537-2797 or 914-434-6871; fax: 914-434-3532).

Older Travelers

Special discounts and more free time are just two factors that have given older travelers a chance to see the world at affordable prices. Many travel suppliers offer senior discounts—sometimes only to members of certain senior citizens organizations (which provide benefits of their own). When considering a particular package, make sure the facilities—and the pace of the tour—match your needs and physical condition.

Publications

Going Abroad: 101 Tips for Mature Travelers (*Grand Circle Travel,* 347 Congress St., Boston, MA 02210; phone: 800-221-2610 or 617-350-7500; fax: 617-423-0445).

The Mature Traveler (PO Box 50820, Reno, NV 89513-0820; phone: 702-786-7419).

Take a Camel to Lunch and Other Adventures for Mature Travelers, by Nancy O'Connell (Bristol Publishing Enterprises, PO Box 1737, San Leandro, CA 94577; phone: 510-895-4461 in California; 800-346-4889 elsewhere in the US; fax: 510-895-4459).

Unbelievably Good Deals & Great Adventures That You Absolutely Can't Get Unless You're Over 50, by Joan Rattner Heilman (Contemporary Books, 1200 Stetson Ave., Chicago, IL 60601; phone: 312-782-9181; fax: 312-540-4687).

Organizations

American Association of Retired Persons (*AARP*; 601 E St. NW, Washington, DC 20049; phone: 202-434-2277).

Golden Companions (PO Box 754, Pullman, WA 99163-0754; phone: 208-858-2183).

Mature Outlook (Customer Service Center, 6001 N. Clark St., Chicago, IL 60660; phone: 800-336-6330).

National Council of Senior Citizens (1331 F St. NW, Washington, DC 20004; phone: 202-347-8800; fax: 202-624-9595).

Package Tour Operators

Elderhostel (75 Federal St., Boston, MA 02110-1941; phone: 617-426-7788; fax: 617-426-8351).

Evergreen Travel Service (4114 198th St. SW, Suite 13, Lynnwood, WA 98036-6742; phone: 800-435-2288 or 206-776-1184; fax: 206-775-0728).

Gadabout Tours (700 E. Tahquitz Canyon Way, Palm Springs, CA 92262; phone: 800-952-5068 or 619-325-5556; fax: 619-325-5127).

Grand Circle Travel (347 Congress St., Boston, MA 02210; phone: 800-221-2610 or 617-350-7500; fax: 617-423-0445).

Grandtravel (6900 Wisconsin Ave., Suite 706, Chevy Chase, MD 20815; phone: 800-247-7651 or 301-986-0790; fax: 301-913-0166).

Insight International Tours (745 Atlantic Ave., Suite 720, Boston, MA 02111; phone: 800-582-8380 or 617-482-2000; fax: 617-482-2425).

Interhostel (*University of New Hampshire,* Division of Continuing Education, 6 Garrison Ave., Durham, NH 03824; phone: 800-733-9753 or 603-862-1147; fax: 603-862-1113).

Mature Tours (c/o *Solo Flights,* 63 High Noon Rd., Weston, CT 06883; phone: 800-266-1566 or 203-226-9993).

OmniTours (104 Wilmot Rd., Deerfield, IL 60015; phone: 800-962-0060 or 708-374-0088; fax: 708-374-9515).

Saga International Holidays (222 Berkeley St., Boston, MA 02116; phone: 800-343-0273 or 617-262-2262; fax: 617-375-5950).

Money Matters

The basic unit of currency in France is the French **franc** (abbreviated "F") which is divided into 100 **centimes**. The franc is distributed in coin denominations of 20F, 10F, 5F, 2F, 1F, and ½F, and 20 centimes, 10 centimes, and 5 centimes, and in bills of 500F, 200F, 100F, 50F, and 20F. Although the French use a comma in expressing numerical values where Americans use a decimal point (and vice versa), throughout this book we use the American style of notation. At the time of this writing, the exchange rate for French currency was 5.8 francs to $1 US.

Exchange rates are listed in international newspapers such as the *International Herald Tribune.* Foreign currency information and related services are provided by banks and companies such as *Thomas Cook Foreign Exchange* (for the nearest location, call 800-621-0666 or 312-236-0042; fax: 312-807-4895); *Harold Reuter and Company* (200 Park Ave., Suite 332E, New York, NY 10166; phone: 800-258-0456 or 212-661-0826; fax: 212-557-6622); and *Ruesch International* (for the nearest location, call 800-424-2923 or 202-408-1200; fax: 202-408-1211). In Paris, you will find the official rate of exchange posted in banks, airports, money exchange houses, hotels, and some shops. Since you will get more francs for your US dollar at banks and money exchanges, don't change more than $10 for foreign currency at other commercial establishments. Ask how much commission you're being charged and the exchange rate, and don't buy money on the black market (it may be counterfeit). Estimate your needs carefully; if you overbuy, you lose twice—buying and selling back.

CREDIT CARDS AND TRAVELER'S CHECKS

Most major credit cards enjoy wide domestic and international acceptance; however, not every hotel, restaurant, or shop in Paris accepts all (or in some cases any) credit cards. (Some cards may be issued under different names in Europe; for example, *MasterCard* may go under the name *Access* or *Eurocard,* and *Visa* sometimes is called *Carte Bleue.*) When making purchases with a credit card, note that the rate of exchange depends on when the charge is processed; most credit card companies charge a 1% fee for converting foreign currency charges.

It's also wise to carry traveler's checks while on the road, since they are widely accepted and replaceable if stolen or lost. You can buy traveler's checks at banks and some are available by mail or phone. Keep a separate list of all traveler's checks (noting those that you have cashed) and the names and numbers of your credit cards. Both traveler's check and credit card companies have international numbers to call for information or in the event of loss or theft.

CASH MACHINES

Automated teller machines (ATMs) are increasingly common worldwide, and most banks participate in international ATM networks such as *CIRRUS* (phone: 800-4-CIRRUS) and *PLUS* (phone: 800-THE-PLUS). Cardholders can withdraw cash from any machine in the same network using either a "bank" card or, in some cases, a credit card. For instance, in Paris, ATMs that accept *MasterCard* or *Visa* are quite common. Additional information on ATMs and networks can be obtained from your bank or credit card company.

SENDING MONEY ABROAD

Should the need arise, you can have money sent to you in Paris via the services provided by *American Express MoneyGram* (phone: 800-926-9400 for information; 800-866-8800 for money transfers) or *Western Union Financial Services* (phone: 800-325-6000 or 800-325-4176). If you are down to your last cent and have no other way to obtain cash, the nearest *US Consulate* will let you call home to set these matters in motion.

Accommodations

For specific information on hotels, resorts, and other selected accommodations see *Checking In* in THE CITY. The *French Government Tourist Office* distributes lists of selected, rated Paris hotels, as well as the US representatives of many French hotels.

RELAIS & CHÂTEAUX

Founded in France, the *Relais & Châteaux* association has grown to include hotels (and restaurants) in numerous countries. At press time, there were two members in Paris, and many more throughout France. All maintain very high standards in order to retain their memberships, as they are reviewed annually. An illustrated catalogue of properties is available from *Relais & Châteaux* (11 E. 44th St., Suite 707, New York, NY 10017; phone: 212-856-0115; fax: 212-856-0193).

RENTAL OPTIONS

An attractive accommodations alternative for the visitor content to stay in one spot is a vacation rental. For a family or group, the per-person cost can be reasonable. To have your pick of the properties available, make inquiries at least six months in advance. The *Worldwide Home Rental Guide* (3501 Indian School Rd. NE, Albuquerque, NM 87106; phone/fax: 505-255-4271) lists rental properties and managing agencies. Those who wish to arrange a rental themselves can write or call the *French Government Tourist Office* or contact the *Fédération Nationale des Agents Immobiliers* (129 Rue du Faubourg-St-Honoré, Paris 75008, France; phone: 33-1-44-20-77-00; fax: 33-1-42-25-80-84) for a list of real estate agencies handling property rentals in and around Paris.

Rental Property Agents

B & V Associates (140 E. 56th St., Suite 4C, New York, NY 10022; phone: 800-546-4777 or 212-688-9538; fax: 212-688-9467).

British Travel International (PO Box 299, Elkton, VA 22827; phone: 800-327-6097 or 703-298-2232; fax: 703-298-2347).

Castles, Cottages and Flats (7 Faneuil Hall Marketplace, Boston, MA 02109; phone: 800-742-6030 or 617-742-6030; fax: 617-367-4521).

Chez Vous (220 Redwood Hwy., Suite 129, Mill Valley, CA 94941; phone: 415-331-2535; fax: 415-331-5296).

Europa-Let (92 N. Main St., Ashland, OR 97520; phone: 800-462-4486 or 503-482-5806; fax: 503-482-0660).

The French Experience (370 Lexington Ave., New York, NY 10017; phone: 212-986-1115; fax: 212-986-3808).

Hideaways International (767 Islington St., Portsmouth, NH 03801; phone: 800-843-4433 or 603-430-4433; fax: 603-430-4444).

Hometours International (PO Box 11503, Knoxville, TN 37939; phone: 800-367-4668).

Interhome (124 Little Falls Rd., Fairfield, NJ 07004; phone: 201-882-6864; fax: 201-808-1742).

Keith Prowse & Co. (USA) Ltd. (234 W. 44th St., Suite 1000, New York, NY 10036; phone: 800-669-8687 or 212-398-1430; fax: 212-302-4251).

London Lodgings and Travel (3483 Golden Gate Way, Suite 211, Lafayette, CA 94549; phone: 800-366-8748 or 510-283-1142; fax: 510-283-1154).

Orion (c/o *B & V Associates,* address above).

Property Rentals International (1 Park W. Circle, Suite 108, Midlothian, VA 23113; phone: 800-220-3332 or 804-378-6054; fax: 804-379-2073).

Rent a Home International (7200 34th Ave. NW, Seattle, WA 98117; phone: 206-789-9377; fax: 206-789-9379).

Rent a Vacation Everywhere (*RAVE;* 383 Park Ave., Rochester, NY 14607; phone: 716-256-0760; fax: 716-256-2676).

Sterling Tours (2707 Congress St., Suite 2G, San Diego, CA 92110; phone: 800-727-4359 or 619-299-3010; fax: 619-299-5728).

Vacances en Campagne (22 Railroad St., Great Barrington, MA 10230; phone: 800-533-5405 or 413-528-6610; fax: 413-528-6222).

VHR Worldwide (235 Kensington Ave., Norwood, NJ 07648; phone: 201-767-9393 in New Jersey; 800-633-3284 elsewhere in the US; fax: 201-767-5510).

La Vie de Châteaux (c/o *B & V Associates,* address above).

Villas and Apartments Abroad (420 Madison Ave., Suite 1105, New York, NY 10017; phone: 212-759-1025 in New York State; 800-433-3020 elsewhere in the US; fax: 212-755-8316).

Villas International (605 Market St., Suite 510, San Francisco, CA 94105; phone: 800-221-2260 or 415-281-0910; fax: 415-281-0919).

HOME EXCHANGES

For comfortable, reasonable living quarters with amenities that no hotel could possibly offer, consider trading homes with someone abroad. The following companies provide information on exchanges:

Home Base Holidays (7 Park Ave., London N13 5PG, England; phone/fax: 44-181-886-8752).

Intervac US/International Home Exchange (PO Box 590504, San Francisco, CA 94159; phone: 800-756-HOME or 415-435-3497; fax: 415-386-6853).

Loan-A-Home (2 Park La., Apt. 6E, Mt. Vernon, NY 10552-3443; phone: 914-664-7640).

Vacation Exchange Club (PO Box 650, Key West, FL 33041; phone: 800-638-3841 or 305-294-3720; fax: 305-294-1448).

Worldwide Home Exchange Club (main office: 50 Hans Crescent, London SW1X 0NA, England; phone: 44-171-589-6055; US office: 806 Brantford Ave., Silver Spring, MD 20904; phone: 301-680-8950).

HOME STAYS

United States Servas (11 John St., Room 407, New York, NY 10038; phone: 212-267-0252; fax: 212-267-0292) maintains a list of hosts worldwide willing to accommodate visitors free of charge. The aim of this nonprofit cultural program is to promote international understanding and peace, and *Servas* emphasizes that member travelers should be interested mainly in their hosts, not in sightseeing, during their stays. Another organization offering home stays with French families is *Friends in France* (40 E. 19th St., Eighth Floor, New York, NY 10003; phone: 212-260-9820; fax: 212-228-0576).

Time Zone

France is in the Greenwich Plus 1 time zone—which means that the time is six hours later than it is in East Coast US cities. Like most Western European nations, France moves its clocks ahead an hour in the spring and back an hour in the fall, corresponding to daylight saving time, although the exact dates of the changes are different from those observed in the US. French timetables use a 24-hour clock to denote arrival and departure times, which means that hours are expressed sequentially from 1 AM—for example, in Paris, 1:30 PM would be "13:30 " or "13 h 30" ("13:30 heures" in French, "13:30 hours" in English).

Business and Shopping Hours

In Paris, most businesses and shops are open from 9 AM to 6 or 7 PM. Smaller retail establishments usually are open Tuesdays through Saturdays from 10 AM to noon, and from 2 to between 6 and 7 PM, and also may be open for a full or half day on Mondays. Some shops in Paris are open on Sundays from 9 AM to 5 PM. Department stores and other large emporia are open from about 9:30 AM to 6:30 or 7 PM (usually with no midday break), Mondays through Saturdays, and may stay open as late as 9 or 10 PM one or more days of the week; they also may offer additional hours during busy holiday seasons.

Banks in Paris usually are open weekdays from 9 AM to 4:30 PM, with some staying open until 6PM; some banks also may offer Saturday hours (usually from 9 AM to 3 PM). Money exchange houses, particularly at the airports, may stay open as late as 11 PM, seven days a week.

Holidays

France shuts down even more thoroughly than the US on public holidays. Banks, offices, stores, museums, and public monuments—even most gas stations—are closed tight. Banks and some offices may close as early as *noon* the day before a holiday. Below is a list of the French national holidays and the dates they will be observed this year. (Note that the dates of some holidays vary from year to year; others occur on the same day every year.)

> *New Year's Day* (January 1)
> *Easter Sunday* (April 16)
> *Easter Monday* (April 17)
> *Labor Day* (May 1)
> *V-E Day* (May 8)
> *Ascension Thursday* (May 25)
> *Whitmonday* (June 5)
> *Bastille Day* (July 14)
> *Feast of the Assumption* (August 15)
> *All Saints' Day* (November 1)
> *Armistice Day* (November 11)
> *Christmas Day* (December 25)

Mail

Post offices in France are indicated by signs reading *La Poste* and displaying a picture of a blue bird against a yellow background. The main post office in Paris (52 Rue du Louvre, Paris 75001 France; phone: 33-1-40-28-20-00; fax: 33-1-40-28-20-81) is open weekdays from 8 AM to 7 PM and Saturdays from 8 AM to noon. Branch offices have similar hours. Stamps also are sold at hotels, *tabacs* (tobacco shops), and some newsstands, as well as from public vending machines. Mailboxes (and stamp vending machines) are painted yellow.

Although letters sent to the US from France have been known to arrive in as little as five days, allow at least 10 days for delivery in either direction. If your correspondence is especially important, you may want to send it via an international courier service, such as *Federal Express* (phone: 800-238-5355 in the US; 05-33-33-55, toll-free, in France) or *DHL Worldwide Express* (phone: 800-225-5345 in the US; 05-20-25-25, toll-free, in France).

You can have mail sent to you care of your hotel (marked "Guest Mail, Hold for Arrival") or to a post office (the address should include *"Poste Restante,"* the French equivalent of "General Delivery"). *American Express* offices in Paris also will hold mail for customers ("c/o Client Letter Service"); information is provided in their pamphlet *Travelers' Companion*. Note that *US Embassies* and *Consulates* abroad will hold mail for US citizens *only* in emergency situations.

Telephone

Direct dialing and other familiar services are available in France. In addition, an increasing number of French homes are equipped with a phone computer called a *minitel,* which offers a wide range of services—from standard telephone listings to brief descriptions of films currently playing in Paris.

France is divided into two zones: Paris/Ile-de-France and the rest of the country (the provinces). All French telephone numbers have eight digits. For most destinations in France, these digits include the city code; however, for Paris/Ile-de-France, it is necessary to dial an additional city code of "1" before the eight-digit number. The procedures for making calls to, from, or within Paris and the rest of France are as follows:

> *To call a number in the Paris/Ile-de-France area from the US:* Dial 011 (the international access code) + 33 (the country code for France) + 1 + the local eight-digit number.
>
> *To call a number in the provinces (outside the Paris/Ile-de-France area) from the US:* Dial 011 (the international access code) + 33 (the country code for France) + the eight-digit number.
>
> *To call the US from anywhere in France:* Dial 19 (wait for a dial tone) + 1 (the US country code) + the area code + the local number.
>
> *To call the provinces from the Paris/Ile-de-France area:* Dial 16 (wait for a dial tone) + the eight-digit number.
>
> *To call the Paris/Ile-de-France area from the provinces:* Dial 16 (wait for a dial tone) + 1 + the eight-digit number.
>
> *To call within the Paris/Ile-de-France area:* Dial the eight-digit number (beginning with 4, 3, or 6—no extra "1"required).
>
> *To call between provinces or within a given province:* Dial the eight-digit number.

Public telephones are found in post offices, cafés, and booths on the street. Although some public telephones still take coins, in Paris and other major cities most accept only plastic phone debit cards called *télécartes.* These cards can be purchased at post offices, transportation centers, tobacco shops, and newsstands in France; they also can be purchased in the US from *Marketing Challenges International* (10 E. 21st St., Suite 600, New York, NY 10010; phone: 212-529-9069; fax: 212-529-4838).

Although you can use a telephone company calling card number on any phone, pay phones that take major credit cards (*American Express, MasterCard, Visa,* and so on) are increasingly common. Also available are combined telephone calling/bank credit cards, such as the *AT&T Universal Card* (PO Box 44167, Jacksonville, FL 32231-4167; phone: 800-423-4343). Similarly, *Sprint* (8140 Ward Pkwy., Kansas City, MO 64114; phone: 800-THE-MOST or 800-800-USAA) offers the *VisaPhone* program, through which you can add phone card privileges to your existing *Visa* card. Companies offering long-distance phone cards without additional credit card privileges include *AT&T* (phone: 800-CALL-ATT), *Executive Telecard International* (4260 E. Evans Ave., Suite 6, Denver, CO 80222; phone: 800-950-3800), *MCI* (323 Third St. SE, Cedar Rapids, IA 52401; phone: 800-444-4444; and 12790 Merit Dr., Dallas, TX 75251; phone: 800-444-3333), *Metromedia Communications* (1 International Center, 100 NE Loop 410, San Antonio, TX 78216; phone: 800-275-0200), and *Sprint* (address above).

Hotels routinely add surcharges to the cost of phone calls made from their rooms. Long-distance telephone services that may help you avoid this added expense are provided by a number of companies, including *AT&T* (International Information Service, 635 Grant St., Pittsburgh, PA 15219; phone: 800-874-4000), *MCI* (address above), *Metromedia Communications* (address above), and *Sprint* (address above). Note that even when you use such long-distance services, some hotels still may charge a fee for line usage.

AT&T's Language Line Service (phone: 800-752-6096) provides interpretive services for telephone communications in French and numerous other languages. Additional resources for travelers include the *AT&T 800 Travel Directory* (phone: 800-426-8686 for orders), the *Toll-Free Travel & Vacation Information Directory* (Pilot Books, 103 Cooper St., Babylon, NY 11702; phone: 516-422-2225; fax: 516-422-2227), and *The Phone Booklet* (Scott American Corporation, PO Box 88, W. Redding, CT 06896; no phone).

Important Phone Numbers

For emergency assistance:
    15 for an ambulance.
    17 for the police.
    18 for the fire department.

Local information and operator: 12.
International operator: 19, wait for dial tone, then 3311.

Electricity

France uses 220-volt, 50-cycle alternating current. Travelers from the US will need electrical converters to operate the appliances they use at home, or dual-voltage appliances, which can be switched from one voltage standard to another. (Some large tourist hotels may offer 110-volt current or may have converters available.) You also will need a plug adapter set to deal with the different plug configurations found in France.

Staying Healthy

For up-to-date information on current health conditions, call the Centers for Disease Control's *International Travelers' Hotline*: 404-332-4559.

Travelers to France face few serious health risks. Tap water generally is clean and potable throughout the country—if the water isn't meant for drinking, it should be marked *eau non potable.* Bottled water also is readily available in stores. Milk is pasteurized throughout France, and dairy products are safe to eat, as are fresh fruit, vegetables, meat, poultry, and fish. Because of Mediterranean pollution, however, all seafood should be eaten cooked, and make sure it is *fresh,* particularly in the heat of the summer, when inadequate refrigeration is an additional concern.

France has socialized medicine, and all hospitals are public facilities *(hôpitaux publiques).* Low-cost medical care is available to French citizens; however, visitors from the US and other countries that are not members of the European Economic Community (which provides reciprocal health coverage) will have to pay for most services.

French hospitals fall into three categories. At the top of the list is the *CHRU (Centre Hôpital Régional et Universitaire,* or Central Regional University Hospital), a large, full-service hospital associated with a major medical university. Others are the *CHR,* which designates a full-service regional hospital, and the *CH,* which means that the hospital is the central one in its town or city (and probably has 24-hour emergency service). There also are some private clinics *(cliniques privées),* which are like small hospitals and can provide medical aid for less serious conditions.

French drugstores, called *pharmacies,* are identified by a green cross out front. There should be no problem finding a drugstore in Paris; one that is open 24 hours is *Pharmacie Derhy* (in the *Galerie Les Champs,* 84 Av. des Champs-Elysées, Paris 75008; phone: 33-1-45-62-02-41; fax: 33-1-45-63-83-79). In France, night duty may rotate among local pharmacies—those that are closed provide the addresses of the nearest all-night drugstores in the window. Telephone operators and local hospitals also may have this information.

In Paris, the *American Hospital* (63 Bd. Victor Hugo, Neuilly-Sur-Seine 92200; phone: 33-1-46-41-25-25) provides advanced equipment and 24-hour emergency service; it also offers dental services. All of the staff speaks English and the hospital maintains an extensive network of English-speaking specialists.

Should you need non-emergency medical attention, ask at your hotel for the house physician or for help in reaching a doctor. Referrals also are available from the *US Embassy* or a *US Consulate.* In addition, *SOS Médecins* provides 24-hour house calls by doctors (phone: 33-1-47-07-77-77). English-speaking dentists in Paris include Dr. Edward Cohen (20 Rue de la Paix, Paris 75002, France; phone: 33-1-42-61-65-64) and Dr. Gérard Gautier (47 Av. Hoche, Paris 75008, France; phone: 33-1-47-66-17-10).

In an emergency: Go directly to the emergency room of the nearest hospital, dial one of the emergency numbers provided in *Telephone*, above, or call an operator for assistance. If possible, someone who can translate into French should make the call.

Additional Resources

InterContinental Medical (2720 Enterprise Pkwy., Suite 106, Richmond, VA 23294; phone: 804-527-1094; fax: 804-527-1941).

International Association for Medical Assistance to Travelers (*IAMAT;* 417 Center St., Lewiston, NY 14092; phone: 716-754-4883; and 40 Regal Rd., Guelph, Ontario N1K 1B5, Canada; phone: 519-836-0102; fax: 519-836-3412).

International Health Care Service (440 E. 69th St., New York, NY 10021; phone: 212 746-1601).

International SOS Assistance (PO Box 11568, Philadelphia, PA 19116; phone: 800-523-8930 or 215-244-1500; fax: 215-244-2227).

Medic Alert Foundation (2323 Colorado Ave., Turlock, CA 95382; phone: 800-ID-ALERT or 209-668-3333; fax: 209-669-2495).

Travel Care International (*Eagle River Airport,* PO Box 846, Eagle River, WI 54521; phone: 800-5-AIR-MED or 715-479-8881; fax: 715-479-8178).

TravMed (PO Box 10623, Baltimore, MD 21285-0623; phone: 800-732-5309 or 410-296-5225; fax: 410-825-7523).

Consular Services

The American Services section of the *US Consulate* is a vital source of assistance and advice for US citizens abroad. If you are injured or become seriously ill, the consulate can direct you to sources of medical attention and notify your relatives. If you become involved in a dispute that could lead to legal action, the consulate can provide a list of English-speaking attorneys. In cases of natural disasters or civil unrest, consulates handle the evacuation of US citizens if necessary.

The *US Embassy* is located at 2 Av. Gabriel, Paris 75008, France (phone: 33-1-42-96-12-02 or 33-1-42-61-80-75; fax: 33-1-42-66-97-83 or 33-1-42-65-05-33). The *Embassy*'s consular section is located at 2 Rue St. Florentin, Paris 75001, France (same phone and fax numbers as the *Embassy*).

The *US State Department* operates an automated 24-hour *Citizens' Emergency Center* travel advisory hotline (phone: 202-647-5225). You also can reach a duty officer at this number from 8:15 AM to 10 PM, eastern standard time on weekdays, and from 9 AM to 3 PM on Saturdays. At all other times, call 202-647-4000. For faxed travel warnings and other consular information, call 202-647-3000 using the handset on your fax machine; instructions will be provided. With a PC and a modem, you can access the consular affairs electronic bulletin board (phone: 202-647-9225).

Entry Requirements and Customs Regulations

ENTERING FRANCE

A valid US passport generally is the only document a US citizen needs to enter France, although immigration officers in French airports *may* ask for proof that you have sufficient funds for your trip, or to see a return or ongoing ticket. As a general rule, a passport entitles the bearer to remain in France for up to 90 days as a tourist. A visa is required for study, residency, work, or stays of more than three months. Proof of means of independent financial support is pertinent to the acceptance of any long-term–stay application. US citizens should contact the *French Embassy* or *Consulate* well in advance of their trip. Note that individuals for whom a visa is necessary also must obtain a *Carte de Séjour* (residency permit) at the local police prefecture upon arrival in France.

You are allowed to enter France with the following items duty-free: 200 cigarettes or 250 grams of tobacco; 50 cigars; up to 2 liters of wine and either 2 liters of liquor under 38.8 proof or 1 liter over 38.8 proof; 50 grams of perfume; a quarter of a liter of cologne; 500 grams of coffee; and 40 grams of tea. Items designated as gifts and valued at less than 300F (about $52 at press time) per item also can be brought into France duty-free; children under 15 can bring in gift items valued at less than 150F (about $26).

DUTY-FREE SHOPS

Located in international airports, duty-free shops provide bargains on the purchase of goods imported to France from other countries. But beware: Not all foreign goods are automatically less expensive. You *can* get a good deal on some items, but know what they cost elsewhere. Also note that although these goods are free of the duty that *French Customs* normally would assess, they will be subject to US import duty upon your return to the US (see below).

VALUE ADDED TAX (VAT)

Called *taxe à la valeur ajoutée (TVA)* in France, this sales tax (typically 18.6%) is applicable to most goods and services. Although everyone must pay the tax, foreigners often can obtain a partial refund if their purchases in a single store total at least 2,000F (about $345 at press time). Note that a refund is *not* applicable to purchases of certain goods such as food, wine, medicine, tobacco, and antiques and works of art worth over 30,000F— although the rules regarding artwork vary, depending on the age of the item.

Many stores participate in the *Europe Tax-Free Shopping (ETFS)* program, which enables visitors to obtain cash refunds at the airport upon departure. The procedure is as follows: Request a tax-free shopping voucher at the store when you make your purchase. At the airport, have this voucher stamped by *French Customs* officials, and then take it to the cash refund desk or agent (customs officials can direct you) for your refund.

If you purchase goods at a store that does not participate in the *ETFS* program, you still may be able to obtain a refund, although the procedure is somewhat more complicated and, unfortunately, subject to long delays. Request special refund forms for this purpose when making your purchase. These must be stamped by *French Customs* officials at the airport upon departure, and then mailed back to the *store,* which processes the refund. The refund will arrive—eventually—in the form of a check (usually in francs) mailed to your home or, if the purchase was made with a credit card, as a credit to your account.

Note that stores are under no obligation to participate in either of the VAT refund programs, so ask if you will be able to get a refund *before* making any purchases. For additional information, contact the French office of *Europe Tax-Free Shopping* (90 Rue Anatole France, Levallois 92300, France; phone: 33-1-47-48-03-22; fax: 33-1-47-48-04-96) or the French tourist authorities.

RETURNING TO THE US

You must declare to the *US Customs* official at the point of entry everything you have acquired in France. The standard duty-free allowance for US citizens is $400. If your trip is shorter than 48 continuous hours, or if you have been outside the US within 30 days of your current trip, the duty-free allowance is reduced to $25. Families traveling together may make a joint customs declaration. To avoid paying duty unnecessarily on expensive items (such as computer equipment) that you plan to take with you on your trip, register these items with *US Customs* before you depart.

A flat 10% duty is assessed on the next $1,000 worth of merchandise; additional items are taxed at a variety of rates (see *Tariff Schedules of the United States* in a library or any *US Customs Service* office). Some articles are duty-free only up to certain limits. The $400 allowance includes one carton of (200) cigarettes, 100 cigars (not Cuban), and one liter of liquor or wine (for those over 21); the $25 allowance includes 10 cigars, 50 cigarettes, and four ounces of perfume. With the exception of gifts valued at $50 or less sent directly to the recipient, *all* items shipped home are dutiable.

Antiques (at least 100 years old) and paintings or drawings done entirely by hand are duty-free. However, to take archaeological finds or other artifacts worth more than 998,100 francs (over $170,000) out of France, you must obtain a certificate from the *Musée de France* (60 Rue des Francs-Bourgeois, Paris 75003, France; phone: 33-1-40-27-60-96; fax: 33-1-40-27-66-45), and bring this certificate to the *Service des Titres du Commerce*

Extérieur (*SETICE;* 8 Rue de la Tour des Dames, Paris 75436, France; phone: 33-1-44-63-25-25; fax: 33-1-44-63-26-59), which will issue you an "authorization of exportation" permit.

FORBIDDEN IMPORTS

Note that US regulations prohibit the import of some goods sold abroad, such as fresh fruits and vegetables, most meat products (except certain canned goods), and dairy products (except for fully cured cheeses). Also prohibited are articles made from plants or animals on the endangered species list.

FOR ADDITIONAL INFORMATION Consult one of the following publications, available from the *US Customs Service* (PO Box 7407, Washington, DC 20044): *Currency Reporting; Importing a Car; International Mail Imports; Know Before You Go; Pets and Wildlife;* and *Pocket Hints. Travelers' Tips on Bringing Food, Plant, and Animal Products into the United States* is available from the *United States Department of Agriculture, Animal and Plant Health Inspection Service* (*USDA-APHIS:* 6505 Belcrest Rd., Room 613-FB, Hyattsville, MD 20782; phone: 301-436-7799; fax: 301-436-5221). For recorded information on customs-related topics, call 202-927-2095 from any touch-tone phone.

For Further Information

Branches of the *French Government Tourist Office* in the US are the best sources of travel information. Offices generally are open on weekdays, during normal business hours. Note, however, that these offices do not accept telephone inquiries. For information by phone, call the *French Government Tourist Office*'s telephone information line, *France on Call* (phone: 900-990-0040); the cost is 50¢ per minute. (There is no charge for information requested in person or by mail from tourist office branches.) A number of free publications also are available from the *French Government Tourist Office,* including the 1995 *France Discovery Guide* and the *American Express Welcome Center Directory.*

Once you have arrived in France, you can take advantage of a computerized information system called *minitel.* Computer terminals are available in the lobbies of most French hotels rated two stars or above, as well as in many post offices. In addition, *American Express* provides an English-language travel information hotline (phone: 05-20-12-02, toll-free, throughout France).

For information on entry requirements and customs regulations, contact the *French Embassy* or a *French Consulate* in the US.

The French Government Tourist Offices

California: 9454 Wilshire Blvd., Suite 715, Beverly Hills, CA 90212 (phone: 310-271-6665; fax: 310-276-2835).

Illinois: 676 N. Michigan Ave., Suite 3360, Chicago, IL 60611 (phone: 312-751-7800; fax: 312-337-6339).

New York: walk-in office: 628 Fifth Ave., Suite 222, New York, NY 10020 (phone: 212-757-1125; fax: 212-247-6468); mailing address: 610 Fifth Ave., New York, NY 10020.

The French Embassy and Consulates in the US

Embassy

Washington, DC: 4101 Reservoir Rd. NW, Washington, DC 20007 (phone: 202-944-6000; fax: 202-944-6212).

Consulates

California: *Consulate General,* 10990 Wilshire Blvd., Suite 300, Los Angeles, CA 90024 (phone: 310-479-4426; fax: 310-312-0704); *Consulate General,* 540 Bush St., San Francisco, CA 94108 (phone: 415-397-4330; fax: 415-433-8357).

Florida: *Consulate General,* 1 Biscayne Tower, 2 S. Biscayne Blvd., Suite 1710, Miami, FL 33131 (phone: 305-372-9798; fax: 305-372-9549).

Georgia: *Consulate General,* Marquis Tower II, 285 Peachtree Center Ave., Suite 2800, Atlanta, GA 30303 (phone: 404-522-4226; fax: 404-880-9408).

Illinois: *Consulate General,* 737 N. Michigan Ave., Suite 2020, Chicago, IL 60611 (phone: 312-787-5359, 312-787-5360, or 312-787-5361; recorded visa information: 312-787-7889; fax: 312-664-4196).

Louisiana: *Consulate General,* 300 Poydras St., Suite 2105, New Orleans, LA 70130 (phone: 504-523-5772; fax: 504-523-5725).

Massachusetts: *Consulate General,* visa applications: 20 Park Plaza, Suite 1123, Boston, MA 02116 (phone: 617-482-2864; fax: 617-426-9236); all other business: 3 Commonwealth Ave., Boston, MA 02116 (phone: 617-266-1680; fax: 617-437-1090).

New York: 934 Fifth Ave., New York, NY 10021 (phone: 212-606-3688; recorded visa information: 212-606-3644, 212-606-3652, or 212-606-3653; fax: 212-606-3670).

Texas: 2777 Allen Pkwy., Suite 650, Houston, TX 77019 (phone: 713-528-2181; fax: 713-528-1933).

The City

Paris

Victor Hugo, the great French poet and novelist, captured the true spirit of his native city when he called it "the heir of Rome, the mundane pilgrim's home away from home." If Rome, for all its earthly exuberance, never lets a visitor forget that it is the spiritual home of the West, Paris—with its supreme joie de vivre and its passion for eating, drinking, and dressing well—belongs unabashedly to the material world.

Paris always has attracted visitors and exiles from all corners of the earth. At the same time, it remains not so much a cosmopolitan city as a very French one, and a provincial one at that. Paris has its own argot, and each neighborhood retains its peculiar character, so that the great capital is still very much a city of 20 villages.

But parochialism aside—and forgetting about the consummate haughtiness of Parisians (someone once remarked that Parisians don't even like themselves)—the main attraction of the City of Light is its beauty. When you speak of the ultimate European city, it must be Paris, if only for the view from the Place de la Concorde or the *Tuileries* up the Champs-Elysées toward the *Arc de Triomphe,* or similarly striking sights beside the Seine. Here is the fashion capital of the world and the center of gastronomic invention and execution. Here the men all seem to swagger with the insouciance of privilege, and even the humblest shop girl dresses with the care of an haute couture mannequin. Paris is the reason "foreign" means "French" to so many travelers.

Paris, roughly elliptical in shape, is in the north-central part of France, in the rich agricultural area of the Seine River valley. With a population of over two million people, it is France's largest city, an industrial and commercial hub, an important river port, as well as an undisputed center for arts and culture. The city has more than doubled in size in the last century; however, the population has decreased during the past decade as residential buildings are converted to offices and the city becomes too expensive for all but the very rich. The ring of mid-19th-century fortifications that once were well beyond its boundaries now serves as the city limits. At the western edge of Paris is the vast *Bois de Boulogne* and to the east is the *Bois de Vincennes*—two enormous parks. Curving through Paris, the Seine divides the city into the northern Rive Droite (Right Bank) and southern Rive Gauche (Left Bank). The Rive Droite extends from the *Bois de Boulogne* on the far west, through Place Charles-de-Gaulle (also known as Place de l'Etoile), which surrounds the *Arc de Triomphe,* farther east to the *Jardin des Tuileries* (Tuileries Gardens) and the fabulous *Louvre,* and on to the stately Marais district. North of the *Louvre* is the area of the Grands Boulevards, centers of business and fashion; farther north is the district of Montmartre, built on a hill and crowned by the domed *Basilique du Sacré-*

Coeur (Basilica of the Sacred Heart), an area that has attracted artists since the days of Monet and Renoir.

The Rive Gauche sweeps from the *Tour Eiffel* (Eiffel Tower) in the west through the Quartier Latin (Latin Quarter), with its university and bohemian and intellectual community. Southwest of the Latin Quarter is Montparnasse, once inhabited by artists and intellectuals and laborers, now a large urban renewal project that includes a suburban-style shopping center around the *Tour Montparnasse* (Montparnasse Tower). To the south of Montparnasse are charming, turn-of-the-century, middle class residential districts.

In the middle of the Seine are two islands, the Ile de la Cité and the Ile St-Louis, the oldest parts of Paris. It was on the Ile de la Cité (in the 3rd century BC) that Celtic fishermen known as Parisii first built a settlement they named Lutetia, or "place surrounded by water." Caesar conquered the city for Rome in 52 BC, and in about AD 300, Paris was invaded by Germanic tribes, the strongest of which were the Franks. In 451, when Attila the Hun threatened to overrun Paris, a holy woman named Geneviève promised to defend the city by praying. She seems to have succeeded—the enemy decided to spare the capital—and Geneviève became the patron saint of Paris. Clovis I, the first Christian King of the Franks, made Paris his capital in the 6th century. As recently as last year, the city has yielded up evidence of this first ruling dynasty, the Merovingians; excavations in central Paris unearthed a spectacular burial site with nearly 60 tombs, including those of high-ranking Frankish dignitaries, dating from the 4th to the 7th centuries. The Merovingians gradually declined, and Paris's fortunes declined with them, until, in the mid-8th century, Pepin the Short took possession of the kingship. Pepin founded a new dynasty, the Carolingians, so named for his son, Charlemagne, who went on to rule not only France, but the entire Western world as head of the Holy Roman Empire. Still, after Charlemagne, relentless Norman sieges, famine, and plague curtailed the city's development, until at the end of the 10th century peace and prosperity were restored when the last of the now ineffectual Carolingian monarchs died, and Hugh Capet ascended the throne. The first of a long line of Capetian kings, Capet made Paris a great cultural center and seat of learning.

The Capetian monarchs contributed much to the growth of the city over the next few centuries. A defensive wall was begun in 1180 by Philip Augustus to protect the expanding Rive Droite business and trading center, as well as the intellectual quarter around the *Sorbonne,* the newly formed university on the Rive Gauche. He then built a new royal palace, the *Louvre,* just outside these ramparts, but never lived there. Medieval Paris was a splendid city, a leader in the arts and intellectual life of Europe. The *Sorbonne* attracted such outstanding scholars as Alexander of Hales, Giovanni di Fidanza (St. Bonaventure), Albertus Magnus, and Thomas Aquinas.

Work began on that splendid monument to medieval Paris, the *Cathédrale de Notre-Dame de Paris,* in 1163, under the direction of the energetic bishop of Paris, Maurice de Sully. The rest of the Ile de la Cité remained a warren of narrow streets and wood and plaster houses, but the banks of the Seine continued to be built up in both directions. Renaissance kings, patrons of the arts, added their own architectural and aesthetic embellishments to the flourishing city. Major streets were laid out; some of Paris's most charming squares were constructed; the Pont-Neuf, the first stone bridge spanning the Seine, was completed; and Lenôtre, the royal gardener, introduced proportion, harmony, and beauty with his extraordinary *Tuileries.*

Louis XIV, who was responsible for many of the most notable Parisian landmarks, including *Les Invalides,* moved the court to Versailles in the late 17th century (for more information on Versailles and the palace Louis XIV built there, see *Celebrated Cathedrals and ·Châteaux Within an Hour of Paris* in DIVERSIONS). Paris nevertheless continued to blossom, and it was under the Sun King's rule that France and Paris first won international prestige. Visitors were drawn to the city, luxury industries thrived, and the *Panthéon, Champ-de-Mars* parade ground, and *Ecole Militaire* were built. In 1785, at age 16, Napoleon Bonaparte graduated from the latter with the notation in his report: "Will go far if circumstances permit!"

French history reflects the conflict between the two extremes of the French character, both equally strong: a tradition of aristocracy and a penchant for revolution. The French aristocracy has erected some of the world's most magnificent palaces—the *Louvre,* the *Palais du Luxembourg,* and *Versailles.* But the French also have mounted their share of insurrections: from 1358, when the mob rebelled against the dauphin, to the Fronde in 1648–49, the 1830 and 1848 revolutions that reverberated throughout Europe, the Paris Commune of 1870–71, and the student rebellion of 1968, which nearly overthrew the Fifth Republic. The most profound uprising of all, of course, was the French Revolution of 1789.

That historic rebellion was set off by the excesses of the French court and the consummate luxury of the *Versailles* of Louis XIV, which cost the French people dearly in taxes and oppression. The Parisians, fiercely independent, forced the French king to his knees with their dramatic storming of the *Bastille* in 1789. Inspired by the ideas of the French and English philosophers of the Enlightenment, just as the American founding fathers were in 1776, the French soon overthrew their monarchy.

During the Revolution, unruly mobs damaged many of the city's buildings, including *Sainte-Chapelle* and *Notre-Dame,* which were not restored until the mid-19th century. Napoleon, who came to power in 1799, was too busy being a conqueror to complete all he planned, though he did manage to restore the *Louvre,* construct the *Arc de Triomphe du Carrousel* (Carrousel Triumphal Arch) and the Place Vendôme victory column, and begin work on the *Arc de Triomphe* and the *Madeleine.* Napoleon's conquests spread the new ideas of the Revolution—including the Code Napoléon, a system of laws embodying the ideals of "Liberty, Equality, Fraternity"—to places as far away as Canada and Moscow.

Later in the 19th century, the great urban planner Baron Haussmann set about reorganizing and modernizing Paris. He instituted the brilliant system of squares as focal points for marvelous, wide boulevards and roads; he planned the Place de l'Opéra, the *Bois de Boulogne* and *Bois de Vincennes,* the railway stations, and the system of 20 *arrondissements* (districts) that make up Paris today. He also destroyed most of the center of the old Cité, displacing 25,000 people.

During the peaceful lull between the Franco-Prussian War and World War I, Paris thrived as never before. These were the days of the Belle Epoque, the heyday of *Maxim's,* the *Folies-Bergère,* and the cancan. Montmartre, immortalized by Henri de Toulouse-Lautrec, was so uninhibited that the foreign press dubbed Paris the "City of Sin."

In the two decades before World War II, this free-spirited city attracted artistic exiles by the dozens: Picasso, Hemingway, Fitzgerald, and Gertrude Stein were just a few. Only in Paris could such avant-garde writers as James Joyce and D. H. Lawrence, and later, Henry Miller, find publishers. Paris witnessed the first Impressionist exhibition in 1874, which introduced Monet, Renoir, Pissarro, and Seurat, and heard the first performance of Stravinsky's revolutionary *Sacre du Printemps* (Rite of Spring) in 1913.

However avant-garde in other areas, Parisians are a conservative lot when it comes to changes in the appearance of their city. When the *Eiffel Tower* was built in 1889, Guy de Maupassant commented, "I spend all my afternoons on the *Eiffel Tower;* it's the only place in Paris from which I can't see it." Not long ago, Parisians grumbled about the ultramodern *Centre Georges-Pompidou,* now a locus for every type of applied and performing art, and about *Le Forum des Halles,* an underground shopping complex in what was once *Les Halles,* the raucous, lively produce market. Today these are popular tourist attractions, symbols of the new, modern Paris. More recent issues that have sparked criticism and controversy include the I. M. Pei glass pyramids that now form the entrance to the *Louvre,* and the project to replace the *Bibliothèque Nationale* with a giant, glass library, due to be completed next year. However, other recent projects have been more popular among Parisians: the face-lift of the formerly rather tacky Champs-Elysées; the creation of a primarily pedestrians-only zone in the glorious Place Vendôme, once virtually clogged with cars; and the ongoing refurbishment of the *Louvre,* which has already resulted in the new *Richelieu Wing,* the elegant, underground *Carrousel du Louvre* shopping complex, and improvements in the surrounding *Jardin des Tuileries.*

Parisians accept innovations reluctantly because they want their city to remain as it has always been. They love their remarkable heritage inordinately, and perhaps it is this love, together with the irrepressible sense of good living, that has made Paris so eternally attractive to others.

Paris At-a-Glance

SEEING THE CITY

It's impossible to single out just one perfect Paris panorama; they exist in profusion. The most popular is the bird's-eye view from the top of the *Eiffel Tower* on the Rive Gauche; there are several places to have snacks and drinks, as well as three restaurants where you can enjoy fine dining while taking in a view (on a clear day) of more than 50 miles. The tops of *Notre-Dame*'s towers offer close-ups of the cathedral's Gothic spires and flying buttresses, along with a magnificent view of the Ile de la Cité and the rest of Paris. The observatory of the *Tour Montparnasse* also presents a striking panorama.

The most satisfying vantage point, if not the highest, is the top of the *Arc de Triomphe*, which commands a view of the majestic sweep of Baron Haussmann's 12 stately avenues radiating from the Place Charles-de-Gaulle, including the splendid vista down the Champs-Elysées to the Place de la Concorde, with the *Louvre* beyond. Visitors can take the elevator or climb the 284 steps up. Other Rive Droite sites offering stunning views are the terrace of *Sacré-Coeur*, the landing at the top of the escalator at the *Centre Georges-Pompidou*, and the observation deck of *La Samaritaine*, the six-floor department store at the foot of the Pont-Neuf (see *Shopping*). For details on the other sites described above see *Special Places*.

Another spectacular cityscape can be seen from the *Grande Arche de la Défense*, to the west of the city (1 Cour de la Défense, Puteaux; phone: 49-07-27-57). The *Grande Arche* completes the axis that starts at the *Louvre* and runs through the Champs-Elysées and the *Arc de Triomphe*. It is open daily. There's an admission charge.

SPECIAL PLACES

Getting around this sprawling metropolis isn't difficult once you understand the layout of the 20 *arrondissements* (districts). A good way to orient oneself is to take one of the many excellent sightseeing tours offered by *Cityrama* or *Paris Vision* (see *Tours,* below, for details on both). Most bookshops and newsstands stock *Paris Indispensable* and *Plan de Paris par Arrondissement.* These little lifesavers list streets alphabetically and indicate the nearest *Métro* station on individual maps and an overall plan. Now you're ready to set out by foot (the most rewarding approach) or by *Métro* (the fastest and surest) to discover Paris for yourself.

Street addresses of the places mentioned throughout this chapter are followed by their *arrondissement* number.

JUST THE TICKET

The *Carte Musées et Monuments* (Museum and Monuments Pass) allows sightseers and art lovers to bypass ticket lines at 65 museums in and near

Paris (though it's not valid for certain special exhibits). Available in one-, three-, or five-day passes, the *carte* is sold in *Métro* stations, museums, at the *Office du Tourisme de Paris,* and at tourist office branches in major train stations (see *Tourist Information* for more on tourist offices). It's also available in the US from *Marketing Challenges International* (10 E. 21st St., Suite 600, New York, NY 10010; phone: 212-529-9069; fax: 212-529-4838). The *Caisse Nationale des Monuments Historiques et des Sites* (see *Le Marais,* below) offers a card good for a year of free visits to monuments and sites both in Paris and throughout France.

LA RIVE DROITE (THE RIGHT BANK)

ARC DE TRIOMPHE AND PLACE CHARLES-DE-GAULLE This monumental arch (165 feet high, 148 feet wide) was built between 1806 and 1836 to commemorate Napoleon's victories (it was then the largest monument of its kind in the world). Note the frieze and its six-foot-high figures—the 10 impressive sculptures symbolizing triumph, peace, and resistance, and especially Rude's *La Marseillaise,* on the right as you face the Champs-Elysées. Also note the arches inscribed with the names of Bonaparte's victories, as well as those of Empire heroes. Beneath the arch is the *Sépulture du Soldat Inconnu* (Tomb of the Unknown Soldier) with its eternal flame, which is rekindled daily at 6:30 PM. Inside the arch, there's a small museum featuring documents and engravings and an audiovisual presentation on the arch's history. A 284-step climb up to the platform at the top is rewarded by a magnificent view of the city, including the Champs-Elysées and the *Bois de Boulogne.* (The platform also can be reached by elevator.) The arch is the center of Place Charles-de-Gaulle, once Place de l'Etoile (Square of the Star), so called because it is the center of a "star," whose radiating points are the 12 broad avenues, including the Champs-Elysées, planned and built by Baron Haussmann in the mid-19th century. The arch is open daily. Admission charge. Pl. Charles-de-Gaulle, 8e (phone: 43-80-31-31).

CHAMPS-ELYSÉES Paris's legendary promenade, the "Elysian Fields," was swampland until 1616. It once was synonymous with all that was glamorous in the city, but the "Golden Arches" and schlocky shops have replaced much of the old *élégance.* Happily, the restoration and greening of what Parisians call the "Champs" have brought back some of the avenue's former cachet. The Champs-Elysées stretches for more than 2 miles between the Place de la Concorde and the Place Charles-de-Gaulle. The broad avenue, lined with rows of chestnut trees, shops, cafés, and cinemas, still is perfect for strolling, window shopping, and people watching. The area from the Place de la Concorde to the Rond-Point des Champs-Elysées is a charming park, where Parisians often bring their children. On the north side of the gardens is the *Palais de l'Elysée* (Elysée Palace), the official home of the President of the French Republic. Ceremonial events, such as the *Bastille Day Parade* (July 14), frequently take place along the Champs-Elysées.

GRAND PALAIS (GREAT PALACE) Off the Champs-Elysées, on opposite sides of Avenue Winston-Churchill, are the elaborate turn-of-the-century *Grand Palais* and *Petit Palais* (see below), built of glass and stone for the *1900 World Exposition.* With its stone columns, mosaic frieze, and flat glass dome, the *Grand Palais* contains the *Galeries Nationales,* a large area devoted to temporary exhibits, as well as the *Palais de la Découverte,* a science museum and planetarium. Parts of the *Grand Palais* will be closed for structural repairs throughout this year. The *Galeries Nationales* are closed Tuesdays; the *Palais de la Découverte* is closed Mondays. Admission charge for both. Av. Winston-Churchill, 8e (phone: 44-13-17-17).

PETIT PALAIS (LITTLE PALACE) Built at the same time as the *Grand Palais,* it has exhibits on the city's history and a variety of fine and applied arts, plus special shows. Closed Mondays and holidays. Admission charge. Av. Winston-Churchill, 8e (phone: 42-65-12-73).

PLACE DE LA CONCORDE Surely one of the most magnificent in the world, this square is grandly situated in the midst of equally grand landmarks: the *Louvre* and the *Tuileries* on one side, the Champs-Elysées and the *Arc de Triomphe* on another, the Seine and the Napoleonic *Palais Bourbon* on a third, and the pillared façade of the *Madeleine* on the fourth. Designed by Gabriel for Louis XV, the elegant square was where his unfortunate successor, Louis XVI, lost his head to the guillotine, as did Marie-Antoinette, Danton, Robespierre, Charlotte Corday, and others. It was first named for Louis XV, then called Place de la Révolution by the triumphant revolutionaries. Its present name, "Concorde," or "peace," signifies France's hope of overcoming the violent history that the square symbolized. Ornamenting the square, the eight colossal statues represent important French provincial capitals, while the 3,300-year-old, 220-ton, 75-foot-high *l'Obélisque de Louqsor* (Obelisk of Luxor) was a gift from Egypt in 1831.

JARDIN DES TUILERIES (TUILERIES GARDENS) Carefully laid out in patterned geometric shapes, with clipped shrubbery and formal flower beds, statues, and fountains, this is one of the finest examples of French garden design (in contrast to informal English gardens, exemplified by the *Bois de Boulogne*). It is currently undergoing extensive renovations, due to be completed in 1997. Along the Seine, between the Place de la Concorde and the *Louvre.*

ORANGERIE A museum on the southwestern edge of the *Jardin des Tuileries,* it displays Monet's celebrated paintings of water lilies, plus the art collection of Jean Walter and Paul Guillaume, with works by Cézanne, Renoir, Matisse, Picasso, and others. Closed Tuesdays. Admission charge. Pl. de la Concorde and Quai des Tuileries, 1er (phone: 42-97-48-16).

JEU DE PAUME (THE TENNIS COURT) This building was refurbished and reopened as a gallery for contemporary art in 1991 as part of the *Louvre* renovation project that began with the opening of the I. M. Pei pyramids. Facing the Place de la Concorde on the northeastern corner of the *Tuileries* opposite the *Orangerie*—and originally an indoor tennis court for France's royalty—the *Jeu de Paume* is the site where, in 1789, delegates met to declare their independence, marking the beginning of the French Revolution (perhaps best commemorated in Jacques-Louis David's famous painting *The Tennis Court Oath,* which hangs in the *Louvre*). Previously home to the *Louvre*'s Impressionist collection (now in the *Musée d'Orsay; see below*), the extensively modernized museum houses exhibitions of contemporary works from 1960 on, including those of Takis, Broodthears, and Dubuffet. It also has video and conference areas, as well as a bookstore and cafeteria. Closed Mondays and weekday mornings. Admission charge. Pl. de la Concorde, 1er (phone: 47-03-12-50).

RUE DE RIVOLI Running along the north side of the *Louvre* and the *Jardin des Tuileries,* this elegant but car-clogged old street has perfume shops, souvenir stores, boutiques, bookstores, cafés, and such hotels as the *Meurice* and the *Inter-Continental* under its 19th-century arcades. The section facing the *Tuileries,* from the Place de la Concorde to the *Louvre,* is an especially good place to explore on rainy days, although much of the merchandise sold here is not of the highest quality.

LOUVRE This colossus on the Seine, born in 1200 as a fortress and transformed over the centuries from Gothic mass to Renaissance palace, served as the royal residence in the 16th and 17th centuries. It was then supplanted by suburban *Versailles,* becoming a museum in 1793 after the Revolution. It was Napoleon who later turned it into a glittering warehouse of artistic booty from the nations he conquered. Today, its 200 galleries cover some 40 acres; to view all 297,000 items in the collections in no more than the most cursory fashion, it would be necessary to walk some 8 miles.
In addition to the *Mona Lisa, Venus de Milo,* and the *Winged Victory of Samothrace,* the *Louvre* has many delights that are easily overlooked—Vermeer's *Lace Maker* and Holbein's *Portrait of Erasmus,* for instance; not to mention van der Weyden's *Braque Triptych,* Ingres's *Turkish Bath,* Dürer's *Self-Portrait,* Cranach's naked and red-hatted *Venus,* and the exquisite 4,000-year-old Egyptian woodcarving known as the *Handmaiden of the Dead.* More of our favorites include Michelangelo's *The Dying Slave* and *The Bound Slave,* Goya's *Marquesa de la Solana,* Watteau's clown *Gilles* and his *Embarkation for Cythera,* Raphael's great portrait *Baldassare Castiglione,* Veronese's *Marriage at Cana,* Titian's masterpiece *Man with a Glove,* both *The Penitent Magdalen* and *The Card Sharps* by Georges de la Tour, Rembrandt's *Bathsheba,* and Frans Hals's *Bohemian Girl.* Also be sure to save time for any one of David's glories: *Madame Récamier, The Oath of the Horatii, The Lictors Bringing Back to Brutus the Body of His Son,* or *The*

Coronation of Napoleon and Josephine. And don't miss *Liberty Leading the People* and *The Bark of Dante,* both by Delacroix, and Courbet's *The Artist's Studio, Burial at Ornans,* and *Stags Fighting.*

Nor is the outside of this huge edifice to be overlooked. Note especially the *Cour Carrée* (the courtyard of the old *Louvre*), the southwest corner of which is the oldest part of the palace (dating from the mid-1550s) and a beautiful example of the Renaissance style that François I had so recently introduced from Italy. Renovation of the *Cour Carrée* and other sections of the museum are in progress and will continue through 1997, but most of the external walls have already been cleaned. Note, too, the *Colonnade,* which forms the eastern front of the *Cour Carrée,* facing the Place du Louvre; classical in style, it dates from the late 1660s, not too long before the Sun King left for *Versailles.* Newer wings of the *Louvre* embrace the palace gardens, in the midst of which stands the *Arc de Triomphe du Carrousel,* erected by Napoleon. From here, the vista across the *Tuileries* and the Place de la Concorde and on up the Champs-Elysées to the *Arc de Triomphe* is one of the most beautiful in Paris. I. M. Pei's glass pyramids, completed in 1989, sit center stage in the *Louvre*'s grand interior courtyard, and the largest of the trio now is the museum's main entrance. The controversial structure houses the *Louvre*'s underground shops and galleries connecting the north and south wings (the addition increased the museum's exhibition space by nearly 80%). Last year, the new *Richelieu Wing* opened, a stunning example of museum architecture just off the main *Louvre* entrance beneath the pyramid, as did the upscale *Carrousel du Louvre* shopping complex under the *Arc de Triomphe du Carrousel* (see *Shopping*).

Good guided tours in English, covering the highlights of the *Louvre,* are frequently available, but be sure to check in advance. Closed Tuesdays. Admission charge. Pl. du Louvre, 1er (phone: 40-20-51-51 for recorded information in French and English; 40-20-50-50 for more detailed information).

FINE PRINTS

For a modest price, you can take home your own work of art from the *Louvre.* The museum's 200-year-old *Chalcographie du Louvre* (Department of Chalcography) houses a collection of 16,000 engraved copper plates—renderings of monuments, battles, coronations, Egyptian pyramids, and portraits—dating from the 17th century. Prints made from these engravings come reproduced on thick vellum, embossed with the *Louvre*'s imprint. The *Chalcographie du Louvre* (closed mornings and Tuesdays) is one flight up from the *Porte Barbet de Jouy* entrance on the Seine side of the *Louvre.*

PLACE VENDÔME Just north of the *Tuileries* is one of the loveliest squares in Paris, the octagonal Place Vendôme, designed by Mansart in the 17th century. Now primarily a pedestrian zone, its arcades contain world-famous jewelers, perfumers, and banks, the *Ritz* hotel, and the *Ministère de Justice* (Ministry of Justice). The 144-foot column in the center is covered with bronze from the 1,200 cannon that Napoleon captured at Austerlitz in 1805. Just off Place Vendôme is the famous Rue du Faubourg-St-Honoré, one of the oldest streets in Paris, which now holds elegant shops selling the world's most expensive made-to-order items. To the north is the Rue de la Paix, noted for its jewelers.

LA MADELEINE Starting in 1764, the *Eglise Ste-Marie-Madeleine* (Church of St. Mary Magdalene) was built and razed twice before the present structure was commissioned by Napoleon in 1806 to honor his armies. The design of the recently cleaned and restored church is based on that of a Greek temple, with 65-foot-high Corinthian columns supporting the sculptured frieze. The bronze doors are adorned with illustrations of the Ten Commandments, and inside there are many distinctive murals and sculptures. From its portals, the view extends down Rue Royale to Place de la Concorde and over to the dome of *Les Invalides.* Nearby are some of Paris's most tantalizing food shops. Open daily. Free concerts are held two Sundays per month at 4 PM. Pl. de la Madeleine, 8e (phone: 42-65-52-17).

OPÉRA/PALAIS GARNIER When it was completed in 1875, this imposing rococo edifice was touted as the largest theater in the world (though with a capacity of only 2,156, it holds fewer people than the *Vienna Opera House* or *La Scala* in Milan). Designed by Charles Garnier, it covers nearly three acres and took 13 years to complete. The façade is decorated with sculpture, including a copy of Carpeaux's *The Dance* (the original is now in the *Musée d'Orsay*). The ornate interior has an impressive grand staircase, a beautiful foyer, lavish marble from every quarry in France, and Marc Chagall's controversially decorated dome. These days, the opera house is home to the *Ballet de l'Opéra de Paris,* while most operatic performances are now held at the *Opéra de la Bastille* (below). At press time, the *Opéra* was closed for renovations through March 1996 at the earliest. Daytime visits may still be possible through the early part of this year. Call ahead for the current status of the renovations. Pl. de l'Opéra, 9e (phone: 40-01-24-93).

BASILIQUE DU SACRÉ-COEUR (BASILICA OF THE SACRED HEART) AND MONTMARTRE Built on the Butte Montmartre—the highest of Paris's seven hills—the white-domed *Basilique du Sacré-Coeur* provides an extraordinary view from its steps, especially at dawn or sunset. The church's Byzantine interior is rich and ornate, though light and well proportioned. Note the huge mosaics, one depicting Christ and the Sacred Heart over the high altar; another, the Archangel Michael and Joan of Arc; and a third, Louis XVI and his family. One of the largest and heaviest bells (19 tons) in Christendom is housed in the tall bell tower to the north. The church, including the cupola, is open daily. 35 Rue Chevalier-de-la-Barre (phone: 42-51-17-02).

The area around *Sacré-Coeur* was the artists' quarter of late 19th- and early 20th-century Paris, and the streets still look the same as they do in the paintings of Utrillo. The site of the last of Paris's vineyards (a boisterous fete is held here during October harvest), Montmartre contains old houses, narrow alleys, steep stairways, and carefree cafés enough to provide a full day's entertainment. And at night the district still comes alive as it did in the days of Toulouse-Lautrec, who immortalized Montmartre's notoriously frivolous Belle Epoque nightlife, particularly the dancers and personalities at the *Moulin Rouge,* in his paintings. The Place du Tertre, where Braque, Dufy, Modigliani, Picasso, Rousseau, and Utrillo once lived, is still charming, but go early in the day; later, it fills up with tourists and mostly under-talented artists. Spare yourself most of the climb to *Sacré-Coeur* by taking the modern glass funicular, for which the fare is one *Métro* ticket, or the Montmartre bus (marked with an icon of *Sacré-Coeur* on the front instead of a number) from Place St-Pierre. Butte Montmartre, 18e.

LES HALLES The *Central Market* ("the Belly of Paris") that once stood on this 80-acre site northeast of the *Louvre* was razed in 1969. Gone are the picturesque early-morning fruit-and-vegetable vendors, butchers in blood-spattered aprons, and truckers bringing the freshest produce from all over France. In their places are the trendy shops and galleries of youthful entrepreneurs and artisans, small restaurants with lots of charm, the world's largest subway station, acres of trellised gardens and playgrounds, and *Le Forum des Halles,* a vast, mainly underground complex of boutiques, as well as concert space and movie theaters. Touch-sensitive locator devices, which help visitors find products and services, are placed strategically throughout the complex. Rue Pierre-Lescot and Rue Rambuteau, 1er. Also see *Walk 6: Beaubourg, Les Halles, and the Hôtel de Ville* in DIRECTIONS.

LE CENTRE NATIONAL D'ART ET DE CULTURE GEORGES-POMPIDOU (GEORGES POMPIDOU NATIONAL ART AND CULTURAL CENTER) Better known as "Beaubourg," after the street it faces and the *quartier* it replaced, this stark, six-level creation of steel and glass, with its exterior escalators and blue, white, and red pipes, created a stir the moment its construction began. Outside, a computerized digital clock ticks off the seconds remaining until the 21st century. The wildly popular cultural center brings together contemporary art in all its forms—painting, sculpture, industrial design, music, literature, cinema, and theater—under one roof. In addition to housing the *Musée National d'Art Moderne* (National Museum of Modern Art) and the *Centre de Création Industrielle* (Industrial Design Center), it also boasts a public information library and the *Institut de Recherches et de Coordination Acoustique/Musique* (IRCAM; Institute for Acoustic and Musical Research). The scene in the front courtyard, which serves as an impromptu stage for jugglers, mimes, acrobats, and magicians, often rivals the exhibits inside, which this year include special exhibitions of the work of Constantin Brancusi and Louise Bourgeois. On the fifth floor there's a cafeteria-style restaurant, and you can step outside for one of the most exciting views in Paris.

A massive renovation project, expected to cost more than $100 million, begins this year with work on the exterior of the center and on adjoining areas and buildings. Work on the interior is not slated to begin until 1997. The center as a whole will remain open throughout the project; sections under renovation will close in turn. Closed Tuesdays, weekday mornings, and May 1. Admission charge for the *Musée National d'Art Moderne* and for special exhibitions only; no admission charge on Sundays. Entrances on Rue de Beaubourg and Rue St-Martin, 4e (phone: 44-78-12-33).

LE MARAIS A marshland until the 16th century, this district east of the *Louvre* in the 4th *arrondissement* became a fashionable neighborhood during the 17th century. As the aristocracy moved on it fell into disrepair, but over the last 30 years the Marais has been enjoying a complete face-lift. Preservationists have lovingly restored more than 100 of the magnificent old *hôtels* (in this sense the word means private mansions or townhouses) to their former grandeur. Exquisitely beautiful, with muraled walls and ceilings, many host theater and music performances in their courtyards during the summer *Festival du Marais*. Among the *hôtels* to note are the *Hôtel Salé*, which now houses the *Musée Picasso* (see below); the *Hôtel de Soubise*, now the *Archives Nationales* (National Archives; 60 Rue des Francs-Bourgeois), with its 14th-century *Porte de Clisson* (58 Rue des Archives); and the *Hôtels d'Aumont* (7 Rue de Jouy); *Guénégaud*, designed by Mansart (60 Rue des Archives); *de Rohan* (87 Rue Vieille-du-Temple); *de Sens* (1 Rue du Figuier); and *de Sully* (62 Rue St-Antoine). The *Caisse Nationale des Monuments Historiques et des Sites* (National Commission for Historic Monuments and Sites), housed in the *Hôtel de Sully*, offers tours on weekends plus a pass good for a year of free visits to sites of interest in Paris and throughout France (phone: 44-61-21-50 for general information; 44-61-21-69/70 for information on tours). Also see *Walk 7: The Marais* in DIRECTIONS.

PLACE DES VOSGES In the Marais district, the oldest square in Paris—and also one of the most beautiful—was completed in 1612 by order of Henri IV, with its houses elegantly "built to a like symmetry." Though many of the houses have been rebuilt inside, their original façades remain, and the restored square is one of Paris's enduring delights. Corneille and Racine lived here, and at No. 6 is the *Maison de Victor Hugo*, once the writer's home and now a museum. It's closed Mondays and holidays. Admission charge (phone: 42-72-10-16).

MUSÉE CARNAVALET Also in the Marais, this once was the home of Mme. de Sévigné, a noted 17th-century writer, and is now a museum with beautifully arranged exhibits covering the history of the city of Paris from the days of Henri IV to the present. The museum's name is derived from that of an earlier owner of the building, the widow of François de Kernevenoy (corrupted to Carnavalet), tutor to Henri III, who bought the *hôtel* in 1572. It was built in 1550 by the architect Pierre Lescot, and over the years had many embellishments added by other architects. The museum's expansion through the *lycée* next door and into the neighboring *Hôtel Le Peletier de Saint-Fargeau* doubled the exhibition space, making it the largest museum in the world devoted to the history of a single capital city. The expansion created space for a major permanent exhibit on the French Revolution, and a new wing is set to open to house recent archaeological finds, including Neolithic canoes discovered during excavations at the Bercy development. Also watch for special exhibitions and occasional concerts. The gift shop offers a wealth of interesting items, from T-shirts to objets d'art; there's also an excellent bookstore. Closed Mondays. No admission charge on Sundays. 23 Rue de Sévigné, 3e (phone: 42-72-21-13).

MUSÉE PICASSO A portion of the collection with which Picasso could never bring himself to part is displayed here in the beautiful, 17th-century *Hôtel Salé* (the building is as interesting as the artwork it houses). More than 200 paintings, 3,000 drawings and engravings, and other objets d'art related to the great artist are arranged here in chronological order. These works provide a panoramic overview of the career of perhaps the century's greatest artist, from the contemplative self-portrait painted in shades of blue in 1921, through the Cubist newspapers and guitars, to the 1961 iron-sheet sculpture of a soccer player that looks like an ice cream on a stick. Especially interesting is Picasso's own collection of works by other artists, including Cézanne, Braque, and Rousseau. There are also films on Picasso's life and work. Be sure to see the lovely fountain by Simounet in the formal garden. Closed Tuesdays. Admission charge. 5 Rue de Thorigny, 3e (phone: 42-71-25-21).

OPÉRA DE LA BASTILLE In sharp contrast to Garnier's *Opéra* is the curved glass façade of 20th-century architect Carlos Ott's opera house. Set against the historic landscape of the Bastille quarter, this austere, futuristic structure houses over 30 acres of multipurpose theaters, shops, and urban promenades. It looks a lot like its namesake, the prison-fortress the storming of which ignited the French Revolution. Pl. de la Bastille, 11e (phone: 44-73-13-00).

AMERICAN CENTER AND BERCY A Parisian venue for performing artists from the US since 1931, the *American Center* reopened last year (after a seven-year hiatus) in a futuristic new building designed by Frank Gehry. The center (51 Rue de Bercy, 12e; phone: 44-73-77-77; fax: 44-73-77-55) comprises a theater, a cinema, a restaurant, a bookstore, classrooms, and performance and gallery spaces. Through an eclectic program of avant-garde dance, music, film, and art, it aims to encourage cross-cultural relations between the US and the rest of the world. It's closed Tuesdays. Admission charge for performances and special exhibits.

The *American Center* is located in eastern Paris's Bercy development, formerly a wine depot, now also the site of France's *Ministère des Finances* and the *Palais Omnisports de Paris-Bercy,* a large sports complex. The much-talked-about new *Bibliothèque Nationale* (National Library) is slated to open here next year.

BOIS DE VINCENNES Designed as a counterpart to the *Bois de Boulogne* (see below), this park and zoological garden was laid out during Napoleon III's time on the former hunting grounds of the 14th-century *Château de Vincennes,* which encompassed 2,300 acres on the city's east side. Visit the château and its lovely chapel, the large garden, and the zoo, with animals in their natural habitats. Located on the eastern edge of the *Bois de Vincennes* is the *Musée des Arts Africains et Océaniens* (Museum of African and Polynesian Art; see *Museums*).

CIMETIÈRE PÈRE-LACHAISE (PÈRE-LACHAISE CEMETERY) With over 100,000 tombs, sepulchers, and monuments, this is the most famous of France's cemeteries. Set in a wooded park, it's the final resting place of such illustrious personalities as Oscar Wilde, Edith Piaf, Marcel Proust, and Sarah Bernhardt. Purchase a map at the entrance before following the bizarre parade of adoring fans to the grave of rock star Jim Morrison of the *Doors.* (Section 27). It's hard to miss the legions of resident cats. Open daily. No admission charge. Bd. de Ménilmontant at Rue de la Roquette, 20e (phone: 43-70-70-33).

LA VILLETTE The *Cité des Sciences et de l'Industrie* (City of Sciences and Industry), a celebration of technology, stands in the *Parc de la Villette* on the northeastern edge of the capital and houses a planetarium, the spherical *Géode* cinema (see *Film*), lots of hands-on displays, and a half-dozen exhibitions at any given time. Also here is the *Cinaxe,* a movie theater that simulates a rocket launch—a must for children, as is a nearby futuristic playground. The *Cité de la Musique* (see *Museums*) and several restaurants and snack bars are also on the park grounds. Closed Mondays. Admission charge. 30 Av. Corentin-Cariou, 19e (phone: 40-05-70-00).

BOIS DE BOULOGNE Originally part of the Forest of Rouvre, on the western edge of Paris, this 2,140-acre park was planned along English lines by Napoleon. It's a great place to ride a horse or a bike, row a boat, trap shoot, go bowling, picnic on the grass, see horse races at *Auteuil* and *Longchamp,* visit a children's amusement park (*Jardin d'Acclimatation*) or a zoo, see a play, walk to a waterfall, or just smell the roses. A particularly lovely spot is the *Bagatelle* château and park; a former residence of Marie-Antoinette, it boasts a magnificent rose garden (on the Rte. de Sèvres in Neuilly, 16e; phone: 40-67-97-00). Avoid the *Bois* after dark, when it becomes a playground for prostitutes and transvestites who actively solicit passersby. Recent attempts by the French government to stop the nighttime activity by banning cars from the park have begun to alleviate the situation. The park is open daily; the château is closed November through mid-March. Admission charge to the château.

PALAIS DE CHAILLOT Built for the *Paris Exposition of 1937* (on the site of the old *Palais du Trocadéro* left over from the *Exposition of 1878*), this structure houses a theater, a *Cinémathèque* (phone: 47-04-24-24), and four museums—the *Musée du Cinéma* (Film Museum; phone: 45-53-74-39); the *Musée de l'Homme* (Museum of Man; phone: 44-05-72-72) with anthropological exhibits; the *Musée de la Marine* (Maritime Museum; phone: 45-53-31-70); and the *Musée des Monuments Français* (Museum of French Monuments; phone: 44-05-39-10), featuring reproductions of monuments. The terraces offer excellent views across gardens, fountains, and the Seine to the *Eiffel Tower* on the Rive Gauche. Closed Tuesdays and major holidays. Admission charge. Pl. du Trocadéro, 16e.

LA RIVE GAUCHE (THE LEFT BANK)

TOUR EIFFEL (EIFFEL TOWER) It is impossible to imagine the Paris skyline without this mighty symbol, yet what has been called Gustave Eiffel's folly was never meant to be permanent. Originally built for the *Universal Exposition of 1889,* it was due to be torn down in 1909, but was saved because of the development of the wireless—the first transatlantic wireless telephones were operated from the 984-foot tower in 1916 (the addition of television antennae in 1957 brought the tower's height up to 1,051 feet). It was the tallest building in the world until New York's Empire State Building (1,284 feet) was completed in 1930. Extensive renovations have taken place in more recent years (including modernized elevators); and a post office, three restaurants, and a few boutiques have opened on the first-floor landing. We recommend the one-Michelin-star *Jules Verne* restaurant, though it is pricey and requires reservations a month or two in advance. It's open daily (phone: 45-55-61-44; fax: 47-05-29-41). On a really clear day, it's possible to see for 50 miles. Open daily. Admission charge. *Champ-de-Mars,* 7e (phone: 45-50-34-56).

LES INVALIDES Founded by Louis XIV in the 1670s as an asylum for wounded and aged soldiers, this vast structure was initially intended to house 4,000; it more often was a refuge for twice that number. The classically balanced buildings were designed by Libéral Bruant and have more than 10 miles of corridors. The royal *Eglise du Dôme* (Church of the Dome), part of the complex, was constructed from 1675 to 1706 and is topped by an elaborate golden dome designed by Mansart. Besides being a masterpiece of the 17th century, the church contains the impressive red-and-green granite *Tombeau de Napoléon Ier* (Tomb of Napoleon; admission charge). The monument is surrounded by 12 huge white marble statues, interspersed with 54 flags, each symbolizing one of Napoleon's victories. The church also has an impressive courtyard and noteworthy frescoes. In addition, at *Les Invalides* is the *Musée de l'Armée,* one of the world's richest museums, displaying arms and armor along with mementos of French military history. For yet another splendid Parisian view, approach the building from the Pont Alexandre III (Alexander III Bridge). Open daily. Admission charge. Av. de Tourville, Pl. Vauban, 7e (phone: 45-55-37-70).

MUSÉE RODIN This is one of France's most complete and satisfying museum experiences. By ambling through one of the great 18th-century Parisian aristocratic homes and its grounds, it's possible to follow the evolution of the career of Auguste Rodin, that genius of modern sculpture. Along the broad terraces and in the serene and elegant gardens are scattered fabled statues such as The Thinker and the *Bourgeois de Calais;* the superb statues of Honoré de Balzac and Victor Hugo; the stunning *Gate of Hell,* on which the master labored a lifetime; *Les Bavardes,* a sculpture by Rodin's mistress Camille Claudel; and more. Rodin's celebrated Ugolin group is placed dramatically in the middle of a pond. The museum boutique sells reproductions of the major works. Closed Mondays. Admission charge. 77 Rue de Varenne, 7e (phone: 47-05-01-34).

MONTPARNASSE In the early 20th century, this neighborhood south of the *Jardin du Luxembourg* (Luxembourg Gardens) hosted a colony of avant-garde painters, writers, and Russian political exiles. Here Hemingway, Picasso, and Scott and Zelda Fitzgerald sipped and supped in such bars and cafés as *La Closerie des Lilas* (see *Nightclubs and Nightlife*); *Le Dôme* (108 Bd. du Montparnasse, 14e; phone: 43-35-25-81); *La Rotonde* (105 Bd. du Montparnasse; phone: 43-26-48-26 or 43-26-68-84); and *La Coupole* and *Le Select* (see *Eating Out* for both). The cafés, small restaurants, and winding streets still exist in the shadow of the *Tour Montparnasse* complex (see below).

TOUR MONTPARNASSE (MONTPARNASSE TOWER) This giant complex dominates Montparnasse. Each day the fastest elevator in Europe whisks Parisians and tourists alike up 59 stories (for a fee) to catch a view *down* at the *Eiffel Tower.* The shopping center here boasts all the famous names, and the surrounding office buildings are the headquarters of some of France's largest companies. 33 Av. du Maine, 15e, and Bd. de Vaugirard, 14e (phone: 45-38-52-56).

MUSÉE D'ORSAY This imposing former railway station has been transformed into one of the shining examples of modern museum design. Its eclectic collection includes not only the Impressionist paintings formerly displayed in the *Jeu de Paume* (see above), but also less sacred 19th-century achievements in sculpture, photography, and the applied arts, which together provide an excellent overview of the Victorian aesthetic. Masterpieces by Degas, Toulouse-Lautrec, Monet, and others hang in specially designed spaces, and no detail of light, humidity, or acoustics has been left to chance, making this voyage around the art world a very comfortable one. Don't miss the museum's pièce de résistance—the van Goghs on the top floor, glow-ing under the skylight. Closed Mondays. Admission charge is reduced on Sundays. 1 Rue de Bellechasse, 7e (phone: 40-49-48-14).

EGLISE ST-GERMAIN-DES-PRÉS (CHURCH OF ST.-GERMAIN-IN-THE-FIELDS) AND THE QUARTIER ST-GERMAIN-DES-PRÉS Probably the oldest church in Paris, it once belonged to an abbey of the same name. The original basilica, completed in AD 558, was destroyed and rebuilt many times. The Romanesque steeple and its massive tower date from 1014. Inside, the choir and sanctuary are as they were in the 12th century, and the marble shafts used in the slender columns are 14 centuries old. Pl. St-Germain-des-Prés, 6e (phone: 43-25-41-71).

Surrounding the church is the Quartier St-Germain-des-Prés, long a center for Paris's "fashionable" intellectuals and artists, with art galleries, boutiques, and renowned cafés for people watching (though not necessarily for dining) such as the *Flore* (172 Bd. St-Germain, 6e; phone: 45-48-55-26), Sartre's favorite, and *Les Deux Magots* (6 Pl. St-Germain-des-Prés, 6e; phone: 45-48-55-25), once a Hemingway haunt.

QUARTIER LATIN (LATIN QUARTER) Extending from the *Jardin du Luxembourg* and the *Panthéon* to the Seine, this famous neighborhood still maintains its unique atmosphere. A focal point for *Sorbonne* students since the Middle Ages, it's a mad jumble of narrow streets, old churches, and academic buildings. Boulevard St-Michel and Boulevard St-Germain are its main arteries, both lined with cafés, bookstores, and boutiques of every imaginable kind. There are also some charming old side streets, such as the Rue de la Huchette, off Place St-Michel, and Rue St-André-des-Arts, which starts on the opposite side of Place St-Michel. And don't miss the famous *bouquinistes* (bookstalls) along the Seine, around Place St-Michel on the Quai des Grands-Augustins and the Quai St-Michel.

PALAIS ET JARDIN DU LUXEMBOURG (LUXEMBOURG PALACE AND GARDENS) Built for Marie de Médicis in 1615 in what once were the southern suburbs of Paris, this Renaissance palace became a prison during the Revolution and now houses the French *Sénat* (Senate). The palace is closed to the public except for a group tour organized by the *Caisse Nationale des Monuments Historiques et des Sites* (see *Le Marais,* above) on the first Sunday of each month. The classic, formal gardens, with lovely statues and the famous Médicis fountain, are popular with students who meet under the chestnut trees and also with neighborhood children, who play around the artificial lake or in the special children's park paved with rubber. 15 Rue de Vaugirard, 6e (phone: 42-34-20-60).

PANTHÉON Originally built by Louis XV in 1764 as a church dedicated to Paris's patron saint, Geneviève, in 1791 it was declared a "nonreligious Temple of Fame dedicated to all the gods," where the *grands hommes* of French liberty (the first *grande femme* only arrived in 1885) would be interred. The tombs of Victor Hugo, the Resistance leader Jean Moulin, Rousseau,

Voltaire, and Emile Zola, are among those here. The impressive interior also features murals depicting the life of St. Geneviève. Closed some holidays. Admission charge. Pl. du Panthéon, 5e (phone: 43-54-34-51).

MUSÉE NATIONAL DU MOYEN-AGE/THERMES DE CLUNY (CLUNY NATIONAL MUSEUM OF THE MIDDLE AGES/ROMAN BATHS OF CLUNY) One of the last remaining examples of medieval domestic architecture in Paris, the 15th-century residence of the abbots of Cluny, which was built on the site of 3rd century Gallo-Roman baths and later became the home of Mary Tudor, is now a museum of medieval arts and crafts. The most famous work displayed here is the celebrated *Lady and the Unicorn* tapestry. Closed Tuesdays. Admission charge. 6 Pl. Paul-Painlevé, 5e (phone: 43-25-62-00).

MOSQUÉE DE PARIS (PARIS MOSQUE) Dominated by a 130-foot-high minaret in gleaming white marble, this is one of the most beautiful structures of its kind in the world. Take off your shoes before entering the pebble-lined gardens full of flowers and dwarf trees. The *Salle de Prières* (Hall of Prayer), with its lush Oriental carpets, is open to the public, but it's closed Fridays (the weekly prayer day for Muslims) and during lunch hours. Admission charge. Next door is a restaurant and a patio for sipping Turkish coffee and tasting Oriental sweets. Pl. du Puits-de-l'Ermite, 5e (phone: 45-35-97-33).

EGLISE ST-SÉVERIN (CHURCH OF ST. SÉVERIN) This church still retains its beautiful Flamboyant Gothic ambulatory, considered a masterpiece of its kind, and lovely old stained glass windows dating from the 15th and 16th centuries. The small garden and the restored charnel house also are of interest. 3 Rue des Prêtres, 5e (phone: 43-25-96-63).

EGLISE ST-JULIEN-LE-PAUVRE (CHURCH OF ST. JULIAN THE POOR) One of the smallest and oldest churches (12th to 13th century) in Paris offers a superb view of Notre-Dame from the charming Place René-Viviani. 1 Rue St-Julien-le-Pauvre, 5e (no phone).

ILE DE LA CITÉ

The birthplace of Paris, settled by Gallic fishermen in about 250 BC, this island in the Seine is so rich in historical monuments that an entire day could be spent here and on the neighboring Ile St-Louis (see below). A walk all around the islands, along the lovely, tree-shaded quays on both banks of the Seine, opens up one breathtaking view (of the *Cathédrale de Notre-Dame,* the *Louvre,* the Pont Neuf) after another.

CATHÉDRALE DE NOTRE-DAME DE PARIS (CATHEDRAL OF OUR LADY OF PARIS) It is said that Druids once worshiped on this consecrated ground. Later, the Romans built their temple here, and many Christian churches followed. In 1163, the foundations were laid for the present cathedral, one of the world's finest examples of Gothic architecture. By 1270, when the funeral of Louis IX (St. Louis) was held here, the cathedral was essentially complete, but construction continued, working from the plans of a single anonymous architect, until 1345. Henri IV and Napoleon both were crowned here. At press time, a 10-year restoration project was beginning, the first major work on the cathedral since the mid-19th century. Unfortunately for visitors, scaffolding is expected to cover the exterior throughout this year, while the façade undergoes a high-tech cleaning process. Take a guided tour (offered in English at noon Tuesdays and Wednesdays and in French at noon other weekdays, 2:30 PM Saturdays, and 2 PM Sundays) or quietly explore on your own, but be sure to climb the 225-foot towers (closed during lunch hours) for a marvelous view of the city, and try to see the splendid 13th-century stained glass rose windows at sunset. Open daily. Pl. du Parvis de Notre-Dame, 4e (phone: 43-54-22-63).

PALAIS DE JUSTICE AND LA SAINTE-CHAPELLE (PALACE OF JUSTICE AND HOLY CHAPEL) This monumental complex was first the seat of the Roman military government, then the headquarters of the early kings of the Capetian dynasty, and finally the law courts. In the 13th century, Louis IX built a new palace, adding *Sainte-Chapelle* to house the Sacred Crown of Thorns and other holy relics. Its 15 soaring stained glass windows (plus a later rose window), with more than 1,100 brilliantly colored and exquisitely detailed miniature scenes of biblical life, are among the unquestioned masterpieces of medieval French art, and the graceful, gleaming 247-foot spire is one of the city's most beautiful and understated landmarks—particularly stunning on a sunny day. Closed holidays. Admission charge. 4 Bd. du Palais, 1er (phone: 43-54-30-09).

CONCIERGERIE This remnant of the former royal palace sits like a fairy-tale castle on the Ile de la Cité. It served as a prison during the Revolution, and visitors can still see the cells where Marie-Antoinette, the Duke of Orléans, Mme. du Barry, and others of lesser fame awaited the guillotine. Documents and engravings dating from the time of Ravaillac, the 17th-century assassin of Henri IV, also illustrate the past of this sinister palace. Don't miss the Girondins' chapel, where the moderate Girondin deputies shared their last meal. Closed holidays. Admission charge. 4 Bd. du Palais, 1er (phone: 43-54-30-06).

ILE ST-LOUIS

Walk across the footbridge behind *Notre-Dame* and you're in a charming, tranquil village. This "enchanted isle" has managed to keep its provincial charm despite its central location. Follow the main street, Rue St-Louis-en-l'Ile, down the middle of the island, past courtyards, balconies, old doors, curious stairways, the ornate *Eglise St-Louis* (St. Louis Church), built between 1664 and 1726, and discreet plaques bearing the names of illustrious former residents (including Mme. Curie, Voltaire, Baudelaire, Gautier, and Daumier). Pause along the way for some famous (and fabulous) *Berthillon* ice cream, either at their shop (see *Shopping*) or at one of the other small cafés that serve it. Then take the quay back along the banks of the Seine.

Sources and Resources

TOURIST INFORMATION

For information in the US, contact the *French Government Tourist Office* (see GETTING READY TO GO). In Paris, the *Office du Tourisme de Paris* (127 Champs-Elysées, 8e; phone: 49-52-53-54 for general information; 49-52-53-56 for a recorded message in English on current events and exhibitions) is the place to go for information, brochures, maps, or hotel reservations. It's closed on *New Year's Day,* May 1, and *Christmas* only. If you call the office, be prepared for a four- to five-minute wait before someone answers. Other tourist offices, all closed Sundays, are found at the *Eiffel Tower* (phone: 45-51-22-15; closed October through April) and at train stations: *Gare du Nord* (15 Rue de Dunkerque, 10e; phone: 45-26-94-82); *Gare de Lyon* (Pl. Louis-Armand, 12e; phone: 43-43-33-24); *Gare de l'Est* (Pl. du 11-Novembre 1918, 10e; phone: 46-07-17-73); *Gare Montparnasse* (17 Bd. de Vaugirard, 15e; phone: 43-22-19-19); and *Gare d'Austerlitz* (53 Quai d'Austerlitz, 13e; phone: 45-84-91-70).

LOCAL COVERAGE *Paris Selection,* in both French and English, is the official tourist office magazine. It lists events, sights, tours, some hotels, restaurants, shopping, nightclubs, and other information. Far more complete are the weekly guides *L'Officiel des Spectacles, 7 à Paris,* and *Pariscope.* All are in simple French (*Pariscope* even has a section in English) and are available at newsstands. English-language magazines are *Boulevard,* sold at newsstands; the monthly *WHERE,* distributed in hotels; and, available free at English-language bookstores and other locations, the monthly *Paris Free Voice,* and the biweeklies *Paris City* and *France-USA Contacts.* Among the city's English-language bookstores are *W. H. Smith and Sons, Brentano's,* and *Shakespeare and Company* (see *Shopping* for all three).

TELEPHONE The area code for Paris is 1. For more information on making telephone calls to and from Paris, see GETTING READY TO GO.

GETTING AROUND

BOAT The *Batobus,* operated by *Bateaux Parisiens* (Pont d'Iéna, Port de la Bourdonnais, 7e, phone: 44-11-33-44; and Quai Montebello, 5e, phone: 43-26-92-55), carries passengers along the Seine daily from mid-April through September 26; stops (watch for the signs on the quays) are near the *Eiffel Tower,* the *Musée d'Orsay,* the *Louvre, Notre-Dame,* and the *Hôtel de Ville* (just east of the *Louvre*). The fare is 12F (about $2.10 at press time) for each leg of the trip, or 60F (about $10.35 at press time) for an all-day, unlimited-travel pass; tickets may be purchased at the stops along the quays.

BUS They're slow, but good for sightseeing; a few do not run on Sundays and holidays. *Métro* tickets are valid on all city buses, but you will need a new ticket if you change buses. Unlike the *Métro,* buses charge by distance; two tickets are sometimes needed for a ride across town (into a different zone). The standard fare is about 7F (around $1.20 at press time), but it's best to buy a *carnet* (booklet) of 10 tickets, only 41F (around $7.10 at press time); one of the special tourist passes for short stays in Paris; or a *carte orange,* a pass permitting either a week or a month of unlimited travel (see *Métro,* below, for more on tickets and passes). Bus lines are numbered, and both stops and buses have signs indicating routes. The Paris *Régional Autorité du Transit Provincial* (*RATP;* Regional Rapid Transit Authority; phone: 43-46-14-14 for general information), which operates the *Métro* and bus system, has designated certain bus lines as being of particular interest to tourists; look for a panel on the front of the bus reading (in English), "This bus is good for sightseeing." On Sundays and holidays, a special *RATP* sightseeing bus, the *Balabus,* runs from the *Grande Arche de la Défense,* west of Paris, all the way east to the *Gare de Lyon.* The total trip time is 75 minutes; you can board the bus at any stop marked "Balabus Bb." The *RATP* has tourist offices at Place de la Madeleine, next to the flower market (8e; phone: 40-06-71-45) and on the Rive Gauche at 53 *bis* Quai des Grands-Augustins near Place St-Michel (6e; phone: 40-46-44-50 or 40-46-43-60); both organize bus tours in Paris and the surrounding region.

CAR RENTAL For information about renting a car in Paris, see GETTING READY TO GO.

MÉTRO Operating from 5:30 AM to about 1 AM, the *Métro* system is generally safe (although pickpockets abound in certain areas), clean, quiet, and easy to use, and since the *RATP* has been sponsoring cultural events and art exhibits in some 200 of Paris's 368 *Métro* stations, at times it is even entertaining. Different lines are identified by the names of their terminals at either end. Every station has clear directional maps, some with push-button devices that light up the proper route after a destination button is pushed.

Keep your ticket (you may be asked to show it to one of the controllers who regularly patrol the *Métro*) and don't cheat; there are spot checks. Tickets cost about 7F (around $1.20 at press time); a *carnet* (10-ticket book) is available at a reduced rate, about 41F (around $7.10 at press time). The *RATP* abolished the *Métro*'s long standing first and second class system in 1993; there is now only one class of ticket. The same tickets can be used on buses, but on the *Métro* you will need only one ticket per ride. The *RATP* offers several economical tourist passes: The *Formule I* card is a one-day pass providing unlimited travel on the *Métro,* bus, and suburban trains; the *Paris-Visite* card entitles the bearer to three or five consecutive days of unlimited travel, plus discounts at several Paris attractions. A two-zone *Formule I* card (covering metropolitan Paris) costs 27F (about $4.70 at press time); three-day *Paris-Visite* cards cost 90F (about $15.50 at press time) and five-day cards cost 145F (about $25 at press time). The cards may be purchased upon presentation of your passport at 44 *Métro* stations, the four regional express stations, the six *SNCF* stations (see *Train,* below), or at the *RATP*'s tourist offices (see *Bus,* above); the cards also may be purchased in the US from *Marketing Challenges International* (10 E. 21st St., Suite 600, New York, NY 10010; phone: 212-529-9069; fax: 212-529-4838). The *carte orange,* a commuter pass, is available weekly (beginning on Mondays) or monthly (beginning the first of the month), and, like the tourist passes, provides unlimited travel. Though actually more economical than the tourist passes, the *carte orange* does require a small (passport-size) photo to attach to the card. For a two-zone pass (covering metropolitan Paris), the weekly *carte orange* costs 63F (about $10.90 at press time); the monthly pass sells for 219F (about $37.75 at press time). They are available at all *Métro* stations.

DOUBT-FREE DIRECTIONS

Handy streetside bus and *Métro* directions are now available in some *Métro* stations from *SITU* (*Système d'Information des Trajets Urbains*), a computer that prints out the fastest routing onto a wallet-size piece of paper, complete with the estimated length of the trip, free of charge. High-traffic spots such as the *Châtelet Métro* station, the *Gare Montparnasse,* and the Boulevard St-Germain now sport *SITU* machines.

TAXI Taxis can be found at stands at main intersections, outside train stations and official buildings, and in the streets. A taxi is available if the entire "TAXI" sign is illuminated (with a white light); the small light *beside* the roof light signifies availability after dark; and no light means the driver is off duty. Be aware that Parisian cab drivers are notoriously selective about where they will go and how many passengers they will allow in their cabs. A foursome will inevitably have trouble since, by law, no one may ride in the front seat, but, also by law, a cab at a taxi stand must take you wherever you want to go. (Good news for those who don't appreciate being snubbed by cabbies: The Paris taxi drivers' association has instituted a new program to teach potential drivers good manners, along with a soupçon of English.) You also can call *Taxi Bleu* (phone: 49-36-10-10) or *Radio Taxi* (phone: 47-39-33-33); dispatchers usually speak at least some English. The meter starts running from the time the cab is dispatched, and a tip of about 15% is customary. Fares increase at night and on Sundays and holidays.

TOURS *Cityrama* (4 Pl. des Pyramides, 1er; phone: 42-60-30-14) and *Paris Vision* (214 Rue de Rivoli, 1er; phone: 42-60-31-25) offer well-planned, informative tours on bubble-top, double-decker buses equipped with earphones for commentary in English. Reserve through any travel agent or your hotel's concierge. Both *Cityrama* and *Paris Vision,* among other operators, also offer organized "Paris by Night" group tours, which include at least one *"spectacle"*—a performance featuring women in minimal, yet elaborate, costumes, lavish sets and effects, and sophisticated striptease.

Another great way to see Paris is from the Seine, by boat. Prices are reasonable for a day or evening cruise on a modern, glass-enclosed river rambler, which provides a constantly changing picture of the city. Contact *Bateaux-Mouches* (Pont d'Alma, 7e; phone: 42-25-96-10); *Bateaux Parisiens* (see *Boat*, above); or *Vedettes Pont-Neuf* (Pl. Vert-Galant, 1er; phone: 46-33-98-38). *Paris Canal* (19-21 Quai de la Loire, Bassin de la Villette, 19e; phone: 42-40-96-97) and *Canauxrama* (13 Quai de la Loire, Bassin de la Villette, 19e; phone: 42-39-15-00) offer three-hour barge trips starting on the Seine and navigating through some of the city's old canals and locks (*Paris Canal* offers a subterranean route under the *Bastille*). *Yachts de Paris* (Port de Javel-Hunt, 15e; phone: 44-37-10-20) offers romantic, first class dinner cruises which feature menus devised by two-Michelin-star chef Gérard Besson. For more details on river and canal cruises, see *Cruising Paris's Waterways* in DIVERSIONS.

TRAIN Paris has six main *SNCF* (*Société Nationale des Chemins de Fer*, the French national railroad) train stations, each one serving a different area of the country. Trains heading north depart from *Gare du Nord* (15 Rue de Dunkerque, 10e; phone: 49-95-10-00); east, *Gare de l'Est* (Pl. du 11-Novembre 1918, 10e; phone: 40-18-20-00); southeast, *Gare de Lyon* (Pl. Louis-Armand, 12e; phone: 40-19-60-00); southwest, *Gare d'Austerlitz* (53 Quai d'Austerlitz, 13e; phone: 45-84-14-18); west, *Gare Montparnasse* (17 Bd. de Vaugirard, 15e; phone: 40-48-10-00); west and northwest, *Gare St-Lazare* (20 Rue St-Lazare, 8e; phone: 42-85-88-00). For general information call 45-82-50-50; for reservations, 45-65-60-60 (there's usually someone who can speak English). For additional information in English, contact the tourist office within each station (see *Tourist Information*).

The *TGV (Train à Grande Vitesse)*, the world's fastest train, has cut two hours off the usual four-hour ride between Paris and Lyons; it similarly shortens traveling time from Paris to Marseilles, the Côte d'Azur, the Atlantic Coast, the English Channel at Calais, and Switzerland. Most *TGV*s leave from the *Gare de Lyon*, except for the Atlantic Coast run, which departs from the *Gare Montparnasse*, and the Lille-Calais run, which leaves from the *Gare du Nord* and connects at Calais to the "Chunnel," the trans-Channel tunnel connecting France and Great Britain. Reserved seats are necessary on all *TGV*s; tickets can be purchased from machines in all main train stations. *Orly-Rail* and *Roissy-Rail*, operated by the *RER*, link Paris with the two major airports, *Charles de Gaulle* and *Orly* (for details see GETTING READY TO GO).

The *SNCF* has recently begun computerizing reservations, much in the same way airlines do. Known as *Socrate*, the new system's quirks have made many travelers wish they could give it hemlock. The bugs were still being worked out at press time, but what will not change is that the farther in advance (up to one month) tickets are purchased, the less expensive they are.

LOCAL SERVICES

BABY-SITTING Many hotels arrange baby-sitters. Agencies recommended by the *Paris Tourist Office* are *Baby-sitting Services* (phone: 46-37-51-24); *Baby-sitters, Inc.* (45-30-03-22); and *SOS Maman* (phone: 46-47-89-98), which specializes in last-minute sitters. Whether the sitter is hired directly or through an agency, ask for and check references.

DRY CLEANER/TAILOR Dry cleaners are available throughout the city. Note that many have two different price schedules *(pressings)*, one for "economic" service, another for faster, more expensive service. The less expensive prices may be posted outside, but unless you specify, your clothes will be given the expensive treatment. *John Baillie, Real Scotch Tailor* (1 Rue Auber at Pl. de l'Opéra, 2e; phone: 47-42-49-17) is a reputable firm that offers French-style tailoring, despite its name.

LIMOUSINE SERVICE *Compagnie des Limousines* (37 Rue Acacias, 17e; phone: 43-80-79-41) and *Executive Car/Carey Limousine* (25 Rue d'Astorg, 8e; phone: 42-65-54-20; fax: 42-65-25-93).

MEDICAL EMERGENCY For information on local medical services and pharmacies, see GETTING READY TO GO.

MESSENGER SERVICE Most hotels will arrange for pickups and deliveries.

OFFICE EQUIPMENT RENTAL *International Computer Location* (43 Rue Beaubourg, 3e; phone: 42-72-07-00) offers rentals of Macintosh computers.

PHOTOCOPIES In addition to the numerous small outlets specializing in photocopies, facilities are available in many stationery stores and post offices.

POST OFFICE For information on several local offices, see GETTING READY TO GO.

TELECONFERENCE FACILITIES *Hôtel Méridien* (81 Bd. Gouvion-St-Cyr, 17e; phone: 40-68-34-34), among other hotels.

TELEX AND FAX SERVICES *Poste Publique de Télex* (7 Rue Feydeau, 2e; phone: 42-33-20-12), a special *PTT* office where you can send a fax or telex, is open daily (closed mornings on holidays); faxes also may be sent from any of the city's other post offices. Prices are astronomical (at press time, around $50 for two pages to the US).

TRANSLATOR For a list of accredited translators, contact the *Consulate* of the *American Embassy* (2 Rue St-Florentin, 1er; phone: 42-96-14-88 or 42-61-80-75).

TUXEDO RENTAL *Au Cor de Chasse* (40 Rue de Buci, 6e; phone: 43-26-51-89).

SPECIAL EVENTS

Fashion shows come to Paris in January, when press and buyers pass judgment on the spring and summer haute couture collections; later, in February and March, more buyers arrive for the ready-to-wear shows (fall and winter clothes), which also are open to the trade only. Cat lovers will want to check out the *Exposition Internationale Féline* (International Cat Show) in early January. March brings the year's first *Foire Nationale à la Brocante et aux Jambons* (National Flea Market and Regional Food Products Fair), an event that is repeated in September; it's held on the Ile de Chatou, an island in the Seine west of Paris, accessible by the *RER* suburban train.

The running of the *Prix du Président de la République,* the year's first big horse race, takes place at *Auteuil,* in the *Bois de Boulogne,* in April. Late April through early May brings the *Foire de Paris,* a big international trade fair, to the *Parc des Expositions* (Porte de Versailles, 15e). In late April or May, the *Paris Marathon* is run; late May through early June is the time for the illustrious *Championnats Internationaux de France,* better known as the *French Open* tennis championship (in France it's informally called the *Roland Garros,* after the stadium in which it's held; 16e). Horse races crowd the calendar in June—there's the *Prix de Diane/Hermès* at *Chantilly,* the *Grand Prix de Paris* at *Longchamp,* the *Grande Steeplechase de Paris* at *Auteuil,* and the *Grand Prix de St-Cloud* (see *Horse Racing,* below, for details on all four). In the middle of June, the *Festival du Marais* begins a month's worth of music and dance performances in the courtyards of the Marais district's old townhouses. *Bastille Day* (July 14), which commemorates the fall of the *Bastille* and the beginning of the French Revolution in 1789, is celebrated with music, fireworks, parades (including one that goes down the Champs-Elysées), and dancing till dawn in many neighborhoods.

Cyclists arrive in Paris for the finish of the three-week *Tour de France* in late July. Also in July, press and buyers arrive to view the fall and winter haute couture collections, but the ready-to-wear shows (spring and summer clothes) wait until September and October, because August for Parisians is vacation time. Practically the whole country takes a holiday then, and in the capital the classical concerts of the *Festival Estival* are among the few distractions in July and August. When they finish, the *Festival d'Automne,* a celebration of the contemporary in music, dance, and theater, takes over from mid-September through December (see *Music* for details on both festivals). In even-numbered years, the *Biennale des Antiquaires,* a major antiques event, comes to the *Grand Palais* from late September through early October. Every year on the first Sunday of October, the last big horse race of the season, the *Prix de l'Arc de Triomphe,* is run at *Longchamp* (see *Horse Racing*). The first Saturday in October also brings the *Fête des Vendanges à Montmartre,* a celebration of the harvest of the city's last remaining vineyard, in Montmartre. The *Salon Mondial de l'Automobile* (World Motor Show) takes place at the *Parc des Expositions* in even-numbered years, usually in October. On November 11, ceremonies at the *Arc de Triomphe* and a parade mark *Armistice Day;* the *Open de Paris* tennis tournament is also played this month. The *Salon du Cheval et du Poney* (Horse and Pony Show) comes to the *Parc des Expositions* in early December; then comes *Noël* (Christmas), which is celebrated most movingly with *La Veille de Noël* (Christmas Eve) midnight mass at *Notre-Dame*. At midnight a week later, the *Nouvel An* (New Year) is ushered in with spontaneous street revelry in the Quartier Latin and along the Champs-Elysées.

MUSEUMS

Besides those described in *Special Places,* the following museums and sites may be of interest (unless otherwise indicated, an admission fee is charged).

BIBLIOTHÈQUE-MUSÉE DE L'OPÉRA (OPERA LIBRARY AND MUSEUM) These trace the history of opera in Paris from its 17th-century origins. Closed Sundays, holidays, and two weeks around *Easter. Opéra/Palais Garnier,* Pl. de l'Opéra, 9e (phone: 47-42-07-02).

CATACOMBES (CATACOMBS) Dating from the Gallo-Roman era, these ossuaries contain the remains of Danton, Robespierre, and many others. Filled with thousands of skeletons and skulls, the site is macabre, fascinating, and definitely not for the claustrophobic, in spite of recent renovations. Bring a flashlight. Closed weekday mornings, during lunch hours on weekends, Mondays, and holidays. 1 Pl. Denfert-Rochereau, 14e (phone: 43-22-47-63).

CITÉ DE LA MUSIQUE Comprising concert halls, the *Conservatoire National Supérieur de la Musique,* and other music-related facilities, this complex also contains a music museum with a collection of 700 rare instruments. Closed Mondays. In the *Parc de la Villette,* 211 Av. Jean-Jaurès, 19e (phone: 40-05-80-00).

CRYPTE ARCHÉOLOGIQUE DE NOTRE-DAME (ARCHAEOLOGICAL CRYPT OF NOTRE-DAME) Exhibits in this ancient crypt on which the cathedral was built include floor plans that show the evolution of the cathedral and earlier religious structures built on this spot. Open daily. Under the square in front of *Notre-Dame,* at Parvis de Notre-Dame, 4e (phone: 43-29-83-51).

EGOUTS (SEWERS) This underground city of tunnels has become an incredibly popular attraction, with lines that sometimes take an hour. Open daily. Pl. de la Résistance, in front of 93 Quai d'Orsay, 7e (phone: 47-05-10-29).

MANUFACTURE DES GOBELINS The famous tapestry factory has been in operation since the 15th century. Guided tours of the workshops take place Tuesdays, Wednesdays, and Thursdays (except holidays) from 2 to 3 PM. 42 Av. des Gobelins, 13e (phone: 43-37-12-60).

MÉMORIAL DE LA DÉPORTATION (DEPORTATION MEMORIAL) In a tranquil garden in the shadow of *Notre-Dame* at the tip of Ile de la Cité, this monument is dedicated to the 200,000 French citizens of all religions and races who died in Nazi concentration camps during World War II. Pl. de l'Ile-de-France, 4e.

MÉMORIAL DU MARTYR JUIF INCONNU (MEMORIAL TO THE UNKNOWN JEWISH MARTYR) A moving tribute to Jews killed during the Holocaust, this renovated memorial includes a museum displaying World War II documents and photographs. Closed Saturdays and Jewish holidays; the museum also is closed Sundays and other holidays. 17 Rue Geoffroy-l'Asnier, 4e (phone: 42-77-44-72). The *French Government Tourist Office* has published a booklet, *France for the Jewish Traveler,* which describes this memorial and the *Mémorial de la Déportation,* as well as other places of interest to Jewish tourists visiting France.

MUSÉE DES ANTIQUITÉS NATIONALES (MUSEUM OF NATIONAL ANTIQUITIES) Archaeological specimens from prehistoric through Merovingian times, including an impressive Gallo-Roman collection, are exhibited. Closed during lunch hours and Tuesdays. Pl. du Château, St-Germain-en-Laye (phone: 34-51-53-65).

MUSÉE DES ARTS AFRICAINS ET OCÉANIENS (MUSEUM OF AFRICAN AND OCEANIAN ART) One of the world's finest collections of art from Africa and the Pacific Islands. Closed during lunch hours and Tuesdays. 293 Av. Daumesnil, 12e (phone: 43-43-14-54).

MUSÉE DES ARTS DE LA MODE ET DU TEXTILE (MUSEUM OF FASHION AND TEXTILE ARTS) Adjacent to the *Musée National des Arts Décoratifs* (see below), this museum chronicles the history of the fashion and textile industries with opulent exhibits. Closed Mondays and Tuesdays. 109 Rue de Rivoli, 1er (phone: 42-60-32-14).

MUSÉE DES ARTS ET TRADITIONS POPULAIRES (MUSEUM OF POPULAR ARTS AND TRADITIONS) Traditional arts and crafts from rural France are featured. Closed Tuesdays. 6 Av. du Mahatma-Gandhi, *Bois de Boulogne,* 16e (phone: 44-17-60-00).

MUSÉE BALZAC The house where the writer lived, with a garden leading to one of the prettiest little alleys in Paris. Closed Mondays and holidays. 47 Rue Raynouard, 16e (phone: 42-24-56-38).

MUSÉE CERNUSCHI A collection of Chinese art. Closed Mondays and holidays. 7 Av. Vélasquez, 8e (phone: 45-63-50-75).

MUSÉE DE LA CHASSE ET DE LA NATURE (MUSEUM OF HUNTING AND NATURE) Art, weapons, and tapestries relating to the hunt are displayed in the beautiful 17th-century *Hôtel Guénégaud.* Of particular interest is the courtyard, now decorated with sculpture, where horses once were kept. Closed during lunch hours, Tuesdays, and holidays. 60 Rue des Archives, 3e (phone: 42-72-86-43).

MUSÉE COGNACQ-JAY In a stunningly beautiful mansion in the Marais, this museum displays art, snuffboxes, and watches from the 17th and 18th centuries. Closed Mondays. 8 Rue Elzévir, 3e (phone: 40-27-07-21).

MUSÉE DES COLLECTIONS HISTORIQUES DE LA PRÉFECTURE DE POLICE (MUSEUM OF THE HISTORICAL COLLECTIONS OF THE POLICE PREFECTURE) On the second floor of this modern police station are historic arrest orders (for Charlotte Corday, among others), collections of contemporary engravings, and guillotine blades. Closed Sundays. 1 *bis* Rue des Carmes, 5e (phone: 43-29-21-57).

MUSÉE DAPPER This museum mounts splendid temporary exhibitions of African art in a charming former private house near the *Arc de Triomphe.* Open daily. 50 Av. Victor-Hugo, 16e (phone: 45-00-01-50).

MUSÉE EUGÈNE-DELACROIX A permanent collection of Delacroix's work as well as temporary exhibits of works by his contemporaries are displayed in the former studio and garden of the great painter. The museum was scheduled to reopen early this year after being closed for renovations. Closed Tuesdays. 6 Rue de Fürstemberg, 6e (phone: 43-54-04-87).

MUSÉE GRÉVIN Waxworks of French historical figures, from Charlemagne to present day political leaders and celebrities. 10 Bd. Montmartre, 9e (phone: 47-70-85-05). A branch devoted to the Belle Epoque is in the *Forum des Halles* shopping complex. Pl. Carrée, 1er (phone: 40-26-28-50). Both branches are closed mornings.

MUSÉE GUIMET The *Louvre*'s Far Eastern collection. The museum's boutique, with reproductions inspired by the collection, is also well worth a visit. Closed Tuesdays. 6 Pl. d'Iéna, 16e (phone: 47-23-61-65).

MUSÉE GUSTAVE-MOREAU A collection of works by the early symbolist. Closed Tuesdays and during lunch hours Thursdays through Sundays. 14 Rue de la Rochefoucauld, 9e (phone: 48-74-38-50).

MUSÉE DE L'INSTITUT DU MONDE ARABE (MUSEUM OF THE INSTITUTE OF THE ARAB WORLD) Arab and Islamic arts from the 9th through the 19th century. Closed Mondays. 23 Quai St-Bernard, 5e (phone: 40-51-38-38).

MUSÉE JACQUEMART-ANDRÉ Eighteenth-century French decorative art and European Renaissance treasures, as well as frequent special exhibitions. Closed Mondays and Tuesdays. 158 Bd. Haussmann, 8e (phone: 42-89-04-91).

MUSÉE MARMOTTAN Superb Monets, including the nine masterpieces that were stolen in a daring 1985 robbery. All were recovered in a villa in Corsica and were cleaned, some for the first time, before being rehung. Closed Mondays. 2 Rue Louis-Boilly, 16e (phone: 42-24-07-02).

MUSÉE DE LA MODE ET DU COSTUME (MUSEUM OF FASHION AND COSTUME) A panorama of French contributions to fashion. Closed Mondays and Tuesday mornings. In the elegant *Palais Galliera,* 10 Av. Pierre-Ier-de-Serbie, 16e (phone: 47-20-85-23).

MUSÉE DE LA MONNAIE (MUSEUM OF CURRENCY) More than 2,000 coins and 450 medallions, plus historic coinage machines. Closed mornings, Mondays, and holidays. 11 Quai de Conti, 6e (phone: 40-46-55-35).

MUSÉE DE MONTMARTRE Formerly artist Maurice Utrillo's house, it's now home to a rich collection of paintings, drawings, and documents depicting life in this quarter. Closed Mondays. 12 Rue Cortot, 18e (phone: 46-06-61-11).

MUSÉE NATIONAL DES ARTS DÉCORATIFS (NATIONAL MUSEUM OF DECORATIVE ARTS) Furniture and applied arts from the Middle Ages to the present, Oriental carpets, Dubuffet paintings and drawings, and three centuries of French posters. The *Galerie Art Nouveau–Art Deco* features the celebrated 1920s designer Jeanne Lanvin's bedroom and bath. Closed mornings, Mondays, and Tuesdays. 107 Rue de Rivoli, 1er (phone: 42-60-32-14).

MUSÉE NISSIM DE CAMONDO A former manor house filled with beautiful furnishings and art objects from the 18th century. Closed during lunch hours and Mondays, Tuesdays, and holidays. 63 Rue de Monceau, 8e (phone: 45-63-26-32).

MUSÉE DE SÈVRES Just outside Paris, next door to the Sèvres factory, it boasts one of the world's finest collections of porcelain. Closed Tuesdays. 4 Grand-Rue, Sèvres (phone: 45-34-99-05).

MUSÉE DU VIN (WINE MUSEUM) Housed in a 14th-century abbey whose interior was destroyed during the Revolution, the museum chronicles the history of wine and describes the wine-making process through displays, artifacts, and a series of wax figure tableaux. Closed mornings. Admission charge includes a glass of wine. 5-7 Pl. Charles-Dickens, 16e (phone: 45-25-63-26).

PARISTORIC This 45-minute film on Paris past and present, with an English soundtrack available on headsets, is a well-done capsule portrait of the city's 2,000-year history. Open daily. *Espace Hébertot*, 78 bis Bd. des Batignolles, 17e (phone: 42-93-93-46).

PAVILLON DES ARTS Located in the mushroom-shaped buildings overlooking the *Forum des Halles* complex, this space mounts a variety of art exhibits, from paintings to sculpture, ancient to modern. Closed mornings, Mondays, and holidays. 101 Rue Rambuteau, 1er (phone: 42-33-82-50).

VIDÉOTHÈQUE DE PARIS A treasure trove of information about the City of Light, this extensive computerized video archive contains thousands of films, documentaries, and videos dating from the turn of the century to the present. Closed mornings and Mondays. 2 Grand Galerie, 1er (phone: 44-76-62-00).

GALLERIES

Montparnasse and Montmartre are no longer the enclaves of art they once were. Nowadays, although fine galleries can be found all over the city, Paris's best are clustered on the Rive Droite around the *Centre Georges-Pompidou* and the Place de la Concorde, and on the Rive Gauche on or near the Rue de Seine. Here are some of our favorites:

ADRIEN MAEGHT Works by a prestigious list of artists that includes Miró, Matisse, Calder, and Chagall are displayed in this Rive Gauche gallery. 42 and 46 Rue du Bac, 7e (phone: 45-48-45-15).

AGATHE GAILLARD The best in photography, including works by Cartier-Bresson and the like. 3 Rue du Pont-Louis-Philippe, 4e (phone: 42-77-38-24).

ARTCURIAL Sculptures and prints by early moderns, such as Braque and Delaunay, are featured. The bookshop has an extensive, multilingual collection of art books. 9 Av. Matignon, 8e (phone: 42-99-16-16).

BEAUBOURG Well-known names in the Paris art scene, including Niki de Saint-Phalle, César, Tinguely, and Klossowski are found here. 23 Rue du Renard, 4e (phone: 42-71-20-50).

CAROLINE CORRE Exhibitions by contemporary artists, specializing in unique, handmade artists' books. 53 Rue Berthe, 18e (phone: 42-55-37-76).

CLAUDE BERNARD Francis Bacon, David Hockney, and Raymond Mason are among the artists exhibited here. 5 Rue des Beaux-Arts, 6e (phone: 43-26-97-07).

DANIEL MALINGUE Works by the Impressionists, as well as such notable Parisian artists from the 1930s to the 1950s as Foujita and Fautrier. 26 Av. Matignon, 8e (phone: 42-66-60-33).

DANIEL TEMPLON Major contemporary American and Italian artists. 30 Rue Beaubourg, 3e (phone: 42-72-14-10).

DARTHEA SPEYER Contemporary painting is featured in this gallery run by a former American embassy attaché. 6 Rue Jacques-Callot, 6e (phone: 43-54-78-41).

GALERIE DE FRANCE A prestigious gallery located in a majestic space features the works of historical avant-garde artists such as Brancusi and Gabo, as well as such contemporary artists as Matta, Aillaud, and Arroyo. 52 Rue de la Verrerie, 4e (phone: 42-74-38-00).

HERVÉ ODERMATT CAZEAU Early moderns—among them Picasso, Léger, and Pissarro—and antiques. 85 *bis* Rue du Faubourg-St-Honoré, 8e (phone: 42-66-92-58).

JEAN FOURNIER This dealer defended abstract expressionism in 1955 and remains faithful to the cause in his main gallery, where he also exhibits the works of promising young artists. 44 Rue Quincampoix, 4e (phone: 42-77-32-31).

LELONG The great moderns on view here include Tapiès, Bacon, Alechinsky, Donald Judd, and Voss. 13-14 Rue de Téhéran, 8e (phone: 45-63-13-19).

MARWAN HOSS In an elegant space near the *Tuileries* are displayed works by Hartung, Henri Hayden, Julio Gonzalez, and Zao Wou-Ki. 12 Rue d'Alger, 1er (phone: 42-96-37-96).

NIKKI DIANA MARQUARDT A spacious gallery of contemporary work opened by an enterprising dealer from the Bronx, New York. 9 Pl. des Vosges, 4e (phone: 42-78-21-00).

THORIGNY Marcel Duchamp, Man Ray, and other early avant-garde greats are exhibited here along with promising new artists. 13 Rue de Thorigny, 3e (phone: 48-87-60-65).

YVON LAMBERT A dealer with an eye for the avant-avant-garde, he also exhibits the works of major artists from the 1970s and 1980s. 108 Rue Vieille-du-Temple, 3e (phone: 42-71-09-33).

ZABRISKIE Early and contemporary photography by Atget, Brassaï, Arbus, and others. 37 Rue Quincampoix, 4e (phone: 42-72-35-47).

SHOPPING

From street trends to classic haute couture, Paris sets the styles the world copies. Prices are generally high, but more than a few people are willing to pay for the quality of the merchandise, not to mention a Paris label.

The big department stores are excellent places to get an idea of what's available. They include *Galeries Lafayette* (40 Bd. Haussmann, 9e; phone: 42-82-34-56; and other locations); *Printemps* (64 Bd. Haussmann, 9e; phone: 42-82-50-00); *La Samaritaine* (19 Rue de la Monnaie, 1er; phone: 40-41-20-20); *Le Bazar de l'Hôtel de Ville* (*BHV;* 52 Rue de Rivoli, 4e; phone: 42-74-90-00); and *Au Bon Marché,* located in two buildings on Rue de Sèvres (main store, 22 Rue de Sèvres, 7e, phone: 44-39-80-00; and the supermarket annex, *La Grande Epicerie,* 38 Rue de Sèvres, phone: 44-39-81-00).

Both *Galeries Lafayette* and *Printemps* hold excellent fashion shows that are open to the public at no charge. The former has shows on Wednesdays year-round; there are additional shows on Fridays from May through October. Reservations are necessary and should be made as early as possible through the direct Paris reservations number (phone: 42-82-30-25) or in the US through *ACRC Corporation* (730 Fifth Ave., 9th Floor, New York, NY 10019; phone: 212-333-3680; fax: 212-977-5931). *Printemps* holds fashion shows every Tuesday, and, from March through October, also on Fridays. Admittance can be arranged in the US through *Marketing Challenges International* (10 E. 21st St., Suite 600, New York, NY 10010; phone: 212-529-9069; fax: 529-4838). The *Annemarie Victory Organization* (136 E. 64th St., New York, NY 10021; phone: 212-486-0353) sponsors trips for style-savvy travelers every January and July that include entrance to the haute couture shows of such designers as Chanel, Givenchy, Nina Ricci, Vicky Tiel, Ungaro, and Valentino.

Three major shopping centers—*Porte Maillot* (Pl. de la Porte Maillot, 16e and 17e; phone: 45-74-29-09); *Maine Montparnasse* (at the intersection of Bd. du Montparnasse and Rue de Rennes, 6e); and the *Forum des Halles* (Rue Pierre-Lescot and Rue Rambuteau, 1er; phone: 44-76-96-56)—also are worth a visit, as is the lovely *Galerie Vivienne* (main entrance at 4 Rue des Petits-Champs, 2e; phone: 42-60-08-23), one of Paris's glass-roofed *galeries,* the 19th-century precursors of the modern-day shopping mall. Two new luxury shopping venues have opened recently: The *Carrousel du Louvre,* an underground complex beneath the museum, ranks among the world's most elegant shopping malls, with 50 fine stores and a central atrium containing an inverted version of the I. M. Pei pyramids (main entrance at 99 Rue de Rivoli, beneath the *Arc de Triomphe du Carrousel,* 1er; phone: 46-92-47-47); the complex is closed Tuesdays, when the museum is also closed. And *Passy Plaza,* located in the posh Passy district, is one of Paris's largest shopping centers (53 Rue de Passy, 16e; phone: 40-50-09-07).

In addition to elegant designer boutiques for fashion, shoes, and leather goods, the best (and most expensive) antiques dealers are along the Rue du Faubourg-St-Honoré on the Rive Droite. On the Rive Gauche, there's *Le Carré Rive Gauche,* an association of more than 100 antiques shops in the area bordered by Quai Voltaire, Rue de l'Université, Rue des Sts-Pères, and Rue du Bac (all 7e). Antiques and curio collectors also should explore Paris's several flea markets, which include the *Puces de la Porte de Montreuil* (Av. de la Porte de Montreuil, 11e), which is held weekends and Mondays year-round and is especially good for secondhand clothing; *Puces de la Porte de Vanves* (at Avenues Georges-Lafenestre and Marc-Sangnier, 14e, *Métro:* Porte de Vanves), held weekends year-round, for furniture and fine bric-a-brac (try to arrive early on Saturday morning); and the largest and best known, *Marché aux Puces de St-Ouen* (more commonly called the *Puces de Clignancourt;* between Porte de St-Ouen and Porte de Clignancourt, 18e), which is held weekends and Mondays year-round and offers an admirable array of antiques. The *Marché Biron* is one of the best of the smaller markets that make up the *Puces de Clignancourt;* it is especially good for fine bric-a-brac. Bargaining is a must at all the flea markets. For more information, see *Antiques Hunting in Paris* in DIVERSIONS.

What follows is a sampling of the wealth of shops in Paris, many of which have more than one location in the city. For a list of the variety of goods for which Paris is famous—and the best areas in which to purchase them—see *Shopping Spree* in DIVERSIONS. And for a detailed description of the gastronomic cornucopia that is *Fauchon,* see *Quintessential Paris* in DIVERSIONS. Standard shopping hours are listed in GETTING READY TO GO.

TIPS FOR SAVVY SHOPPERS

In Paris, *soldes* (sales) take place during the first weeks in January and in late June and July. Any shop labeled *dégriffé* (the word means "without the label") offers year-round discounts on brand-name clothing, often last season's styles. Discount shops also are known as "stock" shops. The French Value Added Tax (VAT) can be refunded on most purchases made by foreigners, provided a minimum is spent in one store. For more information, see GETTING READY TO GO.

Absinthe Chic is the word here—everything from one-of-a-kind silk hats to the latest clothes from up-and-coming designers. Near the Place des Victoires, at 74 Rue Jean-Jacques Rousseau, 1er (phone: 42-33-54-44).

Accessoire Very feminine footwear, often seen on the pages of *Elle* magazine. 6 Rue du Cherche-Midi, 6e (phone: 45-48-36-08) and other locations.

Agatha One of the best sources for chic costume jewelry. In the *Carrousel du Louvre* complex, entrance at 99 Rue de Rivoli, 1er (phone: 42-96-03-09) and other locations.

Agnès B Supremely wearable, trendy, casual clothes. Five stores on the block-long Rue du Jour, 1er: menswear at No. 3 (phone: 42-33-04-13); clothes for young children and infants at No. 4 (phone: 40-39-96-88); articles for the home at No. 5 (phone: 49-53-52-80); womenswear at No. 6 (phone: 45-08-56-56); and *Lolita,* for girls, at No. 10 (phone: 40-26-36-87). Also at 17 Av. Pierre-Ier-de-Serbie, 16e (phone: 47-20-22-44); 81 Rue d'Assas, 6e (phone: 46-33-70-20); and a new location with women's and children's clothing at 6 Rue Vieux-Colombier, 6e (phone: 44-39-02-60).

Après-Midi de Chien Women's and children's wear in what the French call "Anglo-Saxon"-style: tweedy jackets, jodhpurs, and print skirts. 10 Rue du Jour, 1er (phone: 40-26-92-78) and other locations.

Arnys Elegant, conservative men's clothing. 14 Rue de Sèvres, 6e (phone: 45-48-76-99).

Azzedine Alaïa Clothing by the Tunisian designer who redefined "body-conscious." 7 Rue de Moussy, 4e (phone: 42-72-19-19).

Baccarat High-quality porcelain and crystal. 30 *bis* Rue de Paradis, 10e (phone: 47-70-64-30), and 11 Pl. de la Madeleine, 8e (phone: 42-65-36-26).

La Bagagerie Perhaps the best bag and belt boutique in the world. 12 Rue Tronchet, 8e (phone: 42-65-03-40), and other locations.

Au Bain-Marie Beautiful kitchenware and table accessories, with an emphasis on Art Deco designs. 8 Rue Boissy-d'Anglas, 8e (phone: 42-66-59-74).

Balenciaga Ready-to-wear and haute couture from the classic design house. 10 Av. George-V, 8e (phone: 47-20-21-11).

Barthélémy In a city of great cheese stores, this is at the top of almost everyone's *fromagerie* list. Platters of assorted cheeses are available. 51 Rue de Grenelle, 7e (phone: 45-48-56-75).

Berthillon Heavenly ice cream—Parisians often line up outside. Flavors, which change with the season, include wild strawberry, calvados crunch, and candied chestnut. Closed Mondays, Tuesdays, school holidays, and the month of August. 31 Rue St-Louis-en-l'Ile, 4e (phone: 43-54-31-61). Several cafés on the Ile St-Louis also serve scoops of Berthillon.

Biba Designer-label women's clothes, such as Gaultier and Junko Shimada. 18 Rue de Sèvres, 6e (phone: 45-48-89-18).

Boucheron One of several fine jewelers clustered around the elegant Place Vendôme. 26 Pl. Vendôme, 1er (phone: 42-61-58-16).

Boutique Le Flore You'll find silver-plated eggcups and other bistro accoutrements in this annex of the celebrated *Café de Flore*. 26 Rue St-Benoît, 6e (phone: 45-44-33-40).

Brentano's A variety of British and American fiction and nonficton, including travel, technical, and business books. 37 Av. de l'Opéra, 2e (phone: 42-61-52-50).

Cacharel Fashionable ready-to-wear in great prints for children and adults. 34 Rue Tronchet, 8e (phone: 47-42-12-61); 5 Pl. des Victoires, 1er (phone: 42-33-29-88); and other locations.

Carel Beautiful shoes. 12 Rond-Point des Champs-Elysées, 8e (phone: 45-62-30-62), and other locations.

Carita Paris's most extensive—and friendliest—beauty/hair salon. 11 Rue du Faubourg-St-Honoré, 8e (phone: 42-68-13-40).

Cartier The legendary jeweler. 11-13 Rue de la Paix, 2e (phone: 42-61-58-56), and other locations.

Castelbajac Trendy designer clothes for men and women. 31 Pl. du Marché St-Honoré, 1er (phone: 42-60-78-40), and other locations.

Caves Taillevent One of Paris's best and most fairly priced wine shops, run by the owners of the three-star restaurant of the same name. 199 Rue du Faubourg-St-Honoré, 8e (phone: 45-61-14-09).

Céline A popular high-fashion women's boutique for clothing and accessories. 24 Rue François-Ier, 8e (phone: 47-20-22-83); 3 Av. Victor-Hugo, 16e (phone: 45-01-70-48); and other locations.

Cerruti For women's clothing, 15 Pl. de la Madeleine, 8e (phone: 47-42-10-78); for men's, 27 Rue Royale, 8e (phone: 42-65-68-72).

Chanel Classic women's fashions, inspired by the late, legendary Coco Chanel, now under the direction of Karl Lagerfeld. There are three individual buildings (one for shoes, another for clothing and cosmetics, and a third for watches) at 42 Av. Montaigne, 8e (phone: 47-23-74-12). Other locations include 29-31 Rue Cambon, 1er (phone: 42-86-28-00), headquarters for haute couture as well as ready-to-wear and accessories, and 5 Pl. Vendôme, 1er (phone: 42-86-28-00), which sells only Chanel watches.

Chantal Thomass Ultra-feminine fashions and sexy lingerie. Near the *Palais-Royal*, at 1 Rue Vivienne, 1er (phone: 40-15-02-36), and other locations.

Charles Jourdan Sleek, high-fashion footwear. 86 Av. des Champs-Elysées, 8e (phone: 45-62-29-28); 5 Pl. de la Madeleine, 1er (phone: 42-61-50-07); and other locations.

Charley Featuring an excellent selection of lingerie, plus personal attention and relatively low prices. 14 Rue du Faubourg-St-Honoré, 8e (phone: 47-42-17-70).

Charvet Paris's answer to Jermyn Street. An all-in-one men's shop, where shirts (they stock more than 4,000) and ties are the house specialties. 28 Pl. Vendôme, 1er (phone: 42-60-30-70).

La Châtelaine Where all of Paris shops for exquisite (and costly) toys and clothing for children. 170 Av. Victor-Hugo, 16e (phone: 47-27-44-07).

Chaumet Crownmakers for most of Europe's royalty. Expensive jewels, including antique watches covered with semiprecious stones. 12 Pl. Vendôme, 1er (phone: 42-60-32-82), and 46 Av. George-V, 8e (phone: 49-52-08-25).

Chloé Fashion for women. 54-56 Rue du Faubourg-St-Honoré, 8e (phone: 44-94-33-00).

Christian Dior One of the most famous couture houses in the world. Men's fashion, articles for the home, cosmetics, and *Baby Dior* (clothing for infants) are also here. 28-30 Av. Montaigne, 8e (phone: 40-73-54-44).

Christian Lacroix This designer offers the "hautest" of haute couture. 26 Av. Montaigne, 8e (phone: 47-23-44-40), and 73 Rue du Faubourg-St-Honoré, 8e (phone: 42-65-79-08).

Christofle The internationally famous silversmith. 9 Rue Royale, 8e (phone: 49-33-43-00).

Claude Montana Ready-to-wear and haute couture from this au courant designer. For both men's and women's clothes, 3 Rue des Petits-Champs, 1er (phone: 40-20-02-14); for women's clothes only, 31 Rue de Grenelle, 7e (phone: 42-22-69-56).

Coesnon Arguably one of Paris's finest charcuteries—in spite of its diminutive size—with the very best terrines, pâtés, *boudin blanc aux truffes,* and other temptations. 30 Rue Dauphine, 6e (phone: 43-54-35-80).

Commes des Garçons Asymmetrical-style clothing for both *des filles* and *des garçons.* 40-42 Rue Etienne-Marcel, 1er (phone: 42-33-05-21).

Comptoirs de la Tour d'Argent Glassware, napkins, silver items, and other objects bearing the celebrated restaurant's logo. 2 Rue de Cardinal-Lemoine, 5e (phone: 46-33-45-58).

Corinne Cobson The daughter of the founders of *Dorothée Bis* (see below) is making a name for herself with her youthful, cheerfully sexy women's clothing. 43 Rue de Sèvres, 6e (phone: 40-49-02-04).

Courrèges Another bastion of haute couture. 40 Rue François-Ier, 8e (phone: 47-20-70-44), and 46 Rue du Faubourg-St-Honoré, 8e (phone: 42-65-37-75).

Cristalleries de Saint Louis Handmade lead crystal at good prices. They will pack and ship purchases. 13 Rue Royale, 8e (phone: 40-17-01-74).

Dalloyau Fine purveyor of pastries and inventor of the incredibly delicious *gâteau opéra,* a confection of coffee and chocolate cream frosted with the darkest of chocolate and topped with edible gold leaf. 99-101 Rue du Faubourg-St-Honoré, 8e (phone: 43-59-18-10); 2 Pl. Edmond-Rostand, 6e (phone: 43-29-31-10); and other locations.

Debauve et Gallais The decor of this shop, housed in a building dating from 1800, is as fine as the delicious chocolates sold here. 30 Rue des Sts-Pères, 7e (phone: 45-48-54-67).

Didier Lamarthe Elegant handbags and accessories. 219 Rue du Faubourg-St-Honoré, 1er (phone: 42-96-09-90).

Diners En Ville Irresistible antique glassware, dishes, and tablecloths. 27 Rue de Varenne, 7e (phone: 42-22-78-33).

Dominique Morlotti A current favorite of Paris's best-dressed men. 25 Rue St-Sulpice, 6e (phone: 43-54-89-89).

Dorothée Bis Colorful women's knit sportswear. 33 Rue de Sèvres, 6e (phone: 42-22-02-90), and other locations.

Les Drugstores Publicis A uniquely French version of the American drugstore, with an amazing variety of goods—perfume, books, records, foreign newspapers, magazines, film, cigarettes, food, and more, all wildly overpriced. 149 Bd. St-Germain, 6e (phone: 42-22-92-50); 133 Av. des Champs-Elysées, 8e (phone: 47-23-54-34); and 1 Av. Matignon, 8e (phone: 43-59-38-70).

E. Dehillerin An enormous selection of professional cookware. 18-20 Rue Coquillière, 1er (phone: 42-36-53-13).

Elle A clothes and home furnishings boutique run by the magazine that sums up Parisian feminine style. 30 Rue St-Sulpice, 6e (phone: 43-26-46-10).

Emmanuel Ungaro Haute couture for women. 2 Av. Montaigne, 8e (phone: 47-23-61-94).

Emmanuelle Khanh Feminine clothes in lovely fabrics, including embroidered linen. 2 Rue de Tournon, 6e (phone: 46-33-41-03).

Erès Avant-garde sportswear, including chic bathing suits, for men and women. 2 Rue Tronchet, 8e (phone: 47-42-24-55).

Floriane Smart and well-made clothes for children and infants. 45 Rue de Sèvres, 6e (phone: 45-49-97-61), and other locations.

Franck et Fils A department store for women's designer clothes, ranging from Yves Saint Laurent to Thierry Mugler. 80 Rue de Passy, 16e (phone: 46-47-86-00).

Fratelli Rossetti All kinds of shoes, made from buttery-soft leather, for men and women. 54 Rue du Faubourg-St-Honoré, 8e (phone: 42-65-26-60).

Galignani This shop, with books in English and French, has been run by the same family since the early 19th century. 224 Rue de Rivoli, 1er (phone: 42-60-76-07).

Georges Rech One of the most popular makers of classy, very Parisian styles, and at more affordable prices than other similar labels. 273 Rue du Faubourg-St-Honoré, 1er (phone: 42-61-41-14); 54 Rue Bonaparte, 6e (phone: 43-26-84-11); and other locations.

Gianni Versace This mega-store adorned with Empire antiques sells the designer's men's, women's, and children's lines. Across from the *Palais de l'Elysée* at 62 Rue du Faubourg-St-Honoré, 8e (phone: 47-42-88-02). A smaller Rive Gauche outlet featuring only women's clothing is located at 66 Rue des Sts-Pères, 6e (phone: 45-49-22-66).

Giorgio Armani The legendary Italian designer has two shops on the elegant Place Vendôme, 1er: No. 6 (phone: 42-61-55-09), for his top-of-the-line clothes, and *Emporio Armani,* No. 25 (phone: 42-61-02-34), for his less expensive line.

Givenchy Beautifully tailored clothing by the master couturier. 3 and 8 Av. George-V, 8e (phone: 47-20-81-31).

Guerlain For fine perfume and cosmetics. 2 Pl. Vendôme, 1er (phone: 42-60-68-61); 68 Champs-Elysées, 8e (phone: 45-62-52-57); 29 Rue de Sèvres, 6e (phone: 42-22-46-60); and 93 Rue de Passy, 16e (phone: 42-91-60-02).

Guy Laroche Classic, conservative couture. 30 Rue du Faubourg-St-Honoré, 8e (phone: 42-65-62-74), and 29 Av. Montaigne, 8e (phone: 40-69-69-50).

Hanae Mori The grande dame of Japanese designers in Paris. 9 Rue du Faubourg-St-Honoré, 8e (phone: 47-23-52-03), and 5 Pl. de l'Alma, 8e (phone: 40-70-05-73).

Hédiard A pricey but choice food shop, notable for its assortment of coffees and teas. There's a chic tearoom upstairs. 21 Pl. de la Madeleine, 8e (phone: 42-66-44-36).

Hermès For very high quality classic clothes, ties, scarves, handbags, shoes, saddles, and other accessories. 24 Rue du Faubourg-St-Honoré, 8e (phone: 40-17-47-17).

Hôtel des Ventes Drouot-Richelieu Paris's huge auction house often offers good buys. 9 Rue Drouot, 9e (phone: 48-00-20-20).

Hugo Boss Fine men's clothes and accessories at reasonable prices. 2 Pl. des Victoires, 1er (phone: 40-28-91-64).

IGN (French National Geographic Institute) All manner of maps—ancient and modern, foreign and domestic, esoteric and mundane—are sold here. 136 *bis* Rue Grenelle, 7e, and 107 Rue La Boëtie, 8e (phone for both: 42-56-06-68).

Inès de la Fressange The former Chanel model has opened this chic shop, which sells everything from classic white silk shirts to furniture gilded with her signature oak leaf. 14 Av. de Montaigne, 8e (phone: 47-23-08-94).

Issey Miyake An "in" shop, selling women's clothing made by the Japanese artist-designer. Miyake's latest collections are at 3 Pl. des Vosges, 4e (phone: 48-87-01-86); a lower-priced line is featured at *Plantation,* 17 Bd. Raspail, 7e (phone: 45-48-12-32).

Jean-Paul Gaultier Designer clothes for men and women. 6 Rue Vivienne, 2e (phone: 42-86-05-05).

Jil Sander The first boutique in Paris for the leading German womenswear designer. 52 Av. Montaigne, 8e (phone: 44-95-06-70).

John Lobb What are said to be the finest men's shoes in the world (and probably the most expensive) are sold here. 51 Rue François-Ier, 8e (phone: 45-62-06-34).

Junko Shimada Formfitting clothes from the chic Japanese designer. 54 Rue Etienne-Marcel, 2e (phone: 42-36-36-97).

Karl Lagerfeld Women's clothing in a more adventurous spirit than those he designs for Chanel. 19 Rue du Faubourg-St-Honoré, 8e (phone: 42-66-64-64).

Kenzo Avant-garde fashions by the Japanese designer. A *Kenzo* children's shop is located in the passageway next to the store. 3 Pl. des Victoires, 1er (phone: 40-39-72-03). *Kenzo Studio,* with a lower-priced sportswear line, is at 60 Rue de Rennes, 6e (phone: 45-44-27-88).

Kitchen Bazaar Specializes in everything imaginable for the smart kitchen. 11 Av. du Maine, 15e (phone: 42-22-91-17). A second store, *Kitchen Bazaar Autrement,* features kitchen utensils from all over the world. 6 Av. du Maine, 15e (phone: 45-48-89-00).

Lalique The famous crystal. 11 Rue Royale, 8e (phone: 42-66-52-40), and in the *Carrousel du Louvre,* entrance at 99 Rue de Rivoli, 1er (phone: 42-86-01-51).

Lanvin Another fabulous designer, with several spacious, colorful boutiques under one roof. For women's and men's clothes, 15 and 22 Rue du Faubourg-St-

Honoré, 8e (phone: 44-71-33-33); for men's clothes only, 2 Rue Cambon, 1er (phone: 42-60-38-83).

Legrand Fille et Fils Fine wines and spirits and articles for the *cave* and table, such as *rattes* (wrought-iron candle holders used in real wine cellars), plus excellent maps of French wine regions. 1 Rue Banque, 2e (phone: 42-60-07-12).

Lenôtre Specializes in pastries and other desserts—from exquisite éclairs and fruit mousses to charlottes and chocolates. 44 Rue d'Auteuil, 16e (phone: 45-24-52-52), and several other locations.

Lescêne-Dura Everything for the wine lover or maker, except the wine itself. 63 Rue de la Verrerie, 4e (phone: 42-72-08-74).

Limoges-Unic Two stores on Rue de Paradis (10e), the first selling more expensive items, the second offering many varieties of Limoges china as well as a good selection of typically French Porcelaine de Paris. No. 12 (phone: 47-70-54-49), and No. 58 (phone: 47-70-61-49).

Lolita Lempicka Iconoclastic, formfitting womenswear. 3 *bis* Rue de Rosiers, 4e (phone: 42-74-42-94), and other locations.

Louis Vuitton High-quality luggage and handbags. The agreeable, efficient, and well-mannered staff at the modern Avenue Montaigne branch are a pleasure after the chilly reception at the original Avenue Marceau shop. 54 Av. Montaigne, 8e (phone: 45-62-47-00), and 78 *bis* Av. Marceau, 8e (phone: 47-20-47-00).

Lumicrystal In the building where artist Jean-Baptiste-Camille Corot lived and died, this fine china and crystal store carries Baccarat, Daum, Limoges, and Puiforcat. 22 Rue de Paradis, 10e (phone: 47-70-27-97).

La Maison du Chocolat Robert Linxe, perhaps the most talented chocolate maker in Paris, produces delicate, meltingly delicious confections. 225 Rue du Faubourg-St-Honoré, 8e (phone: 42-27-39-44).

La Maison de l'Escargot This shop prepares (and sells) more than 10 tons of snails annually, following a well-guarded secret recipe. 68 Rue Fondary, 15e (phone: 45-77-93-82).

Maison de la Truffe The world's largest retailer of truffles. There are fresh black truffles from November through March, and the fresh white variety are offered from mid-October through December; the rest of the year they're preserved. 19 Pl. de la Madeleine, 8e (phone: 42-65-53-22).

Maria Luisa Haute couture and daring new looks from Paris's top designers are the stock in trade here. 2 Rue Cambon, 1er (phone: 47-03-96-15).

Marie Mercié Fashionable hats, including turbans and velvet berets. 56 Rue Tiquetonne, 2e (phone: 40-26-60-68), and 23 Rue St-Sulpice, 6e (phone: 43-26-45-83).

Marithée & François Girbaud Not just jeans at this shop for men and women. 38 Rue Etienne-Marcel, 2e (phone: 42-33-54-69).

Maud Frizon Sophisticated, imaginative shoes and handbags. 83 Rue des Sts-Pères, 6e (phone: 42-22-06-93).

Max Mara Carries six distinct collections of Italian ready-to-wear, from classic chic to trendy, at surprisingly affordable prices. 37 Rue du Four, 6e (phone: 43-29-91-10); 265 Rue du Faubourg-St-Honoré, 1er (phone: 40-20-04-58); and other locations.

Michel Swiss The best place to buy perfume in the city, offering a voluminous selection, cheerful service, and excellent discounts. American visitors who spend more than 2,700F (about $466 at press time) get a refund of 25%; the VAT refund brings the total discount to almost 44%. 16 Rue de la Paix, 2e (phone: 42-61-71-71).

Miss Maud High-style shoes for young folks' feet. 90 Rue du Faubourg-St-Honoré, 8e (phone: 42-65-27-96), and other locations.

Missoni Innovative Italian knitwear. 43 Rue du Bac, 7e (phone: 45-48-38-02).

Moholy-Nagy The grandson of Bauhaus artist László Moholy-Nagy creates superb shirts, most in cotton, for men and women. 2 *Galerie Vivienne,* 2e (phone: 40-15-05-33).

M.O.R.A. One of Paris's "professional" cookware shops, though it sells to amateurs as well. Just about any piece of equipment you can imagine, and an interesting selection of cookbooks in French. 13 Rue Montmartre, 1er (phone: 45-08-19-24).

Morabito Magnificent handbags and luggage at steep prices. 1 Pl. Vendôme, 1er (phone: 42-60-30-76).

Motsch et Fils Fine hatmaker for men and women since 1887—the film star Jean Gabin was a customer. 42 Av. George-V, 8e (phone: 47-23-79-22).

Muriel Grateau An eclectic shop, with silk blouses and fine table linen. *Jardin du Palais-Royal,* under the arcade, 1er (phone: 40-20-90-30).

Les Must de Cartier Actually two boutiques, on either side of the *Ritz* hotel, offering such Cartier items as lighters and watches at prices that, though not low, are almost bearable when you deduct the 25% VAT. 7-23 Pl. Vendôme, 1er (phone: 42-61-55-55).

Au Nain Bleu The city's greatest toy store. 408 Rue du Faubourg-St-Honoré, 8e (phone: 42-60-39-01).

Nina Ricci Women's fashions, as well as the famous perfume. 39 Av. Montaigne, 8e (phone: 49-52-56-00).

L'Olivier Olives and olive products, with a variety of olive oils, plus other fine cooking oils, from hazelnut to walnut. 23 Rue de Rivoli, 4e (phone: 48-04-56-59).

Paco Rabanne Men's and women's clothes by a French designer famous for dresses mixing fabric and metals. 7 Rue du Cherche-Midi, 6e (phone: 42-22-87-80).

Papier Plus One of Paris's finest *papeteries* (stationery stores). 9 Rue du Pont Louis-Philippe, 4e (phone: 42-77-70-49).

Per Spook One of the city's best younger designers. 40 Av. Montaigne, 8e (phone: 42-99-60-00), and other locations.

Au Petit Matelot Classic sportswear, outdoor togs, and nautical accessories for men, women, and children. Especially terrific are their Tyrolean-style olive or navy loden coats. 27 Av. de la Grande-Armée, 16e (phone: 45-00-15-51).

Pierre Balmain Women's fashions from the classic couturier. 44 Rue François-Ier, 8e (phone: 47-20-98-79), and other locations.

Pierre Cardin The famous designer's own boutique. 27 Av. de Marigny, 8e (phone: 42-66-92-25), and other locations.

Poilâne Considered by many French to sell the best bread in the country; the large and crusty, round country-style loaves dubbed *pain Poilâne* are delicious with soup, pâté, cheese, or cassoulet. 8 Rue du Cherche-Midi, 6e (phone: 45-48-42-59).

Popy Moreni Unusually designed unisex clothes inspired by commedia dell'arte costumes. On one of the loveliest squares in the city. 13 Pl. des Vosges, 4e (phone: 42-77-09-96).

Porthault Expensive but exquisite bed and table linen. 18 Av. Montaigne, 8e (phone: 47-20-75-25).

Puiforcat Art Deco tableware in a beautiful setting. 22 Rue François-Ier, 8e (phone: 47-20-74-27).

Robert Clergerie Among Paris's finest footwear, these slightly chunky, thick-soled shoes and boots will actually stand up to the perils of cobblestone streets. 5 Rue du Cherche-Midi, 6e (phone: 45-48-75-47), and other locations.

Romeo Gigli Men's and women's arty ready-to-wear and haute couture. 46 Rue de Sévigné, 3e (phone: 48-04-57-05).

Shakespeare and Company This legendary English-language bookstore, opposite *Notre-Dame,* is something of a tourist attraction in itself. 37 Rue de la Bûcherie, 5e (phone: 43-26-96-50).

Sidonie Larizzi Heavenly handmade women's shoes. 8 Rue Marignan, 8e (phone: 43-59-38-87).

Sonia Rykiel Stunning sportswear and knits. 175 Bd. St-Germain, 6e (phone: 49-54-60-60), and other locations.

Souleiado Vibrant, traditional Provençal fabrics made into scarves, shawls, totes, tableware, even bathing suits. 78 Rue de Seine, 6e (phone: 43-54-62-25), and 83 Av. Paul-Doumer, 16e (phone: 42-24-99-34).

Stéphane Kélian High-fashion, high-quality, and high-priced (but not completely unreasonable) men's and women's shoes. 66 Av. des Champs-Elysées, 8e (phone: 42-25-56-96), and other locations.

Tartine et Chocolat Clothing for children, from infancy to 12 years old, and dresses for moms-to-be. 90 Rue de Rennes, 6e (phone: 42-22-67-34).

Ted Lapidus A compromise between haute couture and fine ready-to-wear. 23 Rue du Faubourg-St-Honoré, 8e (phone: 44-60-89-91); 35 Rue François-Ier, 8e (phone: 47-20-56-14); and other locations.

Thierry Mugler Dramatic ready-to-wear for women. 10 Pl. des Victoires, 2e (phone: 42-60-06-37), and other locations.

Trussardi Italian ready-to-wear from a designer whose leather goods and canvas carryalls are much appreciated by the French and Japanese. 21 Rue du Faubourg-St-Honoré, 8e (phone: 42-65-11-40).

La Tuile à Loup Crafts from the provinces, including Burgundy pottery and Normandy lace. 35 Rue Daubenton, 5e (phone: 47-07-28-90).

Valentino Ready-to-wear and haute couture fashions for men and women from the Italian designer. 17-19 Av. Montaigne, 8e (phone: 47-23-64-61).

Van Cleef & Arpels One of the world's great jewelers. 22 Pl. Vendôme, 1er (phone: 42-61-58-58).

Vicky Tiel Strapless evening gowns decorated with beads and bows, as well as contemporary sweaters and baseball jackets. 21 Rue Bonaparte, 6e (phone: 44-07-15-99).

Victoire Ready-to-wear from up-and-coming designers such as André Walker, with attractive accessories and jewelry. 10 and 12 Pl. des Victoires, 2e (phone: 42-60-96-21 or 42-61-09-02), and other locations.

Virgin Megastore The British have taken over the Parisian market in CDs, audiocassettes, and videocassettes. Though the selection is staggering, the store is usually so crowded that browsing is impossible. 56-60 Champs-Elysées, 8e, and in the *Carrousel du Louvre,* entrance at 99 Rue de Rivoli, 1er (phone: 49-53-50-00 for both stores).

Walter Steiger Some of the capital's most expensive footwear for men and wom
The flagship shop displays satin slippers like precious jewels—with pri
to match. 83 Rue du Faubourg-St-Honoré, 8e (phone: 42-66-65-08).

W. H. Smith and Sons The largest English-language bookstore in Paris (with more
space now that the upstairs tearoom has been converted into additional
shelf space). It sells the Sunday *New York Times,* in addition to many British
and American magazines. 248 Rue de Rivoli, 1er (phone: 42-60-37-97).

Yohji Yamamoto This Japanese designer offers highly unusual outerwear. For
women, 25 Rue du Louvre, 1er (phone: 42-21-42-93); for men, 47 Rue
Etienne-Marcel, 1er (phone: 45-08-82-45).

Yves Saint Laurent The world-renowned designer's flagship boutique is here, on
the Rue du Faubourg-St-Honoré. 38 Rue du Faubourg-St-Honoré, 8e
(phone: 42-65-74-59); 6 Pl. St Sulpice, 6c (phone: 43-29-43-00); and other
locations.

BEST DISCOUNT SHOPS √ √

If you (like us) are among those shoppers who believe that the eighth deadly
sin is buying retail, you'll treasure the following inexpensive outlets, including some of Paris's best *dépôt-vente* shops, where merchandise is sold on
consignment, at a discount. Several discount designer fashion outlets line
the Rue d'Alésia (14e), from *Sonia Rykiel* at No. 64, to *Chevignon* at No.
122. Also, Rue de Paradis (10e) is the best area to shop for crystal and
porcelain—Baccarat, Saint-Louis, Haviland, Bernardaud, and Villeroy &
Boch—at amazing prices. Try *Boutique Paradis,* No. 1 *bis; L'Art et La Table,*
No. 3; *Porcelain Savary,* No. 9; *Arts Céramiques,* No. 15; and *Cristallerie
Paradis,* No. 17.

Anna Lowe Yves Saint Laurent, Valentino, and others, at a discount. 35 Av.
Matignon, 8e (phone: 43-59-96-61).

Anne Parée Great buys on French perfume, Dior scarves, men's ties, Limoges
china, and Vuarnet sunglasses. A 40% discount (including VAT) is given
on purchases totaling 1,500F (about $260 at press time) or more. Mail order,
too. 10 Rue Duphot, 1er (phone: 42-60-03-26).

Bab's High fashion at reasonable prices. 29 Av. Marceau, 16e (phone: 47-20-84-
74), and 89 *bis* Av. des Ternes, 17e (phone: 45-74-02-74).

Bidermann Menswear from Kenzo, Courrèges, and more in a warehouse of a store
in the Marais. 114 Rue de Turenne, 3e (phone: 44-61-17-00).

Boëtie 104 Good buys on men's and women's shoes. 104 Rue La Boëtie, 8e (phone:
43-59-72-38).

Cacharel Stock Surprisingly current Cacharel fashions at about a 40% discount.
114 Rue d'Alésia, 14e (phone: 45-42-53-04).

Catherine Baril Women's ready-to-wear by designers such as Chanel and Jean-Louis Scherrer. 14 Rue de la Tour, 16e (phone: 45-20-95-21). The men's store down the street carries labels such as Armani and Hermès. 25 Rue de la Tour, 16e (phone: 45-27-11-46).

Chercheminippes One of the best Parisian *dépôt-vente* shops for high-quality children's clothes. The women's *dépôt-vente* collections just down the street are also worth a visit. Children's clothes, 160 Rue du Cherche-Midi, 6e (phone: 42-22-33-89), plus two stores for women, at No. 109 (phone: 42-22-45-23) and No. 111 (phone: 42-22-53-76).

Dépôt des Grandes Marques A third-floor shop near the stock market, featuring up to 50% markdowns on Louis Féraud, Cerruti, Renoma, and similar labels. 15 Rue de la Banque, 2e (phone: 42-96-99-04).

Dorothée Bis Stock The well-known sportswear at about 40% off. 74 Rue d'Alésia, 14e (phone: 45-42-17-11).

Eiffel Shopping Another bastion of fine French perfumes at discounted prices, it also stocks Lalique crystal, watches, and upscale costume jewelry. 9 Av. de Suffren, 7e (phone: 45-66-55-30).

Eve Cazes Bijoux d'Occasion A gem expert has opened a *dépôt-vente* for pre-owned fine jewelry, including pieces by Chaumet and Van Cleef & Arpels. Prices are about 40% lower than new. 20 Rue de Miromesnil, 8e (phone: 42-65-95-44).

Jean-Louis Scherrer Haute couture labels by Scherrer and others at about half their original prices. 29 Av. Ledru-Rollin, 12e (phone: 46-28-39-27).

Kashiyama Check out the upper level of this store for the previous season's clothes from Paris's hottest young designers, sold at a discount here. 80 Rue Jean-Jacques-Rousseau, 1er (phone: 40-26-46-46).

Mendès Less-than-wholesale prices on haute couture, especially Saint Laurent and Lanvin. 65 Rue Montmartre, 2e (phone: 42-36-83-32).

Miss Griff The very best of haute couture in small sizes (up to size 10) at small prices. Alterations, too. 19 Rue de Penthièvre, 8e (phone: 42-65-10-00).

Mouton à Cinq Pattes Ready-to-wear clothing for men, women, and children at 50% off original prices. 8 and 18 Rue St-Placide, 6e (phone: 45-48-86-26), and other locations.

Nina Ricci Stock Discounted fashions by this designer. 17-19 Rue François-Ier, 8e (phone: 47-23-78-88).

Réciproque Billed as the largest *dépôt-vente* in Paris, this outlet features names like Chanel, Alaïa, Lanvin, and Scherrer, as well as fine objets d'art. Several hundred square yards of display area are arranged by designer and by size. Five locations on the Rue de la Pompe, 16e: No. 89 for artwork; No. 93 for women's eveningwear; No. 95 for women's sportswear; No. 103 for men's clothing and accessories (phone: 47-04-30-28 for these four); and No. 123 for women's coats and accessories (phone: 47-27-30-28).

Soldes Trois Lanvin fashions at about half their normal retail cost. 3 Rue de Vienne, 8e (phone: 42-94-99-67).

Sonia Rykiel Rykiel's clothes at half price. 64 Rue d'Alésia, 14e (phone: 43-95-06-13).

SECOND BESTS

If haute couture prices paralyze your pocketbook, several shops in the city offer pre-owned, high-style clothes with down-to-earth price tags. *L'Astucerie* (105 Rue de Javel, 15e; phone: 45-57-94-74) offers designerwear and accessories, from Hermès scarves and Kelly bags to Vuitton luggage; *La Marette* (25 *Galerie Vivienne*, 2e; phone: 42-60-08-19) carries designer items including a selection of stylish children's outfits and accessories; *Dider Ludot*, under the arcades of the *Jardin du Palais-Royal* (19-24 Galerie Montpensier, 1er; phone: 42-96-06-56), offers an array of museum-quality designer fashions, most from the 1940s, '50s, and '60s; and *Troc'Eve* (25 Rue Violet, 15e; phone: 45-79-38-36) also has an impressive stock of pre-owned designer clothes in perfect condition.

SPORTS AND FITNESS

BICYCLING Rentals are available in the *Bois de Boulogne* and the *Bois de Vincennes,* or contact *Paris-Vélo* (2 Rue du Fer-à-Moulin, 5e; phone: 47-07-67-45). For a membership fee, you can take advantage of group outings in Paris and the surrounding region, maps of cycling routes in the area, and other information especially for cyclists from the *Fédération Française de Cyclotourisme* (*FFCT;* 8 Rue Jean-Marie-Jégo, 13e; phone: 44-16-88-88); contact them for a detailed brochure in English. In addition to renting bicycles, both *Bicyclub* (8 Pl. de la Porte-de-Champerret, 17e; phone: 47-66-55-92) and *Paris by Cycle* (78 Rue de l'Ouest, 14e; phone: 40-47-08-04 for rentals and for excursions outside Paris; 48-87-60-01 for Paris tours) offer organized bicycle tours. *Bicyclub* can arrange group and individual tours in Paris and the surrounding region, while *Paris by Cycle* arranges guided group tours of the city and of Versailles, as well as bike trips alternating with horseback rides. *Mountain Bike Trip* (6 Pl. Etienne-Pernet, 15e; phone: 48-42-57-87 or 49-29-93-91) also arranges group rides in and around Paris. The world-famous *Tour de France* bicycle race takes place in July, ending in Paris.

FITNESS CENTERS The *Gymnase Club* (208 Rue de Vaugirard, 15e; phone: 47-83-99-45; and many other locations); *Club Quartier Latin* (19 Rue de Pontoise, 5e; phone: 43-54-82-45); *Club Jean de Beauvais* (5 Rue de Jean-de-Beauvais, 5e; phone: 46-33-16-80); *Espace Beaujon* (208 Rue du Faubourg-St-Honoré,

8e; phone: 42-89-12-32); and *Espace Vit'Halles* (48 Rue Rambuteau; phone: 42-77-21-71) are open daily to non-members for a fee.

GOLF Although there are no 18-hole courses within the city, several major layouts are close by. The *Fédération Française de Golf* (69 Av. Victor-Hugo, 16e; phone: 45-02-13-55) and the *French Ministry of Tourism* have set up a system whereby travelers and others who are not members of a local golf club can play. Greens fees vary according to the day and season, but are usually higher on weekends. Call ahead to reserve. For information on golf courses just outside of Paris, see *Great Golf Nearby* in DIVERSIONS.

In addition, there is a nine-hole municipal course at the *St-Cloud* racecourse (1 Rue du Camp Canadien, St-Cloud; phone: 47-71-39-22), west of the city.

HORSE RACING If Paris has a sporting passion, it's horses. The French invented the pari-mutuel betting system (based on equally distributed winnings) and in and around the city there are eight tracks, a half-dozen racing sheets, and several hundred places to bet during a season that runs year-round. Here are our odds-on favorites for a great day at the races.

WINNING TRACKS

Auteuil Opened in 1870 for steeplechase only, *Auteuil* is not like any other park; there are over 40 permanent obstacles spread across 30 acres. More than 60,000 Parisians turn out for the fashionable *Grande Steeplechase de Paris* on the third Sunday in June (this is where Hemingway took Ezra Pound to the races). The best tip for this track is a reservation at the *Panoramique de l'Hippodrome* restaurant (phone: 45-24-00-38). Or take your winnings over to the neighboring *Pré Catelan* (see *Eating Out*) for a singular, if pricey, dining experience. *Bois de Boulogne* (phone: 45-27-12-25).

Longchamp A temple of thoroughbred racing since 1855, this is Paris's most prestigious racetrack and the one for which hopeful entries train at nearby *Maisons-Laffitte, Enghien, Chantilly, Evry,* and *St-Cloud*. The track's two highlight events are the *Grand Prix de Paris* in late June, which carries a purse of one million francs, and the *Prix de l'Arc de Triomphe* in early October, which at five million francs is one of Europe's most lucrative races. *Bois de Boulogne* (phone: 44-30-75-00).

St-Cloud This course offers flat racing from spring to fall, with the prestigious *Grand Prix de St-Cloud* held the first Sunday in July. West of Paris, in the chic suburb of St-Cloud (phone: 46-02-62-29).

Vincennes A taxi ride into the woods, the *Champs de Courses de Vincennes* is the scene of night racing, particularly trotting. Popular with diehard bettors, the track has a rough reputation and caters to a working-class clientele: red wine at the bar, corn-yellow cigarettes, and spicy *merguez* (sausage) sandwiches. The major highlight of the Vincennes season is the *Prix d'Amérique* for trotters, in the dead cold of January. Reservations are advised for the track restaurant, *Le Paddock* (phone: 43-68-64-94). *Bois de Vincennes* (phone: 49-77-17-17).

From late April through early September, a number of other historic tracks around Paris open for selected racing dates. In late spring, races are scheduled in Fontainebleau, and the French equivalent of *Ascot,* the *Prix de Diane/Hermès,* is held at *Chantilly* (phone: 44-62-91-00), about 25 miles (40 km) north of Paris, as part of the *Grande Semaine. Chantilly,* which many consider the most beautiful racetrack in the world, also has inaugurated a magnificent horse racing museum. Legend has it that one of the 17th-century dukes who lorded over the *Château de Chantilly* believed he would be reincarnated as a horse and ordered stables fit for a king—or, at least, a duke—built for his next life. Though never used, the stables have now been converted into the *Musée Vivant du Cheval.* It's open daily in May and June; closed Tuesday mornings in July and August; Tuesdays in April, September, and October; mornings and Tuesdays November through March; and the first two weeks of December. There's an admission charge (phone: 44-57-13-13). After these spring events, the Parisian racing crowd moves on to summer racing at *Deauville* (about two hours from Paris). The best way to find out times, dates, and racing tips is by reading *Paris-Turf, Tiercé, France-Soir,* or *L'Equipe,* all available at newsstands.

OFF-TRACK BETTING

The words "win," "place," and "show" are as dear to a Frenchman's heart as liberty, fraternity, and equality. Identifiable by their bright green and red logos, there are over 7,000 *PMU (Pari-Mutuel Urbaine)* outlets in French cafés and tobacco shops for off-track betting. The overall system is the third-largest public service industry in France, and is easier to play than the lottery. The traditional system involves marking an entry card for the day's feature race. A minimum bet is 6F (about $1 at press time) for the *tiercé* (picking the first three horses to cross the finish line), or 10F (about $1.70 at press time) for a simple winner. More modern developments are course cafés. These neighborhood betting parlors, which charge an admission fee, offer satellite broadcasts of a full slate of day or night racing direct from trackside, and payouts are immediate. The food is often good, and the ambience convivial. There are presently about two dozen of these cafés in Paris, and their numbers are growing rapidly. Try the *Boul' Mich*

(116 Bd. St-Germain at Carrefour de l'Odéon, 6e; phone: 46-33-76-66), where the barman usually has a winning tip.

JOGGING The streets and sidewalks of Paris may be ideal for lovers, but they're not meant for runners. There are, however, a number of places where you can jog happily; one of the most pleasant is the 2,500-acre *Bois de Boulogne.* Five more centrally located parks are the *Jardin du Luxembourg* and the *Jardin des Tuileries* (see *Special Places* for both); the *Parc du Champ-de-Mars* (behind the *Eiffel Tower,* 7e); *Parc Monceau* (Bd. de Courcelles, 8e); and the *Jardin des Plantes* (Pl. Valhubert, 5e).

SOCCER There are matches from early August through mid-June at *Parc des Princes* (24 Rue du Commandant Guilbaud, 16e; phone: 42-88-02-76).

SQUASH *Stadium Squash Club* (44 Av. d'Ivry, 13e; phone: 45-85-39-06) has 14 air conditioned courts.

SWIMMING Paris boasts a large number of pools for visitors who like to combine sidestrokes with sightseeing. All of the following have an admission charge: the indoor *Piscine des Halles* (10 Pl. de la Rotonde, 1er; phone: 42-36-98-44), open daily; the indoor *Piscine Pontoise* (19 Rue de Pontoise, 5e; phone: 43-54-82-45), open daily; the outdoor *Butte-aux-Cailles* (5 Pl. Paul-Verlaine, 13e; phone: 45-89-60-05), open daily; the outdoor *Stade Nautique Robert-Keller* (14 Rue de l'Ingénieur-Robert-Keller, 15e; phone: 45-77-12-12), closed Mondays; the indoor *Jean-Taris* (16 Rue Thouin, 5e; phone: 43-25-54-03), open daily; the indoor *Tour Montparnasse* (beneath the tower at 66 Bd. du Montparnasse, 15e; phone: 45-38-65-19), open daily; *Piscine Georges-Vallerey* (148 Av. Gambetta, 20e; phone: 40-31-15-20), which is covered, but can be converted to open-air in good weather, open daily; and *Aquaboulevard* (5 Rue Louis-Armand, 15e; phone: 40-60-10-00), a combination health club/water park, with facilities such as a wave pool, manmade beach, and water slides, open daily.

TENNIS Six courts are available in the *Jardin du Luxembourg* for a nominal fee, but be certain to arrive early, as this is a popular spot. For general information on courts in Paris, call the *Ligue Régionale de Paris* (74 Rue de Rome, 17e; phone: 45-22-22-08) or the *Fédération Française de Tennis* (*Stade Roland-Garros,* 2 Av. Gordon-Bennett, 16e; phone: 47-43-48-00). For information on courts outside of Paris, and on obtaining tickets for the *French Open,* see *Game, Set, and Match: Tennis Around Paris* in DIVERSIONS.

THEATER AND OPERA

The most complete listings of theaters, operas, concerts, and movies are found in two weekly publications, *L'Officiel des Spectacles* and *Pariscope,* both available at newsstands. The season generally extends from September through May. Less expensive than in New York, tickets can be obtained at each box office; at any of the large *FNAC* stores (136 Rue de Rennes, 6e, phone: 49-54-30-00; in the *Forum des Halles,* 1er, phone: 40-41-40-00; also other locations); at the two *Virgin Megastores* (56-60 Champs-Elysées, 8e, and the *Carrousel du Louvre* shopping center, 99 Rue de Rivoli, 1er; phone: 49-53-50-00 for both); through brokers (*American Express* and *Thomas Cook* are good ones); or through your hotel's concierge. Tickets can also be purchased at high-tech *Billetel* machines at the *Galeries Lafayette* (see *Shopping*), near the *Centre Georges-Pompidou* (6 Bd. de Sébastopol; phone: 48-04-95-27), and other locations. Insert a credit card into a slot in the *Billetel* and choose from over 100 upcoming theater events and concerts. The device will spew out a display of dates, seats, and prices, from which you can order your tickets, which then will be printed on the spot and charged to your account. Half-price, day-of-performance theater tickets are available at *Kiosque* (15 Place de la Madeleine, 8e); it's closed mornings and Mondays. The curtain usually goes up at 8:30 PM.

The theatrical and operatic map of France has undergone some startling changes in the past decade, and the country literally bristles with first-rate repertory groups and opera companies. The lively arts here are, in fact, livelier than ever. Don't bypass an evening at the theater just because your French is a high school relic; it's a fine way to become a part of local life. In your favor is the current style of splashy, highly visual productions where spectacle trumps text. French-language productions of English classics generally can be found—after all, Paris's most-performed playwright is the *formidable* Guillaume Shakespeare.

What follows is a selection of our favorite Parisian theaters and opera houses.

CENTER STAGE

La Comédie-Française The undisputed dowager queen of French theater, as much a national monument as the *Eiffel Tower,* it presents lavish productions of great classics by Corneille, Racine, Molière, Rostand, and the happy few 20th-century playwrights like Anouilh, Giraudoux, and Sartre who have been received into the inner circle of French culture. The *CF* is polishing up its fin de siècle image (the theater itself was entirely renovated last year), but even at its stodgiest, it's well worth seeing. 2 Rue de Richelieu, 1er (phone: 40-15-00-15). The company also presents contemporary plays in the renovated 350-seat *Théâtre du Vieux-Colombier* (21 Rue du Vieux-Colombier, 6e; phone: 42-22-77-48).

L'Odéon–Théâtre de L'Europe The chameleon-like *Odéon* has, for years, been the joker in the French theatrical pack. After the turbulent period when it hosted the fabled company under the direction of the late Jean-Louis Barrault and Madeleine Renaud and ranked among the most popular houses in the city, it became an annex of the *Comédie-Française.* Now it can be seen in yet another incarnation, as the *Théâtre de l'Europe.* Headed by one of Europe's foremost directors, Giorgio Strehler of Milan's *Piccolo Teatro,* it has become a kind of theatrical Common Market, with original-language productions from all over Europe. Pl. de l'Odéon, 6e (phone: 44-41-36-36).

Opéra in Paris In a futuristic opera house on the Place de la Bastille, the *Opéra de la Bastille* began regular performances in 1990 under the baton of Myung-Whun Chung (no longer with the company), while the *Opéra/Palais Garnier,* at the melodramatic end of Avenue de l'Opéra, hosts the best in ballet (see *Special Places* for details on both opera houses). At press time, the *Opéra-Palais Garnier* was closed for renovations (until at least March 1996); all ballet performances are currently being held at the *Opéra de la Bastille.* The other mainstays of Paris opera are the *Théâtre National de l'Opéra-Comique,* at the *Salle Favart* (Pl. Boïeldieu, 9e; phone: 42-96-12-20), and the *Théâtre du Châtelet/Théâtre Musicale de Paris* (1 Pl. du Châtelet, 1er; phone: 40-28-28-98), in the old *Châtelet* theater. The latter, once the stronghold of the frothy operetta, now does everything from early Offenbach to late Verdi, importing productions from other European opera companies as well. The touch is light and stylish, the accent utterly French. The *Opéra-Comique* isn't especially comic. It's smaller and its performers are generally less well known than those at the *Opéra de la Bastille,* but it has a wider repertoire.

The city has numerous smaller theaters and companies as well. Known for its continually evolving and inventive style, the *Théâtre des Amandiers* (7 Av. Pablo-Picasso; phone: 46-14-70-00) is in Nanterre, a working class suburb of Paris. Recent presentations have included such time-honored classics as the *Oedipus* trilogy by Sophocles, but a trip to the box office can turn up any number of theatrical surprises. The theater is about 20 minutes by the *RER* city-rail from downtown Paris. New formats, odd curtain times, and a constant redefining of theater and its audience are the trademarks of the *Théâtre National de Chaillot* (Pl. du Trocadéro et du 11-Novembre, 6e; phone: 47-27-81-15), whose repertory ranges from *Hamlet* to *Faust* for children—performed by marionettes—to new texts by Algerian workers, plus contemporary musical happenings. And *Théâtre du Soleil* (La Cartoucherie de Vincennes, Rte. du Champ de Manoeuvres, *Bois de Vincennes,* 12e; phone: 43-74-24-08 or 43-74-87-63), housed in an old cartridge factory, always has had a colorful, sweeping style with a popular mood and political overtones. That was true in the dazzling production *1789,* which made the troupe's international reputation during that other year of French upheaval, 1968, and in the more recent Shakespeare series as well. *Bouffes du Nord* (37 *bis* Bd. de la Chapelle, 10e; phone: 46-07-34-50) is a magical place, where the simple stagings and excellent acoustics lend power to the Peter Brook company's productions, from Shakespeare to the *Mahabharata*. The *Théâtre Marie-Stuart* (4 Rue Marie-Stuart, 2e; phone: 45-08-17-80) produces contemporary drama, including some American works (though they're performed in French).

Paris's many café-theaters offer amusing songs, sketches, satires, and takeoffs on topical issues and events. Among them are *Café de la Gare* (41 Rue du Temple, 4e; phone: 42-78-52-51) and *Café d'Edgar* (58 Bd. Edgar-Quinet, 14e; phone: 42-79-97-97). In addition, several vessels moored along the quays offer theatrical performances, ranging from classical French plays to magic shows. The *Péniche Opéra* boat (200 Quai de Jemmapes, 10e; phone: 43-49-08-15) is berthed on the Canal St-Martin on the Rive Droite; it's closed during the summer. Nearby is the *Metamorphosis* (35 Quai de la Tournelle, 5e; phone: 42-61-33-70), which offers magic shows. At the Quai Malaquais, on the Rive Gauche, are *L'Ouragan* (phone: 40-46-01-24) and the *Mare au Diable* (phone: 40-46-90-67).

FILM

With about 200 movie houses, Paris is a real treat for film buffs. No other metropolis offers such a cinematographic feast—current French chic, recent imports from across the Atlantic, grainy 1930s classics, and the best of Third World and Eastern European offerings. In any given week, there are up to 200 different movies shown, the foreign films generally in their original versions with French subtitles. The French often get their favorite American flicks up to six months late, but, then again, many of the front-runners at Cannes hit the screens here well before they wend their way stateside.

Both *Pariscope* and *L'Officiel des Spectacles,* which come out on Wednesday (the day the programs change), are available at newsstands and contain complete listings each week. *Pariscope* has thought of almost every possible way to classify films, sorting them into new releases and revivals, broad subject categories, location by *arrondissement,* late-night showings, and so on.

Films shown with their original-language soundtracks are called *VO (version originale),* worth noting if you want to avoid wincing at a French-dubbed version of an English-language film, called *VF (version française).* Broadly speaking, the undubbed variety of film flourishes on the Champs-Elysées and on the Rive Gauche, and it's a safe bet to avoid the mostly French-patronized houses of the Grands Boulevards north of the *Louvre.* There's more room in the big movie houses on the Champs-Elysées, but the cozier Quartier Latin establishments tend to specialize in the unusual and avant-garde.

The timetables aren't always reliable, so it's worth checking by telephone—if you can decipher the recorded messages that spell out exactly when the five or so showings a day begin. A *séance* (sitting) generally opens with advertisements, and the movie proper begins 15 to 20 minutes later; but since many theaters are small, it's best to arrive on time to ensure getting a seat.

At the *Cité des Sciences et de l'Industrie* complex (see *La Villette* in *Special Places*), the *Géode* (phone: 36-68-29-30 for a recorded message; 40-05-50-50 after 7 PM), the ultimate in high-tech, offers a B-Max hemispherical screen, cupped inside a reflecting geodesic dome. The program is limited, however, to a single scientifically oriented film at any given time. Located in La Défense, west of Paris, *Le Dome Imax* (Parvis de la Défense, La Défense; phone: 46-92-45-45) is billed as the largest of these hemispherical screens in the world.

The *Forum Horizon* (7 Pl. de la Rotonde, 1er; phone: 36-65-70-83), in the underground section of the *Forum des Halles* (see *Shopping*), offers a choice of six first-run movies and has one of the city's best sound systems, while the *Gaumont Kinopanorama* (60 Av. de la Motte-Picquet, 15e; phone: 43-06-50-50) boasts one of the widest screens in Paris. Other big screens are the *Grand Rex* (1 Bd. Poissonnière, 9e; phone: 42-36-83-93) and the *Gaumont Grand Ecran Italie* (30 Pl. d'Italie, 13e; phone: 45-80-77-00). The remodeled *Max Linder Panorama* (24 Bd. Poissonnière, 9e; phone: 48-24-00-47; 48-24-88-88 for a recording of screening times) has a spacious lobby where you can wait in comfort. Some out-of-the-way venues such as the *Olympique Entrepôt* (7 Rue Francis de Pressence, 14e; phone: 45-43-41-63) and the *Lucernaire Forum* (53 Rue Notre-Dame-des-Champs, 6e; phone: 45-44-57-34) are social centers in themselves, incorporating restaurants and/or other theaters.

The *Cinémathèque* at the *Palais de Chaillot* (see *Special Places*) runs a packed schedule of revivals at rates lower than those of commercial cinemas. Daily programs from the museum's eclectic archive of over 20,000 films often include several running concurrently, so that a James Cagney gangster epic can share billing with a 1950s British comedy and a Brazilian thriller; come early, as seating is limited. The *Cinémathèque* also operates theaters in the *Centre Georges-Pompidou* (see *Special Places;* phone: 44-78-12-33) and in the *Palais de Tokyo* (13 Av. President-Wilson, 16e; phone: 47-04-24-24). The *Vidéothèque de Paris* (see *Museums*), in the *Forum des Halles,* is an innovative public video library. Visitors can select individual showings or attend regularly scheduled screenings of films and television programs chronicling Paris's history.

There are two period movie houses almost worth a visit in themselves. *Le Ranelagh* (5 Rue des Vignes, 16e; phone: 42-88-64-44), where both film screenings and live theater performances are held, has an exquisite 19th-century interior. *La Pagode* (57 *bis* Rue de Babylone, 7e; phone: 47-05-12-15), decorated with flying cranes and cherry blossoms, and complete with a tearoom, is built around a Japanese temple shipped over to Paris by a department store owner in the 1920s.

MUSIC

The *Orchestre de Paris* is based at the *Salle Pleyel,* Paris's *Carnegie Hall* (252 Rue du Faubourg-St-Honoré, 8e; phone: 45-63-07-96). The *Nouvelle Orchestre Philharmonic* performs at a variety of venues, including the *Grand Auditorium* at *Maison de Radio France* (116 Av. du Président-Kennedy, 16e; phone: 42-30-22-22). Classical concerts and recitals also take place at the *Salle Gaveau* (45 Rue La Boëtie, 8e; phone: 49-53-05-07); the *Théâtre des Champs-Elysées* (15 Av. Montaigne, 8e; phone: 49-52-50-50); and the *Palais des Congrès* (2 Pl. Porte Maillot, 17e; phone: 40-68-22-22). Special concerts frequently are held in Paris's many places of worship, with moving music at high mass on Sundays.

The *Palais des Congrès* and the *Olympia* (28 Bd. des Capucines, 9e; phone: 47-42-25-49) are the places to see well-known international pop and rock artists. Innovative contemporary music is the province of the *Institut de Recherche et de Coopération Acoustique Musique* (*IRCAM;* 31 Rue du Cloître-St-Merri, 4e; phone: 44-78-48-43), whose musicians can be heard in various auditoriums of the *Centre Georges-Pompidou* (see *Special Places*). The *Musée Carnavalet* (see *Special Places*) rents out its concert hall to various music groups.

During summer and fall, in Paris the word "festival" means something more akin to a musical orgy. From classical to pop rock, it's all here for the listening.

Festival Estival and Festival d'Automne The former, in July and August, brings a musical kaleidoscope of Gregorian chants, Bartók string quartets, Rameau opera, and more to the city's most picturesque and acoustically delightful churches. The *Festival d'Automne,* which takes up where the *Estival* leaves off, concentrates on the contemporary, generally focusing on one or two main themes or composers and including a certain number of new works. Its moving spirit is Pierre Boulez, France's top musical talent. The *Festival d'Automne* also features theater and dance performances. For information, contact the *Festival Estival de Paris* (20 Rue Geoffroy-l'Asnier, Paris 75004; phone: 48-04-98-01) and the *Festival d'Automne* (156 Rue de Rivoli, Paris 75001; phone: 42-96-12-27).

NIGHTCLUBS AND NIGHTLIFE

Typically lavish *Folies-Bergère*–style stage shows are a featured part of the "Paris by Night" group tours offered by a number of tour operators (see *Tours*). In addition, most music halls offer a package (usually far from discount) that includes dinner, dancing, and a half bottle of champagne. To save money, try going to one of these places on your own, skipping dinner and the champagne (both usually are way below par), and sitting at the bar to see the show. The most famous extravaganzas occur nightly at *Crazy Horse* (12 Av. George-V, 8e; phone: 47-23-32-32); *Lido* (116 *bis* Champs-Elysées, 8e; phone: 40-76-56-10); *Moulin Rouge* (Pl. Blanche, 18e; phone: 46-06-00-19); and *Paradis Latin* (28 Rue du Cardinal-Lemoine, 5e; phone: 43-29-07-07). An amusing evening can also be spent at such smaller cabarets as *Au Lapin Agile* (22 Rue des Saules, 18e; phone: 46-06-85-87) and *Michou* (80 Rue des Martyrs, 18e; phone: 46-06-16-04). Reserve a few days in advance for any of the above.

There's one big difference between discotheques and so-called "private" clubs. The latter, fashionable "in" spots such as *Le Palace* (8 Rue Faubourg-Montmartre, 9e; phone: 42-46-10-87); *Régine* (49 Rue de Ponthieu, 8e; phone: 43-59-21-13); *Chez Castel* (15 Rue Princesse, 6e; phone: 43-26-90-22); *Olivia Valère* (40 Rue de Colisée, 8e; phone: 42-25-11-68); *L'Arc* (12 Rue de Presbourg, 16e; phone: 45-00-45-00); and *Les Bains* (7 Rue du Bourg-l'Abbé, 3e; phone: 48-87-01-80) superscreen potential guests. No reason is given for accepting some and turning others away. To gain entrance, go with a member or regular, dress to fit in with the crowd, and show up early and on a weeknight, when your chances of getting past the gatekeeper are at least 50-50. (One expensive way to get into *Régine, Chez Castel,* or *Les Bains* is to have your hotel make dinner reservations there for you.) Just as much fun and usually more hospitable are *Le Balajo* (9 Rue de Lappe, 11e; phone: 47-00-07-87), where the "in" crowd dances to music from rumba to rock; *Keur Samba* (73 Rue de la Boétie, 8e; phone: 43-50-03-10), for an African mood; *Le Café Vogue* (50 Rue de la Chaussée-d'Antin, 9e; phone: 42-80-69-40), a restaurant and disco that is, as its name suggests, a favorite haunt of fashion models and other beautiful people; *Chapelle des Lombards* (19 Rue de Lappe, 11e; phone: 43-57-24-24), for a Brazilian beat; *Le Cirque* (49 Rue de Ponthieu, 8e; phone: 42-25-12-13), a mainly gay nightclub; *Niel's* (27 Av. des Ternes, 17e; phone: 47-66-45-00), chic and popular with the film crowd; and *L'Ecume des Nuits,* in the *Méridien* hotel (see *Checking In*).

A natural choice for an American in Paris is the celebrated *Harry's New York Bar* (5 Rue Daunou, 2e; phone: 42-61-71-14), which has been serving classic cocktails to transatlantic transplants like Ernest Hemingway, Gertrude Stein, and George Gershwin since 1911; a *Harry's* tradition decrees that on the night of a US presidential election, only card-carrying Americans are allowed in the place, where they can watch election returns on the bar's TV set. Other pleasant, popular spots for a nightcap include *Bar de la Closerie des Lilas* (171 Bd. du Montparnasse, 6e; phone: 43-26-70-50); *Fouquet's* (99 Champs-Elysées, 8e; phone: 47-23-70-60); *Ascot Bar* (66 Rue Pierre-Charron, 8e; phone: 43-59-28-15); *Bar Anglais* in the *Plaza-Athénée* hotel (see *Checking In*); and *Pub Winston Churchill* (5 Rue de Presbourg, 16e; phone: 40-67-17-37).

Jazz buffs can choose from among the *Caveau de la Huchette* (5 Rue de la Huchette, 5e; phone: 43-26-65-05); *Le Bilboquet* (13 Rue St-Benoît, 6e; phone: 45-48-81-84); *New Morning* (7-9 Rue des Petites-Ecuries, 10e; phone:45-23-51-41); *La Villa* (in *La Villa* hotel, 29 Rue Jacob, 6e; phone: 43-26-60-00); *Le Petit Journal* (71 Bd. St-Michel, 6e; phone: 43-26-28-59); *Arbuci* (25 Rue de Buci, 6e; phone: 45-23-51-41); *Le Petit Opportune* (15 Rue des Lavandières-Sainte-Opportune; phone: 42-36-01-36); *Le Baiser Salé* (58 Rue des Lombards, 1er; phone: 42-33-37-71); and *Au Duc des Lombards* (42 Rue des Lombards, 1er; phone: 42-33-22-88). *Au Duc des Lombards* and *New Morning* are the best of the bunch.

Enghien-les-Bains, 8 miles (13 km) away in Enghien-les-Bains (3 Av. de Ceinture; phone: 34-12-90-00), is the only casino in the Paris vicinity. Open from 3 PM to about 4AM, it's easily reached by train from the *Gare du Nord.* For more information, see *Casinos Royale* in DIVERSIONS.

Best in Town

CHECKING IN

Paris offers a broad choice of accommodations, from luxurious palaces with every service to more humble budget hotels. Below is our selection from all categories; for a double room, expect to spend $450 or more (sometimes much more) per night in the "palace" hotels, which we've listed as very expensive; from $250 to $450 in the expensive ones; $150 to $250 in the moderate places; and less than $150 in the inexpensive hotels.

Hotel rooms usually are at a premium in Paris. To reserve your first choice, we advise making reservations at least a month in advance, even farther ahead for the smaller, less expensive places. Watch for the dates of special events, when hotels are even more crowded than usual. For information on apartment rentals and other accommodation options, see GETTING READY TO GO.

Street addresses of the hotels below are followed by the number of their *arrondissement* (neighborhood). Unless otherwise noted, all hotels listed feature air conditioning, TV sets, telephones, and private baths in the rooms. Some less expensive hotels may have private baths in only some of their rooms; it's a good idea to confirm whether your room has a private bath when making a reservation. Most of Paris's major hotels have complete facilities for the business traveler. Those hotels listed below as having "business services" usually offer such conveniences as an English-speaking concierge, meeting rooms, photocopiers, computers, translation services, and express check-out, among others. All hotels listed are open year-round and accept major credit cards, unless otherwise indicated.

For an unforgettable experience, we begin with our favorite Paris hostelries, followed by our cost and quality choices, listed by price category.

In an increasingly homogeneous and anonymous world, the fine Parisian hotel remains one of the last bastions of charm and luxury. From the first warm, flaky croissant to the last turned-down eiderdown, a stay in one of them is a study in perpetual pampering that is not to be missed. Such a hotel may have a sleek, urbane lobby that throbs with the pulse of Paris. Or it may be a small, exclusive retreat hidden away on a cobbled Rive Gauche street, whose stone walls have welcomed weary travelers for centuries. Either way, a stay at one of these extra-special spots is sure to be memorable.

Bristol Headquarters to dignitaries visiting the *Palais de l'Elysée* (Elysée Palace, the French White House), just a few steps down the street, this elegant establishment boasts 154 rooms and 41 suites, all beautifully decorated, and a one-Michelin-star restaurant with two dining rooms—one for summer and another for winter. The first is a light, airy glassed-in room overlooking the garden; the second is a richly wood-paneled room, a reassuring reminder of Old World craftsmanship. The open and exquisite elevator recalls an earlier age, the marvelously designed marble bathrooms are veritable oases of comfort, and the service is nothing short of superb. An elegant and comfortable lobby and bar add to the charm; there's also a new fitness center and business center, as well as a heated pool on the sixth-floor terrace, an amenity seldom found in Paris hotels. 112 Rue du Faubourg-St-Honoré, 8e (phone: 42-66-91-45; 800-223-6800; 212-838-3110 in New York City; fax: 42-66-68-68).

Crillon Today's heavy traffic gives the Place de la Concorde a frenetic atmosphere at odds with its 18th-century spirit. But here, within the Sienese marble foyers and the 163 elegant rooms and suites (plus three master suites) of this Relais & Châteaux member, guests are largely insulated from the world outside. Diplomats from nearby Embassy Row, observed by ever-present journalists, buy and sell countries in the bar (considered one of the city's most sophisticated meeting places) or dine in the two restaurants, *L'Obélisque* and the two-Michelin-star *Les Ambassadeurs* (see *Eating Out*). Rooms facing the street, though rather noisy, have a view *sans pareil;* those on the courtyards are just as nice and more tranquil. Business services are available. 10 Pl. de la Concorde, 8e (phone: 42-65-24-24; 800-888-4747; fax: 44-71-15-02).

George V The lobby is a League of Nations of private enterprise; it also seems to be where the *Cannes Film Festival* crowd spends the other 11 months of the year, so numerous are the stars, directors, producers, and other movie folk who stay in the hotel's 298 rooms and 53 suites and dine in its two restaurants, including the one-Michelin-star *Les Princes.* The *Eiffel Tower* is just across the river, the Champs-Elysées down the block, and the *Arc de Triomphe* around the corner; most of the rest of Paris can be seen from the windows of rooms on the higher floors. Even those who can't afford one of them—or the tranquil chambers facing the gracious courtyard—should be sure to stop in for an utterly lyrical croissant at breakfast or a mean martini in the lively and chic bar. Business services are available. 31 Av. George-V, 8e (phone: 47-23-54-00; fax: 47-20-40-00).

Lancaster If location is everything, this charming 19th-century townhouse has it all: It's steps from the Champs-Elysées and two blocks from the Faubourg-St-Honoré. Admired by literati, dignitaries, socialites, Americans in the know, and even the haughtiest of Parisians, this Savoy Group establishment exudes an air of gentility, calm, and, above all, coziness. Aside from its handsome, 18th-century antiques and objets d'art, every one of its only 50 rooms and nine suites (with no more than 10 rooms on each floor) has individual charm. Try to book accommodations on the sixth (top) floor, where there's sure to be a view of the *Eiffel Tower, Sacré-Coeur,* or the hotel's delightful garden from a balcony or a terrace. There's an old-fashioned bar with garden murals, a delightful spot for taking mid-morning coffee, afternoon tea, or a postprandial liqueur, and a relaxed and refined restaurant, with alfresco dining when the weather permits. If the pleasure of truly personal service and gracious surroundings with nary a glimmer of glitz are your preference, this is the place. Business services are available. 7 Rue de Berri, 8e (phone: 40-76-40-76; 800-223-6800; fax: 40-76-40-10).

Lutétia The only real palace hotel on the Rive Gauche, this aristocrat of elegantly ornamented stone with 286 rooms and 21 suites has reigned at the corner of Rue de Sèvres and Boulevard Raspail since 1910. From gray-striped balloon awnings and bowers of sculpted stone flowers framing its graceful arched windows to the regal red lobby appointed with crystal chandeliers, Art Deco skylights, and intricately carved wrought iron, this is a quintessentially Parisian place (owned by the Taillevent family, it's one of the city's few grand hotels still in French hands). It also offers some of the most fantastic views in Paris from its upper floors. The best perspective is from No. 71, a seventh-floor corner room whose balcony commands a view of nearly all of Paris's most famous monuments. There's also a restaurant, the one-Michelin-star *Le Paris,* and a brasserie. A range of business services is available. 45 Bd. Raspail, 6e (phone: 49-54-46-46; fax: 49-54-46-00).

Plaza-Athénée This European hotel is ever elegant and charming—from the 215 rooms and 41 suites done in Louis XV and XVI style to the *Relais Plaza* grill, where *tout Paris* seems to be eternally lunching, and the idyllic one-Michelin-star *Régence* restaurant, which is like a set for some Parisian *Mikado,* with its chirping birds, pools, and bridge. There's also the *Bar Anglais,* a classic Parisian spot for cocktails. A little more sedate and a little more French than the *George V* (above), this is an haute bastion that takes its dignity very seriously (a discreet note in each bathroom offers an unobtrusive route in and out of the hotel for those in jogging togs). Business services are available. 25 Av. Montaigne, 8e (phone: 47-23-78-33; fax: 47-20-20-70).

Ritz The Rive Droite establishment that César Ritz made synonymous with all the finer things in life is such a Paris legend that, seeing it for the first time, it's almost hard to believe it still exists, much less reigns as majestically as ever over the Place Vendôme. Marcel Proust wrote most of *Remembrance of Things Past* here, and Georges-Auguste Escoffier put France at the top of the culinary Olympus from its kitchen, still highly rated today as the two-Michelin-star *L'Espadon* restaurant. The *Ritz Club* is a nightclub and discotheque open to guests and club members only, and there's a deluxe spa. But even if you can't afford to stay in one of the 142 rooms or 45 suites, have a glass of champagne in the elegant bar. Business services are available. 15 Pl. Vendôme, 1er (phone: 42-60-38-30; fax: 42-60-23-71).

VERY EXPENSIVE

Grand Part of the Inter-Continental chain, this property has long been a favorite of Americans abroad, with its "meeting place of the world," the *Café de la Paix.* It has 545 rooms and luxurious suites, plus cheerful bars, two restaurants, and a prime location next to the *Opéra/Palais Garnier.* There is also a fitness center, and a wide range of business services is available. 2 Rue Scribe, 9e (phone: 40-07-32-32; 800-327-0200; fax: 42-66-12-51).

Inter-Continental The 452 rooms and suites have been meticulously restored to re-create turn-of-the-century elegance with modern conveniences. The cozy, top-floor Louis XVI "garret" rooms look out over the *Tuileries.* There's an American-style coffee shop, a grill, and a popular bar. Extensive business services are also offered. 3 Rue de Castiglione, 1er (phone: 44-77-11-11; fax: 44-77-14-60).

Pont Royal Right in the midst of Paris's most exclusive antiques and shopping district, this former 18th-century *hôtel particulier* (private home) has been a well-kept secret. Each of the 78 spacious rooms and suites is tastefully appointed with fine French antiques and sumptuous fabrics. The formal dining room, *Les Antiquaires,* serves first-rate fare, and business services are available. Closed for renovations at press time, the hotel was scheduled to reopen early this year. 7 Rue Montalembert, 7e (phone: 45-44-38-27; fax: 45-44-92-07).

Prince de Galles An excellent location (a next-door neighbor of the pricier *George V*) and impeccable style make this Sheraton member a good choice. All 173 rooms and suites are individually decorated, there's a restaurant and oak-paneled bar, and parking is available. Business services are offered. 33 Av. George-V, 8e (phone: 47-23-55-11; fax: 47-20-96-92).

Raphaël Less well-known among the top Paris hotels is this spacious, stately place, with a Turner in the lobby downstairs and paneling painted with sphinxes in the generous guestrooms. Its 87 rooms, including 38 suites, attract film folk and the like, and for those who savor strolling down the Champs-Elysées, it's only a short walk away. Most, but not all, of the rooms are air conditioned. There's a restaurant, and a wide range of business services is offered. 17 Av. Kléber, 16e (phone: 44-28-00-28; fax: 45-01-21-50).

Relais Carré d'Or For longer stays, this hostelry provides all the amenities of a luxury hotel, plus a variety of accommodations—from studios to multi-room apartments—all with modern kitchens, marble bathrooms, and lovely, understated furnishings. Most have balconies overlooking the hotel's garden or Avenue George V. There's a restaurant, and extensive business services are available. 46 Av. George-V, 8e (phone: 40-70-05-05; fax: 47-23-30-90).

Royal Monceau This elegant, impeccably decorated 180-room, 39-suite hotel has three restaurants (including *Le Jardin du Royal Monceau;* see *Eating Out*), two bars, a fitness center, a pool, a Jacuzzi, and a beauty salon. The rooms are spacious, and the Sunday brunch is a delight. A range of business services is also offered. Not far from the *Arc de Triomphe,* at 37 Av. Hoche, 8e (phone: 45-61-98-00; fax: 45-63-28-93).

La Trémoille Built in 1886, this former *hôtel particulier* is a true gem. Each of the 110 spacious rooms is beautifully appointed. The atmosphere is one of understated elegance, and the location, just off Avenue Montaigne, a bonus. There's a restaurant, and business services are available. 14 Rue de la Trémoille, 8e (phone: 47-23-34-20; fax: 40-70-01-08).

EXPENSIVE

Abbaye St-Germain On a quiet street, this small, delightful place was once a convent. The lobby has exposed stone arches, and the 46 elegant rooms (we especially admire No. 4, whose doors open onto the charming courtyard) are furnished with antiques, tastefully selected fabrics, and marble baths; none is air conditioned. Unfortunately, there continue to be some complaints about the service. There's no restaurant. Some business services are available. 10 Rue Cassette, 6e (phone: 45-44-38-11; fax: 45-48-07-86).

Balzac Very private, this luxurious, charming hotel has 70 rooms and suites, plus the Paris branch of Milan's *Bice* restaurant. The nocturnally inclined can dance until dawn in the discotheque, and business services are available. Ideally located off the Champs-Elysées, at 6 Rue Balzac, 8e (phone: 45-61-97-22; fax: 45-25-24-82).

Colbert Decorated in pastel tones, each of the 34 rooms and two suites in this Rive Gauche hostelry has a balcony and a mini-bar, but no air conditioning. There's no restaurant, but breakfast is included. Limited business services are available. 7 Rue de l'Hôtel-Colbert, 5e (phone: 43-25-85-65; 800-755-9313; fax: 43-25-80-19).

Duc de St-Simon In two big townhouses in a beautiful, quiet backwater off the Boulevard St-Germain, this elegant 29-room, five-suite establishment veritably screams Proust. None of the rooms is air conditioned, and there's no restaurant. Some business services are available. No credit cards accepted. A five-minute walk from the spectacular *Musée d'Orsay,* at 14 Rue de St-Simon, 7e (phone: 45-48-35-66; fax: 45-48-68-25).

L'Hôtel Small, but chic, this Rive Gauche hostelry is favored by experienced international travelers with an eye for the offbeat, and, though it's growing a bit shabby around the edges, it still has great charm. It's also where Oscar Wilde died (room No. 16 is a re-creation of the room in which he lived briefly in 1900) and where the Argentinian writer Jorge Luis Borges lived. The 24 rooms and three suites are tiny, but beautifully appointed with antiques, fresh flowers, and marble baths; they also have mini-bars and safes. The attractive restaurant serves first-rate fare. Business services are available. 13 Rue des Beaux-Arts, 6e (phone: 43-25-27-22; fax: 43-25-64-81).

Jeu de Paume The architect-owner of this former *jeu de paume* (tennis court) has artfully married old and new in this addition to the Ile St-Louis's collection of exclusive hotels. High-tech lighting, modern artwork, and a sleek glass elevator are set against ancient ceiling beams and limestone brick hearths. Each of the comfortable 30 rooms and two suites overlooks the lovely garden; none is air conditioned. There is also a music salon, but no restaurant. Business services are available. 54 Rue St-Louis-en-l'Ile, 4e (phone: 43-26-14-18; fax: 40-46-02-76).

Méridien *Air France*'s modern, well-run hotel is American style, but with all the expected French flair. The 1,025 rooms are on the small side, but they're tastefully decorated, quiet, and boast good views. There are four attractive restaurants (one, *Le Clos Longchamp,* has a Michelin star, while another serves Japanese fare), a shopping arcade, three lively bars, and a chic night-club, *L'Ecume des Nuits.* Business services are available. 81 Bd. Gouvion-St-Cyr, 17e (phone: 40-68-34-34; fax: 40-68-31-31).

Méridien Montparnasse With 952 rooms, this ultramodern giant has a futuristic lobby, efficient service, a coffee shop, two bars, the one-Michelin-star *Montparnasse 25* restaurant, and in summer, a garden restaurant. There is also an excellent, ample Sunday brunch. A full range of business services is available. In the heart of Montparnasse, at 19 Rue du Commandant-René-Mouchotte, 14e (phone: 44-36-44-36; fax: 44-36-49-00).

Meurice Refined Louis XV and XVI elegance and a wide range of services are offered for a franc or two less than at the other "palaces." The hotel, a member of the CIGA chain, has 179 rooms and 35 especially nice suites, a popular bar, the one-Michelin-star restaurant *Le Meurice* overlooking the Rue de Rivoli, and the chandeliered *Pompadour* tearoom. Business services are available. Ideally located at 228 Rue de Rivoli, 1er (phone: 44-58-10-10; fax: 44-58-10-15).

Montaigne This unpretentious establishment is a true find. Each of its 29 rooms is comfortable, clean, and chicly decorated. There's a bar and a breakfast room, but no restaurant. 6 Av. Montaigne, 8e (phone: 47-20-30-50; fax: 47-20-94-12).

Montalembert Privacy is the hallmark of this exquisite little place, whose 56 rooms and suites are available in two styles—traditional, with restored period armoires and sleigh beds, or contemporary, with straight geometric lines and fireplaces. (If you're over six feet tall, ask for one of the modern rooms—the beds are longer.) Bathrooms are small, but high-tech. The hotel's *Le Montalembert* restaurant, which replaced *L'Arpège,* serves delicious fare; there's also a cozy bar, and business services are available. On the Rive Gauche at 3 Rue Montalembert, 7e (phone: 45-48-68-11; 800-628-8929; fax: 42-22-58-19).

Le Parc Victor Hugo A sumptuous 122-room hotel, decorated in the style of an English country house, it features a large interior garden. Its excellent restaurant, *Le Relais du Parc,* was set up by super-chef Joël Robuchon, whose own three-Michelin-star, self-named establishment (see *Eating Out*) is next door. Business services are available. 55 Av. Raymond-Poincaré, 16e (phone: 44-05-66-66; fax: 44-05-66-00).

Paris Hilton International Of the 455 modern rooms here, those facing the river have the best views. *Le Western* serves American staples like T-bone steaks, apple pie à la mode, and brownies (mostly to French diners), and the coffee shop is a magnet for homesick Americans. Complete business services are available. A few steps from the *Eiffel Tower,* at 18 Av. de Suffren, 15e (phone: 42-73-92-00; 800-932-3322; fax: 47-83-62-66).

Pavillon de la Reine Under the same ownership as the *Relais Christine* (see below), the Marais's only luxury hotel is similarly appointed. It's blessed with a supreme location on the elegant Place des Vosges, and the 55 rooms (most are on the small side) look out on a garden or courtyard. There's no restaurant. Some business services are available. 28 Pl. des Vosges, 3e (phone: 42-77-96-40; fax: 42-77-63-06).

Régina This hotel's 116 rooms and 14 suites are spacious and furnished with antiques. The restaurant has a lovely garden, and there's also a bar and a small fitness center. Business services are available. Centrally located, overlooking the *Louvre* and the *Tuileries,* at 2 Pl. des Pyramides, 1er (phone: 42-60-31-10; fax: 40-15-95-16).

Relais Christine Formerly a 16th-century cloister, this lovely place boasts 34 rooms and 17 suites with modern fixtures and lots of old-fashioned charm. Ask for a room with a courtyard or garden view; the suites and the ground-floor room with a private *terrasse* are particularly luxurious. There's no restaurant. Some business services are offered. 3 Rue Christine, 6e (phone: 43-26-71-80; fax: 43-26-89-38).

Relais Médicis With the same owners as the *Relais Saint-Germain* (see below), this elegant 16-room establishment in an 18th-century building boasts marble bathrooms and beamed ceilings. There's no restaurant. 23 Rue Racine, 6e (phone: 43-26-00-60; fax: 40-46-83-39).

Relais Saint-Germain In a 17th-century building, this hostelry with 19 guestrooms and one suite is ideally situated on the Rive Gauche, just steps from the Boulevard St-Germain and the area's best shops, eateries, and galleries. It is attractively decorated and charming down to its massive ceiling beams and huge flower bouquets. A rare find. There's a breakfast parlor, but no restaurant. 9 Carrefour de l'Odéon, 6e (phone: 43-29-12-05; fax: 46-33-45-30).

Résidence Maxim's No expense has been spared to create sybaritic splendor in Pierre Cardin's luxurious venture, a distinguished favorite of the rich and famous (it was Bette Davis's Paris *pied-à-terre*). Its clever decor combines modern statuary with Belle Epoque appointments. There are 37 suites and four rooms, as well as a classic lobby, a secluded bar (*Le Maximin,* open late), and *L'Atmosphere,* a world class restaurant. Complete business services are available. Near the Champs-Elysées and the *Palais de l'Elysée,* at 42 Av. Gabriel, 8e (phone: 45-61-96-33; fax: 42-89-06-07).

Résidence du Roy This establishment offers 36 self-contained studios, suites, and duplexes, complete with kitchen facilities. There's no restaurant, but business services are available. Within easy reach of the Champs-Elysées, at 8 Rue François-Ier, 8e (phone: 42-89-59-59; fax: 40-74-07-92).

St. James Paris Like something out of an Evelyn Waugh novel, this secluded 19th-century château is located in a residential neighborhood within a stroll of the *Bois de Boulogne.* The 17 rooms and 31 suites (including four penthouse suites opening onto a winter garden), the walled courtyard with a regal fountain, the library bar, the health club, the elegant restaurant overlooking a rose garden, and the more relaxed grill—all give one a sense of being a guest at an English country estate. Though the place is billed as a private club, hotel guests are welcome to stay after paying a temporary membership fee of about $10. (Non-members not staying at the hotel, however, may not dine or sip cocktails here.) Business services are available. 5 Pl. Chancelier-Adenauer, 16e (phone: 47-04-29-29; 212-956-0200 in New York City; fax: 45-53-00-61; 212-956-2555 in the US).

San Régis Guests are made to feel at home at this elegant place with a comfortable ambience. There are 34 rooms and 10 suites, all beautifully appointed, as well as a restaurant and bar. Business services are available. 12 Rue Jean-Goujon, 8e (phone: 44-95-16-16; fax. 45-61-05-48).

Sofitel CNIT La Défense The city's sights and pleasures are easily reached from this modern luxury hotel in suburban La Défense. The 147 rooms and six suites are outfitted with mini-bars and other up-to-date amenities. There's also a shopping arcade, a bar, and the one-Michelin-star restaurant, *Les Communautés.* Business services are available. Steps away from the *Centre National des Industries et des Techniques* (*CNIT;* National Center for Industry and Technology) and the *Grande Arche,* at 2 Pl. de la Défense, La Défense (phone: 46-92-10-10; 800-763-4835; fax: 46-92-10-50).

Le Stendhal Named for the famous novelist who died here, this luxurious hostelry's 21 rooms feature antiques, Jacuzzis, and mini-bars. The suites are particularly charming—especially Nos. 52 and 53. There's a cozy bar, but no restaurant. Near the Place Vendôme, at 22 Rue Danielle-Casanova, 2e (phone: 44-58-52-52; fax: 44-58-52-00).

Tuileries With a good location in a "real" neighborhood in the heart of the city, this 26-room, four-suite hotel has a well-tended look and attractive, carved wood bedsteads. All the rooms have mini-bars and safes. There's no restaurant. This is also one of the few Parisian members of the Relais de Silence, an association of hotels that meet requirements for being especially quiet. 10 Rue St-Hyacinthe, 1er (phone: 42-61-04-17 or 42-61-06-94; fax: 49-27-91-56).

Le Vernet Guests staying in the 60 modern rooms and three suites here have complimentary access to the fitness center at the elegant *Royal Monceau* (see above), its sister establishment. There's an excellent restaurant, the one-Michelin-star *Les Elysées,* and business services are available. A few steps from the *Arc de Triomphe,* at 25 Rue Vernet, 8e (phone: 44-31-98-00; fax: 44-31-85-69).

De Vigny A small, elegant 25-room, 12-suite Relais & Châteaux member, it features lots of mahogany and chintz. Suite 504 has its own stairway leading to a glass-roofed *salon* with a spectacular view. There's a bar, but no restaurant; this is one of the few hotels in the neighborhood where nonsmoking rooms and parking are available. 9 Rue Balzac, 8e (phone: 40-75-04-39; fax: 40-75-05-81).

Westminster This establishment, which in recent years has regained some of its lost luster, has a traditional decor complete with wood paneling, marble fireplaces, and parquet floors. Some of the 101 rooms (including 16 suites) overlook the street; others look down into an inner courtyard. There's also a one-Michelin-star restaurant, *Le Céladon,* and a bar. Business services are available. Between the *Opéra/Palais Garnier* and the *Ritz,* at 13 Rue de la Paix, 2e (phone: 42-61-57-46; fax: 42-60-30-66).

MODERATE

Angleterre Its 29 classic, unpretentious rooms and one suite (none with air conditioning) are in what was the British Embassy in the 18th century; the building is now a national monument. There's no restaurant. Some business services are offered. 44 Rue Jacob, 6e (phone: 42-60-34-72; fax: 42-60-16-93).

Bretonnerie This restored, 17th-century townhouse with 28 rooms and one suite (none air conditioned) takes itself seriously, with dark wood furnishings and several beamed attic rooms that overlook the narrow streets of the fashionable Marais area. There's no restaurant. 22 Rue Ste-Croix-de-la-Bretonnerie, 4e (phone: 48-87-77-63; fax: 42-77-26-78).

Brighton This 69-room, one-suite hotel facing the *Tuileries* is decorated in pure 19th-century style; many of the spacious rooms overlook the gardens. Some smaller and less expensive rooms in the charming attic have great views, and the suite, with its gilt mosaic bathroom, is a bargain. There's no restaurant. Some business services are available. 218 Rue de Rivoli, 1er (phone: 42-60-30-03; fax: 42-60-41-78).

Britannique A Quaker mission house during World War I, this friendly hotel now offers 40 rooms, all equipped with mini-bars, hair dryers, and satellite TV, but not air conditioning. There's no restaurant. Within minutes of the *Louvre* and *Notre-Dame,* at 20 Av. Victoria, 1er (phone: 42-33-74-59; 800-755-9313; fax: 42-33-82-65).

Danube St-Germain The 40 rooms and six elegant suites, all with four-poster bamboo beds, are comfortable, and some of them overlook an attractive courtyard typical of the Rive Gauche. None of the rooms is air conditioned, and 10 lower-priced rooms have baths, but shared toilets and no TV sets. There's no restaurant. Some business facilities are available. American Express only accepted. 58 Rue Jacob, 6e (phone: 42-60-34-70; fax: 42-60-81-18).

Deux Continents The cozy red sitting room of this quiet, 40-room establishment on the Rive Gauche looks invitingly onto the street. Eleven of the rooms are air conditioned. There's no restaurant. 25 Rue Jacob, 6e (phone: 43-26-72-46).

Deux Iles On the historic Ile St-Louis, this beautifully restored 17th-century house has a garden with a Portuguese fountain, but no restaurant. Though small, the 17 rooms are nicely decorated with French provincial fabrics and Louis XIV ceramic tiles in the bathrooms; none is air conditioned. Limited business services are available. No credit cards accepted. 59 Rue St-Louis-en-l'Ile, 4e (phone: 43-26-13-35; fax: 43-29-60-25).

Ferrandi This no-frills hostelry with a winding wood staircase and a quiet lounge is popular with international business travelers. The 41 rooms and one suite (none air conditioned) have antique furnishings. There's no restaurant. 92 Rue du Cherche-Midi, 6e (phone: 42-22-97-40; fax: 45-44-89-97).

Fleurie This lovely, family-run hotel in a former 18th-century townhouse has 29 well-equipped rooms with mini-bars and safes. The service is friendly, and there's a bar, but no restaurant. 32-34 Rue Grégoire-de-Tours, 6e (phone: 43-29-59-81; fax: 43-29-68-44).

Grand Hôtel de l'Univers Modern and tucked away on a quiet street, this hotel has 34 rooms, all with mini-bars and safes. There's no restaurant. Near St-Germain-des-Prés and the Quartier Latin, at 6 Rue Grégoire-de-Tours, 6e (phone: 43-29-37-00; fax: 40-51-06-45).

Grandes Ecoles This is the sort of place that people recommend only to the right friends (even the proprietress wants to keep it a secret). Insulated from the street by a delightful courtyard and garden, it is a simple, 19th-century private house that's long on atmosphere even though the 48 rooms offer plain comforts (they lack air conditioning and TV sets, and some do not have private baths). There aren't many like it in Paris, but beware: Booking is difficult, and the owner has been known to give away reserved rooms. There's no restaurant. 75 Rue Cardinal-Lemoine, 5e (phone: 43-26-79-23; fax: 43-25-28-15).

Le Jardin des Plantes In addition to a magnificent setting across from Paris's botanical gardens, near the *Sorbonne,* this hotel offers 33 airy rooms with mini-bars and hair dryers, some with safes; some also have alcoves large enough for extra beds for children. None of the rooms is air conditioned. Art exhibits and classical music concerts are held on Sundays in the vaulted cellar. There's also a sauna in the basement, but no restaurant. 5 Rue Linné, 5e (phone: 47-07-06-20; fax: 47-07-62-74).

Lenox St-Germain Small and tastefully done, this hotel has 32 rooms (none air conditioned) and a cozy bar, but no restaurant. It's popular with the fashion crowd. Between the busy St-Germain area and the boutiques nearby, at 9 Rue de l'Université, 7e (phone: 42-96-10-95; fax: 42-61-52-83).

Littré This 93-room, four-suite Rive Gauche hotel has old-fashioned elegance, spacious rooms (with large beds, a rarity, but no air conditioning) and huge bathrooms. There's no restaurant, but room-service meals are available, and there's an English-style bar. Business services are also offered. No credit cards accepted. 9 Rue Littré, 6e (phone: 45-44-38-68; fax: 45-44-88-13).

Lord Byron On a quiet street off the Champs-Elysées, it has a pleasant courtyard and 31 comfortable, homey rooms (none is air conditioned). The staff is friendly and speaks good English. There's no restaurant. 5 Rue de Chateaubriand, 8e (phone: 43-59-89-98; fax: 42-89-46-04).

Lutèce Here are 23 smallish, but luxurious rooms (one split-level; none air conditioned) on the charming Ile St-Louis. The decor is positively ravishing, with exquisite toile fabric and wallpaper and raw wood beams. There's no restaurant. No credit cards accepted. 65 Rue St-Louis-en-l'Ile, 4e (phone: 43-26-23-52; fax: 43-29-60-25).

Madison This place offers 55 large, bright rooms, with such amenities as mini-bars and safes; some have balconies. There's no restaurant. 143 Bd. St-Germain, 6e (phone: 40-51-60-00; fax: 40-51-60-01).

Des Marroniers An excellent location in the heart of the Rive Gauche makes this 37-room hotel a real bargain. The rooms are not air conditioned. There's a garden courtyard and pretty breakfast room, but no restaurant. No credit cards accepted. 21 Rue Jacob, 6e (phone: 43-25-30-60; fax: 40-46-83-56).

Novanox This 27-room hotel is ultramodern, with high-tech furniture, but it offers old-fashioned extras such as brioches for breakfast, served on an outdoor terrace. All the rooms have mini-bars and safes, but no air conditioning. There's a bar, but no restaurant. Service is exceptionally friendly. 155 Bd. du Montparnasse, 6e (phone: 46-33-63-60; fax: 43-26-61-72).

Odéon Small (29 rooms), modernized, and charming, it's in the heart of the St-Germain area on the Rive Gauche. There's no restaurant. 13 Rue de St-Sulpice, 6e (phone: 43-25-70-11; fax: 43-29-97-34).

Parc St-Séverin An interesting little hotel on the Rive Gauche, it has 27 rooms (none air conditioned), including a top-floor penthouse with a wraparound balcony. The decor is modern but understated, and the overall ambience is appealing, even though the neighborhood is not the quietest in Paris. There's no restaurant. 22 Rue de la Parcheminerie, 5e (phone: 43-54-32-17; fax: 43-54-70-71).

Pavillon Bastille There's a 17th-century fountain in the courtyard of this small, 19th-century *hôtel particulier*. The 24 smallish rooms and one suite are all cheerfully decorated in contemporary style and equipped with mini-bars. There's a bar and a breakfast room, but no restaurant. Conveniently located near the Place de la Bastille, at 65 Rue de Lyon, 12e (phone: 43-43-65-65; fax: 43-43-96-52).

Perreyve This quiet, 30-room hotel with understated, traditional decor is ideally located near the *Jardin du Luxembourg.* There's no restaurant. 63 Rue Madame, 6e (phone: 45-48-35-01; fax: 42-84-03-30).

Pierre et Vacances In a sleepy corner of Montmartre, this residential hotel charges nightly, weekly, and monthly rates. The apartments have kitchens, and some overlook a peaceful garden; none is air conditioned. There's no restaurant. Near the leafy square of the *Théâtre de l'Atelier,* 10 Pl. Charles-Dullin, 18e (phone: 42-57-14-55; fax: 42-54-48-87).

Récamier An amazing bargain for those who manage to reserve a room, this is a simple, clean, and very peaceful 30-room hotel right on the elegant Place St-Sulpice. The rooms are not air conditioned and have no TV sets; eight share baths (though all have private toilet facilities). There's no restaurant. 3 *bis* Pl. St-Sulpice, 6e (phone: 43-26-04-89).

Regent's Garden This small hotel has 39 spacious rooms, some with large marble fireplaces, and three suites; none of the accommodations is air conditioned, but all have amenities such as mini-bars and hair dryers. A country atmosphere pervades, and the young hoteliers who run the place make guests feel completely at home. There's also a garden and parking, but no restaurant. On a quiet street near the *Arc de Triomphe,* at 6 Rue Pierre-Demours, 17e (phone: 45-74-07-30; fax: 40-55-01-42).

Royal St-Honoré Newly renovated, the 68-room, seven-suite hotel is one of the city's best values for this prime location. Some rooms have terraces overlooking the *Jardin des Tuileries.* There's no restaurant, but business services are available. 221 Rue Saint-Honoré, 1er (phone: 42 60 32 79; fax: 42-60-47-44).

St-Germain-des-Prés In the heart of one of Paris's loveliest districts, this comfortable 30-room hotel is a good bargain. Request a room on the courtyard, as the street can be noisy. There's no restaurant. 36 Rue Bonaparte, 6e (phone: 43-26-00-19; fax: 40-46-83-63).

Le St-Grégoire A small 18th-century mansion on the Rive Gauche, this hostelry has an intimate, cozy atmosphere, a warm fire in the hearth, and 19 tastefully furnished rooms and one suite. Two of the rooms have terraces overlooking a garden, and only two of the rooms are air conditioned. There's no restaurant. 43 Rue de l'Abbé-Grégoire, 6e (phone: 45-48-23-23; fax: 45-48-33-95).

St-Louis Marais This tiny hotel is a short walk from the Place des Vosges, the quays along the Seine, and the Bastille-quarter nightclubs. Dating from the 18th century, when it was part of the Celestine Convent, it has 15 small rooms with safes and hair dryers (none has a TV set or air conditioning). There's no restaurant, and historical landmark status has barred the installation of an elevator. No credit cards accepted. On a quiet residential street on the edge of the chic Marais, at 1 Rue Charles-V, 4e (phone: 48-87-87-04; fax: 48-87-33-26).

Sofitel Porte de Sèvres Located in southwest Paris, this modern luxury hotel features 635 comfortably furnished rooms with all the conveniences (such as mini-bars). There's also a glass-enclosed fitness center and pool with marvelous views, the one-Michelin-star *Relais de Sèvres* restaurant, a brasserie, jazz bar, and even a movie theater. Business services are available. Right by the *Parc des Expositions,* at the Porte de Versailles, 8 Rue Louis-Armand, 15e (phone: 40-60-33-11; 800-763-4835; fax: 45-57-04-22).

Solférino A cozy place with Oriental rugs scattered about. The 34 tiny rooms have floral wallpaper; none has air conditioning or a TV set. There's a plant-filled breakfast and sitting room, but no restaurant. 91 Rue de Lille, 7e (phone: 47-05-85-54; fax: 45-55-51-16).

Suède A delightful hotel in a quiet area, just around the corner from the prime minister's residence. All 40 rooms and one suite are beautifully appointed (none has air conditioning or a TV set); those overlooking the garden are smaller but much prettier. There's no restaurant, but breakfast is served in a simple salon or, in good weather, in the beautiful courtyard. 31 Rue Vaneau, 7e (phone: 47-05-18-65; fax: 47-05-69-27).

Villa des Artistes Quiet luxury is the drawing card of this popular Quartier Latin hotel with 59 rooms and its own patio-garden. There's no restaurant. 9 Rue de la Grande-Chaumière, 6e (phone: 43-26-60-86; fax: 43-54-73-70).

INEXPENSIVE

Bersoly's Saint-Germain This quiet hotel near the *Musée d'Orsay* attracts artists and antiques dealers. Each of the 16 rooms (none with air conditioning) is named for a famous painter. There's no restaurant. 28 Rue de Lille, 7e (phone: 42-60-73-79; fax: 49-27-05-55).

Caron de Beaumarchais Named after the 18th-century playwright who once lived on this street, this elegant new hotel in the Marais has 19 rooms, all with fax lines, cable TV, safes, and mini-bars, and some with small balconies. There's a breakfast room that opens onto a small garden, but no restaurant. 12 Rue Vieille-du-Temple, 4e (phone: 42-72-34-12; fax: 42-72-34-63).

Delavigne With a good location (down the street from the *Odéon* theater) and an enlightened manager who says he isn't interested in simply handing out keys, but enjoys introducing foreigners to Paris, this 34-room hotel is a good value. None of the rooms is air conditioned. There's no restaurant. 1 Rue Casimir-Delavigne, 6e (phone: 43-29-31-50; fax: 43-29-78-56).

Deux Avenues A quiet 32-room hotel offering friendly service, near a lively street market. There's no restaurant. 38 Rue Poncelet, 17e (phone: 42-27-44-35; fax: 47-63-95-48).

Esmeralda Some of this hotel's 19 rooms look directly at *Notre-Dame* over the gardens of *Eglise St-Julien-le-Pauvre,* one of Paris's oldest churches. The oak beams and furniture enhance the medieval atmosphere. Don't look for air conditioning or TV sets here, though the rooms do have safes and hair dryers, and all but three have private baths. Small and friendly, it's especially popular with the theatrical crowd. There's no restaurant. No credit cards accepted. 4 Rue St-Julien-le-Pauvre, 5e (phone: 43-54-19-20; fax: 40-51-00-68).

Familia With friendly management and 30 rooms (none air conditioned), this simple hotel is a great bargain. The rooms feature such amenities as mini-bars and hair dryers. There's no restaurant. Near the *Sorbonne,* at 11 Rue des Ecoles, 5e (phone: 43-54-55-27; fax: 43-29-61-77).

Jeanne d'Arc This little place doesn't get top marks for decor, and its facilities are simple, but somehow word of its appeal has spread from Minnesota to Melbourne. It's well placed, near the Place des Vosges, and the management is friendly. There's no restaurant. On a quiet street in the Marais, at 3 Rue de Jarente, 4e (phone: 48-87-62-11; fax: 48-87-37-31).

Marais Ideal for families traveling with children, this simple, 39-room hotel with friendly management has several connecting rooms available. None of the rooms is air conditioned. There's no restaurant. Near the *Bastille,* at 2 *bis* Rue Commines, 3e (phone: 48-87-78-27; fax: 48-87-09-01).

Oriental This simple but comfortable 32-room hotel is near *Notre-Dame.* There's no restaurant. 2 Rue d'Arras, 5e (phone: 43-54-38-12; fax: 40-51-86-78).

Prima-Lepic The cheerful young owners have decorated the 38 rooms in this Montmartre hotel with pretty floral wallpapers and one-of-a-kind furnishings—a wicker chair, a mirrored armoire, a 1930s lamp (no air conditioning, though). No. 56, on the top floor, looks out over Paris, and travelers with children should make special note of room No. 2, which connects to an adjoining room. The public spaces are charming, too. There's no restaurant. 29 Rue Lepic, 18e (phone: 46-06-44-64; fax: 46-06-66-11).

Le Vieux Marais This agreeable Marais hostelry has 30 pretty, if not very large, rooms; none is air conditioned. The breakfast room (there's no restaurant) has an impressive wall-size engraving of the Place des Vosges; the real thing is not far away. Near the *Centre Georges-Pompidou,* at 8 Rue du Plâtre, 4e (phone: 42-78-47-22; fax: 42-78-34-32).

Welcome Overlooking the Boulevard St-Germain, it's simple but comfortable. There are 30 rooms; those on the street are relatively noisy, in spite of double windows, and none is air conditioned. The sixth floor garret rooms are very romantic, with great views. There's no restaurant. No credit cards accepted. 66 Rue de Seine, 6e (phone: 46-34-24-80; fax: 40-46-81-59).

EATING OUT

Paris considers itself the culinary capital of the world, and you will never forget food for long here. Whether you grab a fresh croissant and café au lait for breakfast or splurge on an epicurean fantasy for dinner, this is the city in which to indulge all your gastronomic dreams. Remember, too, that there is no such thing as "French" food; rather, Paris is a gastronomic mosaic, where one can try cuisines from Provence, Alsace, Normandy, Brittany, and other regions.

For a dinner for two, including service, but not wine, a very expensive restaurant will charge $250 or more; an expensive one, $150 to $200; a moderate place, $100 to $150; an inexpensive restaurant, $50 to $100; and a very inexpensive one, $50 or less. A service charge of 15% usually is included in the bill, but it's customary to leave a small additional tip for good service. Street addresses of the restaurants below are followed by their *arrondissement* number. Unless otherwise noted, all restaurants listed below are open for lunch and dinner.

Although the city of Paris has passed a law requiring that all restaurants provide nonsmoking areas, nonsmokers can't claim victory yet. The general dearth of space in Paris restaurants, combined with the large numbers of French people who smoke (around 80% of the population, according to one recent survey), means that nonsmokers are still rarely seated very far from a smoker. And, what's more, compliance with the law is erratic: Ask restaurateurs in Paris about what is known there as the law "*à l'Américaine,*" and most will just laugh!

REMEMBER, CALL AHEAD

To save frustration and embarrassment, always *reconfirm* dinner reservations before noon on the appointed day. (For information about making written dinner reservations see *Useful Words and Phrases*, in the GLOSSARY.) Also remember that some of the better restaurants do not accept credit cards, and many close over the weekend, as well as for part or all of July or August. It's best to check ahead on these matters to avoid disappointment at the restaurant of your choice. It's also worth remembering that many restaurants offer special lunch menus at considerably lower prices.

For an unforgettable culinary experience, we begin with our favorites, followed by our cost and quality choices listed by price category.

HAUTE GASTRONOMIE

L'Ambroisie Promoted to three-star status by Michelin in 1988, this elegant establishment is the showcase for chef Bernard Pacaud's equally elegant cuisine. The menu is limited to only a few sublime entrées, such as a fresh truffle in puff pastry, rack of Pauillac lamb in a truffle crust, and *crème de homard aux Saint-Jacques* (lobster with sea scallops in a cream sauce). Closed Sundays, Mondays, two weeks in February, and the first three weeks in August. Reservations necessary. Major credit cards accepted. 9 Pl. des Vosges, 4e (phone: 42-78-51-45).

Amphyclès A protégé and former sous-chef of super-chef Joël Robuchon (see below), Philippe Groult prepares fine contemporary cuisine, which bears both bourgeois and southern French influences. There are splendid creamy soups, lamb stew with rosemary, lobster salad with sweet red peppers, and a rock lobster risotto. If the brightly lit modern decor of his small two-Michelin-star establishment is forgettably neutral, the food is unquestionably memorable. Closed Saturday lunch, Sundays, and most of July. Reservations necessary. Major credit cards accepted. Near the Place des Ternes, at 78 Av. des Ternes, 17e (phone: 40-68-01-01; fax: 40-68-91-88).

L'Arpège The minimalist decor of this two-Michelin-star establishment belies the succulent, generous cuisine prepared by chef Alain Passard. Peppery tuna filet, veal sweetbreads with rosemary, and lemon soufflé flavored with cloves are just a few of the possibilities. The prix fixe lunch menu is a relative bargain. Closed Saturdays and Sunday lunch. Reservations necessary. Major credit cards accepted. 84 Rue de Varenne, 7e (phone: 45-51-47-33; fax: 44-18-98-39).

Guy Savoy In spite of the fact that he now operates several bistros throughout Paris (see *Le Bistrot de l'Etoile-Lauriston* and *La Butte Chaillot,* below), Savoy, unlike many globe-trotting celebrity chefs, still mans the kitchen at his handsome, two-Michelin-star restaurant. The menu is small and constantly changing, with such recent successes as a peppery, jellied duck foie gras served with celery-root purée, and *volaille confite et laquée au vinaigre* (chicken stewed in and glazed with vinegar). Inventive desserts (which may be ordered in half portions) include a grapefruit terrine with tea-flavored sauce. There had been some complaints about high prices, some disappointing dishes, and chilly service, but the restaurant seems to be back on track now. Closed weekends and most of August. Reservations necessary. Major credit cards accepted. 18 Rue Troyon, 17e (phone: 43-80-40-61; fax: 46-22-43-09).

Joël Robuchon A legend in his own time, Joël Robuchon is already ranked in France among the greatest chefs of any era, alongside Taillevent, Carême, and Escoffier. Robuchon's revolutionary cuisine, which he calls *moderne,* is neither traditional French nor nouvelle cuisine, but a happy medium. Like nouvelle cuisine,

Robuchon's creations are lighter than traditional recipes, employing less butter and cream. They're based on intense reductions of vegetable, fish, and meat essences, as well as highly flavored, typically French ingredients such as truffles (a Robuchon favorite—the finest available pop up frequently in his signature dishes). But Robuchon also favors earthy, bistro-style ingredients that would never find their way onto the usual nouvelle cuisine menu. Mere words can't do justice to menu offerings such as *gratin de macaroni aux truffes et foie gras* (macaroni with truffles and foie gras) and *langouste rôtie au cumin et au romarin* (roast rock lobster with cumin and rosemary), both served topped with aged Parmesan and chopped fresh truffles. Robuchon's three-Michelin-star restaurant now goes by his name (it was formerly *Jamin*) and has a new locale, in a turn-of-the-century townhouse with the warm feel of a Victorian British country estate. Robuchon has said he'll retire in 1996 (at the ripe old age of 50), depriving the world of his genius, so now is the time to experience it. Closed weekends and the month of July. Reservations necessary far in advance. Major credit cards accepted. 55 Av. Raymond-Poincaré, 16e (phone: 47-27-12-27).

Lasserre The waiters are in tails, the ceiling glides open to reveal the stars, the decanted burgundy is poured over the flame of a candle to detect sediment, and the impeccable service makes diners feel that somehow they deserve all this. The two-Michelin-star cuisine—heavy on foie gras, caviar, truffles, and rich sauces—is traditional French at its most heavenly, and the wine cellar is a virtual museum of French oenology. Not surprisingly, making dinner reservations here is akin to booking seats for a sold-out Broadway musical, so think way ahead. Closed Sundays, Monday lunch, and the month of August. Reservations necessary. Major credit cards accepted. 17 Av. Franklin-Roosevelt, 8e (phone: 43-59-53-43; fax: 45-63-72-23).

Lucas-Carton This lush, plush Belle Epoque dining room, under the watchful eye of chef/owner Alain Senderens, is the perfect place to sample a few bites of truffle salad, lobster with vanilla, or anything else on the ever-changing menu. Diners also have the opportunity to order each course with a perfectly matched glass of wine. Senderens' quirky and innovative cooking combines many tenets of nouvelle cuisine with Asian influences, and Michelin lost no time in awarding it three stars. The utensils and serving pieces are almost as alluring as the food. The prix fixe lunch menu is a good value. Closed weekends, most of August, and December 24 through January 3. Reservations necessary. Major credit cards accepted. 9 Pl. de la Madeleine, 8e (phone: 42-65-22-90; fax: 42-65-06-23).

Michel Rostang Rostang seems to be at the top of his form these days, with an inventive repertoire that takes its inspiration from the cuisine of Savoie, Lyons, and Provence. The restaurant has two dining rooms, one of which has a large glass wall overlooking the kitchen. Specialties include *oeufs de caille en coque d'oursin* (quail's eggs in a sea-urchin shell), *feuilleté de canard et foie gras au chou rouge* (duck and foie gras in puff pastry with a red cabbage sauce), and Scottish salmon with sesame seeds and artichokes. Desserts include warm chocolate tart, and pears roasted in sauternes. Closed Saturday lunch, Sundays, and the first two weeks of August. Reservations necessary. Major credit cards accepted. 20 Rue Rennequin, 17e (phone: 47-63-40-77; fax: 47-63-82-75).

Taillevent Named after a famed medieval chef, this three-Michelin-star dining room occupies a distinguished 19th-century mansion complete with fine paintings, porcelain dinnerware, and aristocratic decor, making it look as if the French Revolution was really just a bad dream. Longtime chef Claude Deligne has retired, but the traditions he established and many of his recipes are being kept alive by Philippe Legendre, who also has added new items to the menu. The rabbit in pastry with spinach and *sarriette* (summer savory), the sea-urchin mousse, and the many stunning desserts are sure to please, while the wine list is one of the city's best and most reasonably priced. One of the hardest-to-get restaurant reservations in France—but do try. Closed weekends, part of February, and most of August. Reservations necessary. Major credit cards accepted. 15 Rue Lamennais, 8e (phone: 45-61-12-90; fax: 42-25-95-18).

La Tour d'Argent For many, this place is touristy, overrated, and overpriced, but Paris's senior three-Michelin-star restaurant continues to amaze and entertain with its cuisine and the most romantic view of any restaurant in the city. The gold-toned room brings to mind Cole Porter's "elegant, swellegant party"; in fact, Porter occasionally dined here, as have a host of other luminaries, from Franklin Roosevelt to Paul McCartney, Greta Garbo to the Aga Khan. The specialty is a Charente duck pressed at tableside just as it was a century ago; also not to be missed are the classic quenelles in mornay sauce with fresh black truffles. The spectacular wine list is one of France's best. Because it has a reservations book thicker than the Manhattan telephone directory, it's often impossible to get dinner reservations at certain times of the year. Best tip: Book a windowside table for lunch on a weekday, when there's a prix fixe menu; the view of *Notre-Dame* and the Seine is just as splendid by daylight. Closed Mondays. Reservations necessary. Major credit cards accepted. 15 Quai de la Tournelle, 5e (phone: 43-54-23-31; fax: 44-07-12-04).

Vivarois Claude Peyrot is unquestionably one of France's finest chefs. His small, elegant establishment features *la cuisine du marché,* meaning that offerings vary according to what is available at the market. A splendid grilled turbot with capers is usually on the menu. Michelin has awarded it two stars. Closed weekends and the month of August. Reservations necessary. Major credit cards accepted. 192 Av. Victor-Hugo, 16e (phone: 45-04-04-31; fax: 45-03-09-84).

BEST BISTROS

L'Assiette The chef, Lulu, is very much present in her slightly scruffy bistro, which attracts a fashionable clientele for delicious and generous servings of roast duck, potato salad with fresh truffles, and *coquilles St-Jacques* (sea scallops in cream sauce). The wine list is sublime, the prices astronomical. France's president, François Mitterrand, has been known to dine here. Closed Mondays, Tuesdays, and the month of August. Reservations necessary. Major credit cards accepted. 181 Rue du Château, 14e (phone: 43-22-64-86).

Astier An honest-to-goodness neighborhood spot that always is packed, it offers the staples of bourgeois cooking, lovingly prepared and remarkably inexpensive. Closed weekends, late April through mid-May, and late August through early September. Reservations advised. Major credit cards accepted. 44 Rue Jean-Pierre-Timbaud, 11e (phone: 43-57-16-35).

Le Bistrot d'à Côté Flaubert Michel Rostang, impresario of the topflight restaurant that bears his name (see above), here offers *cuisine de terroir* (back-to-basics regional fare) at moderate prices in a turn-of-the-century bistro. Closed Saturday lunch, Sundays, and the first two weeks of August. Reservations advised. Major credit cards accepted. 10 Rue Gustave-Flaubert, 17e (phone: 42-67-05-81; fax: 47-63-82-75).

Le Bistrot de l'Etoile-Lauriston One of famed chef Guy Savoy's bistros (also see his self-named restaurant, above, and *La Butte Chaillot,* below), this place offers excellent value with innovative variations on classic bistro themes, such as lamb with rosemary and *bisque d'étrilles,* a soup made from tiny crabs. Closed Saturday lunch and Sundays. Reservations advised. Major credit cards accepted. 19 Rue de Lauriston, 16e (phone: 40-67-11-16; fax: 45-00-99-87).

Le Caméléon In a true bistro atmosphere—with marble tables, mole-skin banquettes, and the spirit of 1920s Montparnasse, as well as moderate prices—try the superb casserole-roasted veal and *morue provençale* (salt cod in tomato sauce with garlic mayonnaise). Closed Sundays, Mondays, and the month of August. Reservations advised. No credit cards accepted. 6 Rue de Chevreuse, 6e (phone: 43-20-63-43).

Cartet This tiny, friendly place serves Lyonnaise specialties with a focus on charcuterie and meat, such as *côtes de veau aux morilles* (veal chops with morel mushrooms), at low prices. Closed weekends and the month of August. Reservations advised. Major credit cards accepted. 62 Rue de Malte, 11e (phone: 48-05-17-65).

Chez Benoît A pretty, unpretentious bistro with wonderful, old-fashioned Lyonnais cooking and exquisite wines. Just about at the top of the bistro list (in prices as well as food and atmosphere), it's rated one Michelin star. Closed weekends and the month of August. Reservations necessary. No credit cards accepted. 20 Rue St-Martin, 4e (phone: 42-72-25-76; fax: 42-72-45-68).

Chez Janou The chef/owner of this moderately priced bistro with turn-of-the-century decor serves French home cooking, such as poached eggs with wild mushrooms, game in season, and chicory sorbet for dessert. Closed weekends and holidays. Reservations necessary. MasterCard and Visa accepted. 2 Rue R.-Verlomme, 3e (phone: 42-72-28-41).

Chez Pauline In this quintessential, albeit pricey, bistro, which has earned one Michelin star, ask to be seated in the tiny, wood-paneled downstairs room, brightened by large mirrors and fresh flowers. Try the oysters in a watercress sauce or the assortment of seafood with a saffron sauce, and save room for dessert—the mille-feuille (layered puff pastry) of orange with raspberry sauce is sublime. Closed Saturday dinner, Sundays, the month of July, two weeks in August, and from December 24 through January 2. Reservations advised; make them well in advance. Major credit cards accepted. 5 Rue Villedo, 1er (phone: 42-96-20-70; fax: 49-27-99-99).

Le Grizzli The wonderful food at this moderately priced bistro is southwestern French in accent, featuring duck and plenty of garlic. Closed Sundays and Monday lunch. Reservations advised. Major credit cards accepted. 7 Rue St-Martin, 4e (phone: 48-87-77-56).

Marie et Fils Marie and her son have found a successful formula: great bistro food, an authentic Rive Gauche atmosphere, and reasonable prices. Reservations advised. MasterCard and Visa accepted. Closed Sundays and Monday lunch. 34 Rue Mazarine, 6e (phone: 43-26-69-49).

Le Passage This bistro serves 70 excellent wines by the glass (try the chinon) and has a varied menu of bistro classics like *foie de veau sauté* (sautéed calf's liver), plus friendly service and low prices. Closed Saturday lunch, Sundays, and most of August. Reservations advised. MasterCard and Visa accepted. 18 Passage de la Bonne-Graine, 11e (phone: 47-00-73-30).

Au Petit Marguery Although the prices run rather high in this family-run bistro on the Rive Gauche, the old-fashioned cuisine and *petit crus* wines are excellent. Closed Sundays, Mondays, the month of August, and December 23 through *New Year's Day*. Reservations advised. Major credit cards accepted. 9 Bd. du Port Royal, 13e (phone: 43-31-58-59).

Robert et Louise With a warm, paneled decor, high standards in the kitchen, and moderate prices on the menu, this family-run bistro is a great place to try *boeuf bourguignon* or open-fire–grilled *côte de boeuf*. Also good are the *fromage blanc* and the *vin en pichet*. Closed Sundays, holidays, and the month of August. Reservations advised for Friday and Saturday dinner. No credit cards accepted. 64 Rue Vieille-du-Temple, 3e (phone: 42-78-55-89).

La Rôtisserie d'en Face Comfortably low-key decor, tiled floors, and an open, uncluttered atmosphere provide the backdrop for the bistro fare of noted chef Jacques Cagna's (also see his self-named restaurant, above), such as grilled chicken, roast leg of lamb, and thick steaks, all priced in the moderate range. Closed Saturday lunch and Sundays. Reservations advised. MasterCard and Visa accepted. 2 Rue Christine, 6e (phone: 43-26-40-98; fax: 43-54-54-48).

Le Trumilou The formidable proprietress sets the tone of this robust establishment on the Seine, which serves huge, steaming portions of game in season, *truite aux amandes* (trout with almonds), and chicken, all beneath a frieze of some excruciatingly bad rustic oil paintings and at pleasingly low prices. Try the *charlotte aux marrons* (chestnut parfait) for dessert. The amazingly cheerful service is another plus. Closed Mondays. Reservations unnecessary. Major credit cards accepted. 84 Quai de l'Hôtel-de-Ville, 4e (phone: 42-77-63-98).

VERY EXPENSIVE

Les Ambassadeurs A two-Michelin-star establishment that offers a soul-satisfying meal gracefully presented in an elegant dining room with 20-foot-high ceilings, massive crystal chandeliers, and stunning views of the Place de la Concorde. Delicious dishes such as *gratin dauphinois de homard avec crème au caviar* (potatoes au gratin with lobster in caviar sauce) and veal sweetbreads in a light wine sauce are perfectly complemented by one of the exceptional wines from the *cave*. The prix fixe lunch menu is a good value. Open daily. Reservations necessary. Major credit cards accepted. In the *Crillon Hotel*, 10 Pl. de la Concorde, 8e (phone: 44-71-16-16; fax: 44-71-15-02).

L'Ami Louis The archetypal Parisian bistro, small and charmingly unassuming, but with huge portions of generally marvelous, if extremely expensive food (though these days the place seems to be coasting on its reputation and on its appealing ambience). Specialties include foie gras, roast chicken, spring lamb, ham, and burgundy wines. A favorite among Americans, this is the place to sample authentic French fries. Closed Mondays, Tuesdays, and most of July and August. Reservations necessary. Major credit cards accepted. 32 Rue de Vertbois, 3e (phone: 48-87-77-48).

Le Grand Véfour Established in 1760 in the stately courtyard of the *Palais-Royal*, this restaurant has rich carpets and mirrors framed by ornate frescoes, and the choice two-Michelin-star dishes are named for dignitaries who have discussed affairs of state here since the time of Robespierre. These delectable dishes, such as crayfish with olive oil and spices, or potato-truffle terrine, are every bit as enthralling as the restaurant's rich history. In honor of both, gentlemen still are required to wear jacket and tie. The prix fixe lunch menu is a good value. Closed Saturday lunch, Sundays, and the month of August. Reservations necessary. Major credit cards accepted. 17 Rue de Beaujolais, 1er (phone: 42-96-56-27; fax: 42-86-80-71).

Laurent This *grande luxe* restaurant has regained its former glory under chef Philippe Braun, who trained with super-chef Joël Robuchon. The finest ingredients are cooked to perfection—the freshest fish served with rare morel mushrooms, and game in season—and the wine list is one of Paris's best. Closed Saturday lunch, Sundays, and part of August. Reservations necessary. Major credit cards accepted. Near the Champs-Elysées, at 41 Av. Gabriel, 8e (phone: 42-25-00-39; fax: 45-62-45-21).

Maxim's Paris's most celebrated Belle Epoque restaurant was a century old in 1991; unfortunately, it has seen better days—it's now often half empty, with a façade that could use a face-lift. In fact, there are rumors that owner Pierre Cardin may be thinking of selling. But *Maxim's* will always be *Maxim's,* and with care could recapture its past glory. With scenes like tableaux from Colette around its elegant salons, the gentle rustle of silk, the glow of silver, and the soft strains of a string quartet, there are still few places like it. The service is impeccable, with excellent sommeliers to help with the extensive and intelligent wine list. The food is sometimes surprisingly good; try the *Challans canard aux cerises* (Challans duck with cherries). Fridays remain a strictly black-tie-only tradition, with an orchestra for dancing from 9:30 PM to 2 AM. Closed Sundays in July and August. Reservations necessary. Major credit cards accepted. 3 Rue Royale, 8e (phone: 42-65-27-94; fax: 40-17-02-91).

Pré Catelan This dreamy dinner palace is a wonderful special occasion spot—particularly in summer, when guests can dine on the flower-decked terrace. The food—which has earned two Michelin stars—lives up to the promise of the ambience. Offerings include pumpkin soup with crayfish, braised whole sole, and rack of lamb with coriander. Closed Sunday dinner, Mondays, and two weeks in February. Reservations necessary. Major credit cards accepted. Rte. de Suresnes, Bois de Boulogne, 16e (phone: 45-24-55-58; fax: 45-24-43-25).

EXPENSIVE

Apicius Jean-Pierre Vigato's highly original recipes have earned this restaurant two Michelin stars. Favorites include *tourte de canard* (duck in pastry), potato purée with truffles, and *crème brûlée* made with cherries. Closed weekends and the month of August. Reservations necessary. Major credit cards accepted. 122 Av. de Villiers, 17e (phone: 43-80-19-66; fax: 44-40-09-57).

Auberge des Deux Signes This place was once the cellars of the priory of *St-Julien-le-Pauvre;* try to get an upstairs table overlooking the gardens. Auvergnat cooking (ham, charcuterie, cabbage, and potato dishes) is prepared with a light touch. Closed Saturday lunch, Sundays, and the month of August. Reservations necessary. Major credit cards accepted. 46 Rue Galande, 5e (phone: 43-25-46-56; fax: 46-33-20-49).

Beauvilliers With its intimate dining rooms and hydrangea-rimmed summer terraces, this one-Michelin-star restaurant is one of the most romantic spots in Paris. The rich, generous fare, prepared in the classic tradition of the restaurant's namesake, a famous 18th-century chef, complements the setting. Try the rabbit and parsley terrine, *turbot au jus de jarret* (turbot cooked in veal shank gravy), and the remarkable praline chocolate cake. Closed Sundays and Monday lunch. Reservations necessary. Major credit cards accepted. On the northern slope of the Butte Montmartre, at 52 Rue Lamarck, 18e (phone: 42-54-54-42; fax: 42-62-70-30).

Bistro 121 Hearty food and excellent wines are offered in a modern setting that's always chic and crowded. Try one of the many first-rate fish dishes or an original creation such as *canard au fruit de la passion* (duck with passion fruit). Open daily until midnight. Reservations advised. Major credit cards accepted. 121 Rue de la Convention, 15e (phone: 45-57-52-90).

Le Carré des Feuillants Alain Dutournier of *Au Trou Gascon* (see below) has set up shop in the heart of the city, offering such creations as *perdreau sauvage* (wild partridge) with cumin, apricots, and fresh coriander. Michelin has awarded the establishment two stars. The prix fixe lunch menu is a good value. Closed Saturday lunch, Sundays, and the month of August. Reservations necessary. Major credit cards accepted. 14 Rue de Castiglione, 1er (phone: 42-86-82-82; fax: 42-86-07-71).

Chiberta Elegant and modern, this two-Michelin-star restaurant boasts the nouvelle cuisine of Philippe da Silva. Try the goat cheese ravioli, or the fish with ginger and mango in puff pastry. Closed weekends, the month of August, and December 24 through January 3. Reservations necessary. Major credit cards accepted. 3 Rue Arsène-Houssaye, 8e (phone: 45-63-77-90; fax: 45-62-85-08).

La Coquille This is a classic bistro, where the service is unpretentious and warm, and the food consistent, although the seafood (except the scallops) is usually overcooked. From October through mid-May, as its name suggests, the restaurant specializes in *coquilles St-Jacques,* a version that consists of scallops roasted with butter, shallots, and parsley. Closed Sundays, Mondays, late July through early August, and December 23 through January 3. Reservations advised. Major credit cards accepted. 6 Rue du Débarcadère, 17e (phone: 45-72-10-73).

Le Divellec This bright and airy, two-Michelin-star place serves exquisitely fresh seafood. Try the sea bass, the *rouget* (mullet), or the sautéed turbot. The latter is served with a thick pasta flavored with squid ink—an unusual and delicious concoction. Closed Sundays, Mondays, the month of August, and December 24 through January 3. Reservations necessary. Major credit cards accepted. 107 Rue de l'Université, 7e (phone: 45-51-91-96; fax: 45-51-31-75).

Drouant Founded in 1880, this perennial favorite has an ambitious chef who favors classic French recipes, particularly fish dishes and *agneau de Pauillac,* a traditional lamb specialty from the Médoc region. Last year, Michelin awarded it a coveted second star. Open daily. Reservations necessary. Major credit cards accepted. 18 Rue Gaillon, 2e (phone: 42-65-15-16; fax: 49-24-02-15).

Duquesnoy Jean-Paul Duquesnoy, one of Paris's most promising young chefs, is in his element in this enchanting, two-Michelin-star establishment. Warm, carved woods and tasteful decor set the stage for specialties that include squab with foie gras, and fresh sardines grilled with almond butter; for dessert, the *crème brûlée* with walnuts is a delight. Closed Saturday lunch, Sundays, and three weeks in August. Reservations necessary. Major credit cards accepted. 6 Av. Bosquet, 7e (phone: 47-05-96-78; fax: 44-18-90-57).

Elysée-Lenôtre Arguably one of Paris's most elegant dining rooms, this restaurant in a former private house on the Champs-Elysées serves fine traditional cuisine with a focus on seafood. Closed Saturday lunch and most of August. Reservations advised. Major credit cards accepted. 10 Av. des Champs-Elysées, 8e (phone: 42-65-85-10; fax: 42-65-76-23).

Faucher Chef/owner Gerard Faucher has drawn praise (and one Michelin star) for his light touch with fish dishes and desserts. Closed Saturday lunch, Sundays, and one week in August. Reservations necessary. Major credit cards accepted. 123 Av. Wagram, 17e (phone: 42-27-61-50; fax: 46-22-25-72).

Faugeron Awarded two stars by Michelin, this place combines a nouvelle cuisine approach with bistro influences and more generous portions. Specializing in such simple, but exquisitely prepared, dishes as soft-boiled eggs with truffle purée and slices of sea scallops with lentils, it offers excellent service, a first-rate wine list, and one of Paris's prettiest settings, in what was once a school. Closed weekends (except Saturday dinner October through April), and the month of August. Reservations necessary. Major credit cards accepted. 52 Rue de Longchamp, 16e (phone: 47-04-24-53; phone: 47-55-62-90).

La Ferme St-Simon Among our favorites for wholesome *cuisine d'autrefois* (old-fashioned cooking), this one-Michelin-star place offers nothing very chichi, just well-prepared, authentic dishes—the kinds you'd expect from a traditional Rive Gauche restaurant. Leave room for dessert; the owner once was a top assistant to France's famed pastry chef Gaston Lenôtre. It's also a perfect place for lunch. Closed Saturday lunch, Sundays, and three weeks in August. Reservations advised. Major credit cards accepted. 6 Rue de St-Simon, 7e (phone: 45-48-35-74; fax: 40-49-07-31).

Gérard Besson Michelin has given this small, formal eatery two stars. The service is impeccable and the classic menu includes specialties such as *ris de veau poêlé à la truffe* (veal sweetbreads sautéed with truffles). Closed Sundays, and from September through December for lunch. Reservations necessary. Major credit cards accepted. 5 Rue Coq-Héron, 1er (phone: 42-33-14-74; fax: 42-33-85-71).

Goumard-Prunier Chef Jean-Claude Goumard relies on a network of Breton and Mediterranean fishermen to provide the finest seafood obtainable; his inventive creations, such as scallop mille-feuilles, have earned him two Michelin stars. Closed Sundays and Mondays. Reservations necessary. Major credit cards accepted. 9 Rue Duphot, 1er (phone: 42-60-36-07; fax: 42-60-04-54).

Jacques Cagna This establishment has a quintessentially Rive Gauche look and a mix of nouvelle and classic dishes, which Michelin has awarded two stars. The talented eponymous chef always provides an interesting menu at this charming spot near the Seine. Closed weekends (except Saturday dinner twice a month), three weeks in August, and *Christmas* week. Reservations necessary. Major credit cards accepted. 14 Rue des Grands-Augustins, 6e (phone: 43-26-49-39; fax: 43-54-54-48).

Le Jardin du Royal Monceau With the arrival of chef Bernard Guilhaudin, this attractive garden restaurant in one of Paris's best hotels has begun to reap accolades. Many dishes have an Asian accent, such as crayfish with mango and papaya. Open daily. Reservations advised. Major credit cards accepted. At the *Royal Monceau Hotel,* 35 Av. Hoche, 8e (phone: 45-62-96-02; fax: 45-63-04-03).

Jean-Claude Ferrero This inventive chef prepares eclectic cuisine, from authentic bouillabaisse to chicken with asparagus, and game in season. The restaurant is one of the city's prettiest and is favored by the diplomatic crowd. Closed weekends (except Saturday dinner October through March), two weeks in May, and most of August. Reservations advised. Major credit cards accepted. 38 Rue Vital, 16e (phone: 45-04-42-42).

Ledoyen This grand dowager of Paris restaurants has been given a breath of life by a new chef, Ghislaine Arabian, who favors hearty, classic dishes such as *coquilles St-Jacques* (sea scallops in cream sauce). Last year, her efforts were rewarded with a second Michelin star. There's also an excellent, more moderately priced lunch menu. The view from the upstairs dining room—of the Champs-Elysées, but with trees blocking the traffic—is superb. Closed weekends and most of August. Reservations necessary. Major credit cards accepted. Carré des Champs-Elysées, 8e (phone: 47-42-23-23; fax: 47-42-55-01).

La Marée Its exterior is unobtrusive, but there is great comfort within—also the freshest of fish, the best wine values in Paris, and fabulous desserts. Michelin has awarded it one star. Closed weekends, holidays, and the month of August. Reservations advised. Major credit cards accepted. 1 Rue Daru, 8e (phone: 43-80-20-00; fax: 48-88-04-04).

Miravile Gilles Epié's one-Michelin-star cuisine features such memorable dishes as *lapin aux olives* (rabbit with olives) and other Provençal-inspired recipes. Closed Saturday lunch and Sundays. Reservations necessary. Major credit cards accepted. 72 Quai de l'Hôtel-de-Ville, 4e (phone: 42-74-72-22; fax: 42-74-67-55).

Morot-Gaudry This one-Michelin-star restaurant is perched on the top floor of a 1920s building with a great view of the *Eiffel Tower,* especially from the flowered terrace. Among the inventive dishes is *pigeon en papillote* (squab steamed in its own juices); many dishes have a Mediterranean accent. Closed weekends. Reservations necessary. Major credit cards accepted. 8 Rue de la Cavalerie, 15e (phone: 45-67-06-85; fax: 45-67-55-72).

Le Petit Montmorency In his location near the Champs-Elysées, chef Daniel Bouché presents one of the most consistent menus in Paris, offering such specialties as a fresh truffle roasted in pastry (in winter) and a *soufflé aux noisettes* (hazelnut soufflé). Closed weekends and the month of August. Reservations necessary. Major credit cards accepted. 26 Rue Jean-Mermoz, 8e (phone: 42-25-11-19).

Pile ou Face The name means "heads or tails," but you won't be taking any chances at this one-Michelin-star bistro; super-fresh ingredients come from the owners' own farm. Try the *lapin en marmelade de romarin* (rabbit in a rich, rosemary-flavored sauce). Closed weekends, the month of August, and *Christmas* through *New Year's Day.* Reservations advised. Major credit cards accepted. 52 *bis* Rue Notre-Dame-des-Victoires, 2e (phone: 42-33-64-33; fax: 42-36-61-09).

Le Port Alma This elegant establishment with a view of the *Eiffel Tower* offers some of the finest seafood in town, such as baby clams in a thyme-flavored cream sauce. Closed Sundays and the month of August. Reservations necessary. Major credit cards accepted. 10 Av. de New-York, 16e (phone: 47-23-75-11).

La Timonerie At this one-Michelin-star restaurant, specialties include *filet de maquereau* (mackerel filet) with an herb salad, and a superb chocolate tart. Especially recommended is the very affordable prix fixe lunch. Closed Sundays, Mondays, and one week in August. Reserve at least three days in advance. MasterCard and Visa accepted. 35 Quai de la Tournelle, 5e (phone: 43-25-44-42).

Le Toit de Passy Not only is the food here good (Michelin has awarded chef Yannick Jacquot one star), but the rooftop view in one of Paris's more exclusive districts is spectacular. Try specialties such as *pigeonneau en croûte de sel* (squab in a salt crust) while dining outdoors. Closed Saturday lunch, Sundays, and *Christmas* week. Reservations necessary. Major credit cards accepted. 94 Av. Paul-Doumer, 16e (phone: 45-24-55-37; fax: 45-20-94-57).

Le Train Bleu The pricey traditional cuisine is adequate, but it's really the setting that makes this place worthwhile—in a train station whose Baroque decor is so gorgeous that the spot has been declared a national monument. Open daily. Reservations advised. Major credit cards accepted. *Gare de Lyon,* 20 Bd. Diderot, 12e (phone: 43-43-38-39; fax: 43-43-97-96).

Au Trou Gascon Alain Dutournier created this restaurant's inspired and unusual cooking, featuring southwestern French specialties and augmented by a vast choice of regional wines and armagnacs. He now has set up operations in a more elegant neighborhood at *Le Carré des Feuillants* (see above), while his wife holds down the fort at this one-Michelin-star restaurant. Closed weekends, the month of August, and *Christmas* week. Reservations advised. Major credit cards accepted. 40 Rue Taine, 12e (phone: 43-44-34-26; fax: 43-07-80-55).

Vancouver One of Paris's newest seafood restaurants, this modern establishment has already won a Michelin star for dishes with a Pacific flair, such as sweet and sour shrimp with fresh seaweed, and crayfish wrapped in coriander leaves. Closed weekends and most of August. Reservations advised. Major credit cards accepted. 4 Rue Arsène-Houssaye, 8e (phone: 42-56-77-77; fax: 44-71-15-02).

MODERATE

Ambassade d'Auvergne The young chef here creates delicious, classic Auvergnat dishes with an innovative touch. Try the lentil salad and the sliced ham or the *aligot* (a purée of potatoes and young cantal cheese); for dessert, opt for a slice of one of the wonderful cakes. Closed August 1 through 16. Reservations advised. Major credit cards accepted. 22 Rue du Grenier-St-Lazare, 3e (phone: 42-72-31-22; fax: 42-78-85-47).

Atelier Maître Albert Unlike most other eateries on the Rive Gauche, this one is pleasantly roomy, with a a prix fixe menu of classic French cuisine and a cozy log fire in winter. The spectacle of *Notre-Dame* looming before you as you walk out the door and onto the quay adds the finishing stroke to a charming meal. Closed Sunday dinner. Reservations advised. Major credit cards accepted. 1 Rue Maître-Albert, 5e (phone: 46-33-13-78).

L'Auberge Nicolas Flanel Believed to be the oldest restaurant in Paris (an inn opened in the half-timbered building in 1407), its menu includes such good, simple fare as grilled tuna and leg of lamb. Closed Saturday lunch, Sundays, and the first two weeks in August. Reservations advised. MasterCard and Visa accepted. 51 Rue de Montmorency, 3e (phone: 42-71-77-78).

L'Avenue This chic brasserie, as fashionable as the district, offers grilled meat, raw oysters, and old-fashioned desserts in a dining room with a view of the *Eiffel Tower*. Closed most of August. Reservations advised. Major credit cards accepted. 41 Av. Montaigne, 8e (phone: 40-70-14-91).

Balzar Perhaps because of its location next to the *Sorbonne,* this mirrored brasserie has always attracted well-heeled intellectuals. The steaks and *pommes frites* are definitely worth a visit. Open until midnight; closed the month of August, and *Christmas* through *New Year's Day.* Reservations necessary (and often difficult to get). Major credit cards accepted. 49 Rue des Ecoles, 5e (phone: 43-54-13-67).

Baracane This reasonably priced bistro has excellent cuisine from southwestern France. Try the *lentilles au magret d'oie séché* (lentils with dried goose breast) or the cassoulet. Closed Saturday lunch, Sundays, and most of August. Reservations necessary. MasterCard and Visa accepted. 38 Rue des Tournelles, 4e (phone: 42-71-43-44).

Bistro de la Grille The decor of this old-fashioned spot is right out of a Cartier-Bresson photo, and the excellent food, from the raw oysters to the *andouillette* (grilled tripe sausage), is as classic as the setting. The *première étage* (upstairs) is preferable to the noisy downstairs. Closed most of August. Reservations advised. MasterCard and Visa accepted. In the stylish St-Germain-des-Prés district, at 14 Rue Mabillon, 6e (phone: 43-54-16-87).

Le Bistrot du Sommelier The wine list is sublime in this bistro operated by 1992's *Meilleur Sommelier du Monde* (World's Best Sommelier), and there's hearty bourgeois cuisine to match. The special wine-lover's menu at dinner features six dishes served with six different wines. Closed weekends, the month of August, and *Christmas* through *New Year's Day.* Reservations advised.

Major credit cards accepted. 97 Bd. Haussmann, 8e (phone: 42-65-24-85; fax: 42-94-03-26).

Le Boeuf sur le Toit A haunt of Jean Cocteau, Antoine de St-Exupéry, and other Paris artists and writers in the 1940s, this eatery is managed by the Flo group, well known for good value in atmospheric surroundings, although here these far outrank the classic brasserie fare. The piano bar is open until 2 AM. Open daily. Reservations advised. Major credit cards accepted. Off the Champs-Elysées, at 34 Rue du Colisée, 8e (phone: 43-59-83-80; fax: 45-63-45-40).

Bofinger This magnificent Belle Epoque place is one of Paris's oldest brasseries, and its beauty makes up for the occasionally mediocre food. Ask to be seated on the ground floor, and order onion soup and *choucroute* (sauerkraut)—you won't be disappointed. Open daily. Reservations advised. Major credit cards accepted. 15 Rue de la Bastille, 4e (phone: 42-72-87-82; fax: 42-72-97-68).

Brasserie Lipp This famous brasserie (a beer hall distinguished by its brass dispensers), where the Paris intelligentsia have flocked for over a century, is fashionable for a late supper of *choucroute* and Alsatian beer and for people watching indoors and out, although guests not known to the staff sometimes receive less than welcoming treatment. Closed July and August. Reservations advised. Major credit cards accepted. 151 Bd. St-Germain, 6e (phone: 45-48-53-91).

Brissemoret Popular with Parisians, this pleasant eatery features basic, high-quality food: excellent foie gras, raw salmon marinated in fresh herbs, and great sauces—try the breast of duck in wine sauce. Closed weekends and most of August. Reservations necessary. Major credit cards accepted. 5 Rue St-Marc, 2e (phone: 42-36-91-72).

La Butte Chaillot A starkly modern bistro in a posh district, one of several restaurants operated by celebrated chef Guy Savoy (also see his self-named restaurant and *Le Bistrot de l'Etoile-Lauriston,* above), features such old-fashioned dishes as roast chicken with mashed potatoes, and an unusual lentil soup with crayfish. Closed *Christmas* and *New Year's Day.* Reservations advised. Major credit cards accepted. 112 Av. Kléber, 16e (phone: 47-27-88-88; fax: 47-04-85-70).

La Cagouille This Rive Gauche bistro prepares fish to one-Michelin-star perfection; try the steamed clams or the *bar* (sea bass) with vegetables. Closed three weeks in August and *Christmas* through *New Year's Day.* Reservations advised. Major credit cards accepted. 12 Pl. Constantin-Brancusi, 14e (phone: 43-22-09-01; fax: 45-38-57-29).

Campagne et Provence The bistro alternative to the fine *Miravile* (see above), this tiny Quartier Latin spot has a lovely *tapenade de lapin* (rabbit with olive purée) and a garlicky mixed green salad. Closed Saturday lunch, Sundays, Mondays, and most of August. Reservations necessary. MasterCard and Visa accepted. 25 Quai de la Tournelle, 5e (phone: 43-54-05-17; fax: 42-74-67-55).

Canard'avril This friendly place features such southwestern French specialties as roast duck, cassoulet, foie gras, and potatoes sautéed with garlic; there's also a good selection of fish dishes. Closed weekends. Reservations advised. MasterCard and Visa accepted. 5 Rue Paul-Lelong, 2e (phone: 42-36-26-08).

Le Caroubier A family-run couscous restaurant, it has some of the best hand-rolled couscous grains in town, accompanied by good vegetables, grilled meat, and a delicious *pastilla,* a flaky pastry with a spicy meat filling. Pour the vegetable broth on the delicate couscous, add a little hot pepper sauce, and you'll feel as if you've been transported to Morocco. Closed Sunday dinner, Mondays, and the month of August. Reservations advised. MasterCard and Visa accepted. 122 Av. du Maine, 14e (phone: 43-20-41-49).

Chez Marius A real find—the rotund chef really loves his work, and the three-dish prix fixe dinner is a great deal. Specialties are bouillabaisse and grilled fish. The atmosphere is Old World cozy though there have been complaints of late about the service. Closed Saturday lunch, Sundays, most of August, and a week at *Christmas.* Reservations advised. Major credit cards accepted. 5 Rue Bourgogne, 7e (phone: 47-05-96-19).

La Coupole A big, brassy brasserie, once the haunt of Hemingway, Josephine Baker, and Picasso, it's now owned by the Flo group. The atmosphere is still great, and the food is improving. Open until 2 AM; closed the month of August and *Christmas Eve.* Reservations advised. Major credit cards accepted. 102 Bd. du Montparnasse, 14e (phone: 43-20-14-20; fax: 43-35-46-14).

Fontaine de Mars A simple, family-style restaurant with dishes from southwestern France, such as salad with *magret de canard* (slices of smoked duck breast) and chicken with morel mushrooms. In summer, there's outdoor dining on the patio. Closed Sundays and the month of August. Reservations advised. Major credit cards accepted. Near the *Eiffel Tower,* at 129 Rue St-Dominique, 7e (phone: 47-05-46-44; fax: 45-50-31-92).

Fouquet's Bastille Sister restaurant to the Champs-Elysées institution (see *Cafés,* below), this postmodern brasserie next to the *Opéra de la Bastille* serves traditional fare, such as shellfish platters and simple *plats du jour,* with a modern touch. Closed Saturday lunch, Sundays, and the month of August. Reservations advised. Major credit cards accepted. 130 Rue de Lyon, 12e (phone: 43-42-18-18).

Au Gamin de Paris Combining the coziness of a classic bistro with the chicness of a historic Marais building, it serves well-prepared, imaginative food.

Specialties include grilled salmon and *magret de canard;* for dessert, try the *crème brûlée* or *tarte tatin* (caramelized apple tart). Open daily. Reservations unnecessary. Major credit cards accepted. 51 Rue Vieille-du-Temple, 4e (phone: 42-78-97-24).

Jo Goldenberg The best-known eating house in the Marais's quaint Jewish quarter, with good, albeit overpriced, chopped liver and cheesecake and a range of Eastern European Jewish specialties. Try the mushroom and barley soup. It's also a fine place to sip mint tea at the counter in the middle of a busy day. Open daily. Reservations unnecessary. Major credit cards accepted. 7 Rue des Rosiers, 4e (phone: 48-87-20-16).

Le Maraîcher This tiny Marais eatery has excellent bourgeois cooking (try the cassoulet). Closed Sundays, Monday lunch, the month of August, and *Christmas* week. Reservations advised. Major credit cards accepted. 5 Rue Beautrellis, 4e (phone: 42-71-42-49).

Moissonnier Over the past 30 years little has changed (except the prices) on the menu of this Lyonnaise restaurant, across the street from what was once Paris's wine depot. The seafood, tripe dishes, and beaujolais may not be anything new, but this is bourgeois cuisine par excellence. Closed Sunday dinner and Mondays. Reservations advised. MasterCard and Visa accepted. 28 Rue Fossés-St-Bernard, 5e (phone: 43-29-87-65).

Le Muniche St-Germain's best brasserie is a bustling place with a rather extensive menu. Open daily until 1:30 AM. Reservations advised. Major credit cards accepted. 22 Rue Guillaume-Apollinaire, 6e (phone: 47-34-01-06).

Ostréade Seafood is king at this bustling, loft-like Montparnasse brasserie. Try the salad of potatoes and baby clams or the whole roast fish, and don't miss the tiny Breton oysters known as *boudeuses.* Open daily. Reservations necessary. Major credit cards accepted. 11 Bd. de Vaugirard, 15e (phone: 43-21-87-41).

Le Poquelin The excellent bourgeois cooking includes *magret de canard en croûte d'épices* (duck breast in a spicy crust). Closed Saturday lunch, Sundays, and three weeks in August. Reservations advised. Major credit cards accepted. 17 Rue Molière, 1er (phone: 42-96-22-19; fax: 42-96-05-72).

La Rôtisserie du Beaujolais A de rigueur spot for Paris's "in" set is Claude Terrail's casual canteen on the quay in the shadow of his three-star gastronomic temple, *La Tour d'Argent.* Most of the restaurant's meat, produce, and cheese comes from Lyons; try the offerings with a superb Georges Duboeuf beaujolais. Closed Mondays. No reservations. Major credit cards accepted. 19 Quai de la Tournelle, 5e (phone: 43-54-17-47).

La Tour de Montlhéry This bistro offers great bourgeois cooking. Closed weekends and the month of August. Reservations necessary. MasterCard and Visa accepted. In *Les Halles,* at 5 Rue des Prouvaires, 1er (phone: 42-36-21-82).

Le Valençay A small, popular bistro with classic bourgeois fare and wines by the glass or the bottle. Closed Sundays and the month of August. No reservations. Major credit cards accepted. 11 Bd. du Palais, 4e (phone: 43-54-64-67).

Yvan Creative bistro fare, such as squab with polenta, and sardines with tomatoes, along with a wonderful cheese selection, keeps this restaurant almost always full. The place also boasts a stylish atmosphere and very reasonable prices. Closed Saturday lunch and Sundays. Reservations necessary. Major credit cards accepted. 1 *bis* Rue Jean-Mermoz, 8e (phone: 43-59-18-40; fax: 45-63-78-69).

Les Zygomates This friendly bistro occupies a converted fin de siècle charcuterie with lots of mirrors and marble counters. The menu includes fish, as well as classic bistro meat dishes and gooey chocolate desserts. Closed Saturday lunch, Sundays, most of August, and December 26 through January 4. Reservations necessary. MasterCard and Visa accepted. In an out-of-the-way location, at 7 Rue Capri, 12e (phone: 40-19-93-04).

INEXPENSIVE

L'Ami Jean This place offers good Basque cooking. Closed Saturday dinner and Sundays. No reservations. No credit cards accepted. 27 Rue Malar, 7e (phone: 47-05-86-89).

Auberge de Jarente This Basque restaurant is the place to sample classic *pipérade* (omelette with ham and tomato), and cassoulet. Closed Sundays, Mondays, and the month of August. Reservations advised. Major credit cards accepted. In the heart of the Marais, at 7 Rue de Jarente, 4e (phone: 42-77-49-35).

Brasserie Fernand A nondescript hole-in-the-wall place that produces surprisingly tasty dishes. The pot-au-feu, steaks with shallots, and fish pâté all are first-rate, but the real lure is the huge tub of chocolate mousse served for dessert—a chocoholic's fantasy come true. Open daily for dinner only. Reservations advised. MasterCard and Visa accepted. 13 Rue Guisarde, 6e (phone: 43-54-61-47).

Casa Olympe Dominique Nahmias, the former *doyenne* of *Olympe,* has her own restaurant again, a chic and intimate place in a charming neighborhood. Her copious servings of fine bistro classics with a Mediterranean touch, such as *lapin au pistou* (rabbit with garlic-basil sauce), at reasonable prices (the menu is prix fixe only) have made reservations difficult to get, but keep trying. Closed weekends and most of August. Reservations necessary. Major credit cards accepted. 48 Rue Saint-Georges, 9e (phone: 42-85-26-01; fax: 45-26-49-33).

Le Grand Colbert This restaurant near the lovely *Galerie Vivienne* has murals on the walls, copper light fixtures, and big banquettes—in short, authentic, turn-of-the-century decor—and good brasserie specialties like herring with potatoes in vinaigrette and duck *confit* with garlic-laden potatoes. Closed mid-July to mid-August. Reservations advised. Major credit cards accepted. 2 Rue Vivienne, 2e (phone: 42-86-87-88; fax: 42-86-82-65).

La Lozère Here you'll find authentic country cooking from the Lozère region in the south of France, with an emphasis on charcuterie and cassoulet. Closed Sundays, Mondays, and the month of August. Reservations advised. No credit cards accepted. 4 Rue Hautefeuille, 6e (phone: 43-54-26-64).

Polidor Regulars here, who have included such starving artists as Paul Verlaine, James Joyce, Ernest Hemingway, and, more recently, Jean-Paul Belmondo, still keep their napkins in numbered pigeonholes. The *Collège de Pataphysique,* founded by Raymond Queneau and Eugène Ionesco, continues to meet here regularly for the good family-style food. But a drawback to this customer loyalty is that foreigners are banished to the back room. Closed the month of August. Reservations unnecessary. No credit cards accepted. 41 Rue Monsieur-le-Prince, 6e (phone: 43-26-95-34).

La Route du Beaujolais This is a barn-like workers' bistro serving Lyonnaise specialties and beaujolais wines. Don't miss the charcuterie and the fresh bread here, and try the *tarte tatin* for dessert. Closed Saturday lunch and Sundays. Reservations unnecessary. MasterCard and Visa accepted. On the Rive Gauche, at 17 Rue de Lourmel, 15e (phone: 45-79-31-63).

Thoumieux This family-run bistro has been reliable for decades. Come here for tripe, cassoulet, and *boudin aux châtaignes* (blood sausage with chestnuts). Open daily. Reservations advised. MasterCard and Visa accepted. 79 Rue St-Dominique, 7e (phone: 47-05-49-75; fax: 47-05-36-96).

Aux Tonneaux des Halles Wine by the glass, an old-fashioned setting, and typical bistro dishes like *navarin d'agneau* (lamb stew) make this a popular spot among Parisians. Closed Sundays and Mondays. Reservations advised. MasterCard and Visa accepted. 28 Rue Montorgueil, 1er (phone: 42-33-36-19).

VERY INEXPENSIVE

Bistro de la Gare Michel Oliver's restaurants offer a choice of three appetizers and three main courses with *pommes frites,* excellent for a quick lunch. Open daily. No reservations. Major credit cards accepted. Ten locations, including 1 Rue du Four, 6e (phone: 43-25-87-76); 59 Bd. du Montparnasse, 6e (phone: 45-48-38-01); and 30 Rue St-Denis, 1er (phone: 40-26-82-80).

Chartier This huge, turn-of-the-century place serves lots of down-to-earth food for the price. The famous pot-au-feu is still served on Mondays. Open daily. No reservations. No credit cards accepted. 7 Rue du Faubourg-Montmartre, 9e (phone: 47-70-86-29).

Drouot A favorite of locals, the younger member of the Chartier family (see above) proffers simple fare at bargain prices. To avoid a long wait for a table, arrive before 9 PM. Open daily. No reservations. No credit cards accepted. 103 Rue de Richelieu, 2e (phone: 42-96-68-23).

Le Petit Gavroche A hole-in-the-wall bistro-cum-restaurant with a lively clientele and a classic menu. Closed Sundays. Reservations unnecessary. No credit cards accepted. 15 Rue Ste-Croix-de-la-Bretonnerie, 4e (phone: 48-87-74-26).

Le Petit St-Benoît Here is French cooking at its simplest, in a plain little place with tiled floors and curlicued hat stands. Closed weekends. Reservations unnecessary. No credit cards accepted. 4 Rue St-Benoît, 6e (phone: 42-60-27-92).

Au Pied de Fouet This former coach house has had its habitués, including celebrities as diverse as Graham Greene, Le Corbusier, and Georges Pompidou. Service is fast and friendly, and the daily specials are reliably good. Save room for the marvelous desserts, such as *charlotte au chocolat.* Arrive early; it closes at 9 PM. Closed Saturday dinner, Sundays, two weeks at both *Easter* and *Christmas,* and the month of August. No reservations. No credit cards accepted. 45 Rue de Babylone, 7e (phone: 47-05-12-27).

FAUCHON FARE

Although we've noted *Fauchon* as a shopping destination in *Quintessential Paris* (see DIVERSIONS), we would be remiss in omitting it here. On the first floor of the 30 Place de la Madeleine location is *Le 30,* a charming, garden restaurant that serves first-rate seafood and veal dishes, along with spectacular desserts. And for nonpareil pastries, coffee, and a variety of light lunches or snacks, folks in the know head for the basement. Mornings begin at 8 AM here with an American- or French-style breakfast (with over 40 different types of coffee). For lunch there are reasonably priced daily specials which attract shoppers from nearby department stores (this can mean long lines for the cafeteria-style service and no available tables, so try to avoid the 1 to 2 PM crush). In the afternoons (until about 5 PM), the basement serves as a tearoom, offering the house's celebrated pastries: chocolate *opéra* cakes, macaroons in many hues, as well as mille-feuilles and other custardy concoctions.

CAFÉS

Paris without cafés would be like Madrid without tapas bars, Dublin without pubs, or New York without delis. The corner café is the glue that holds the French neighborhood together; it's a place for coffee and gossip, or just a spot in which to sit and watch the world go by. Reservations are never needed; just claim a table, and it's yours for as long as the spirit moves you. And, possibly best of all, it's almost always easy on the wallet. Of the more than 5,000 cafés in Paris, the following are our favorites:

Café Costes Philippe Starck's postmodern design, inspired by Fritz Lang's *Metropolis,* helped make this café the trendiest of trendsetters for *branché* ("with-it") Parisians; now its fame is such that it has rated a mention in *Time* magazine. Open daily. Major credit cards accepted. In the Beaubourg district, near the *Centre Georges-Pompidou,* at 4 Rue Berger, 1er (phone: 45-08-54-38/9).

Café de la Paix Designed by Charles Garnier to complement his baroque *Opéra,* this grande dame is best for afternoon tea; keep your eye out for the elusive pastry cart (the service in general can be elusive at times). Open daily until 1:30 AM. Major credit cards accepted. Two entrances, at 12 Bd. des Capucines and 2 Rue Scribe, 9e (phone: 40-07-32-32).

Fouquet's Arguably Paris's best-located café—it's part of the eponymous regal restaurant, now an official historic monument—this institution on the Champs-Elysées is far from perfect: The drinks are too expensive; the sidewalk is often too crowded; and the downstairs dining is forgettable one night and downright mediocre the next. But if there is still magic in the world, it can be found here at dusk, when the lights come up on the *Arc de Triomphe.* Open daily 9 PM to midnight. Major credit cards accepted. 99 Av. des Champs-Elysées, 8e (phone: 47-23-70-60).

Ma Bourgogne Set beneath the vaulted arcades of the Place des Vosges, this is a great spot for an afternoon stop, not so much for the food as for the view of Paris's most beautiful square; it was also the favorite hangout of Simenon's fictional Inspector Maigret. Try their specialty of sausages from Auvergne with a glass of burgundy or bordeaux. Closed Mondays. MasterCard and Visa accepted. 19 Pl. des Vosges, 4e (phone: 42-78-44-64).

La Palette A Rive Gauche hangout on a tiny square, with outdoor tables during the summer, it stays lively with a young crowd until 2 AM. Closed Sundays, holidays, and the month of August. No credit cards accepted. 43 Rue de Seine, 6e (phone: 43-26-68-15).

Le Piano Zinc Tiny and authentic, this hole-in-the-wall place with a classic, zinc-topped, horseshoe-shaped bar has a regular and eclectic clientele of artists and workers. Central to Marais shopping, museums, designer boutiques, and the *Hôtel de Ville,* it's well worth a detour. Closed the month of August. No credit cards accepted. 49 Rue des Blancs-Manteaux, 3e (phone: 42-74-32-42).

La Rhumerie This longtime hangout of Rive Gauche literati has a pleasant elevated terrace, salads and Caribbean-style cuisine for light lunches, and 15 varieties of mostly rum-based punch. Open daily until 2 AM. MasterCard and Visa accepted. 166 Bd. Saint-Germain, 6e (phone: 43-54-28-94).

Le Select Opened in 1925 at the height of the Jazz Age, this was the first Montparnasse café to stay open all night. Edna St. Vincent Millay, Erik Satie, and Leonard Foujita adored the place; in 1927 Isadora Duncan got into a fistfight here with an American newspaperman. (History records the dancer won by a decision.) The café hasn't changed much since, and it has some of the liveliest early-morning and late-night scenes imaginable. Open daily until 2 AM. MasterCard and Visa accepted. 99 Bd. du Montparnasse, 6e (phone: 42-22-65-27 or 45-48-38-24).

Le Voltaire An often-overlooked gem, this tiny café along the Seine has a rich literary history: It's where Baudelaire wrote *Les Fleurs du Mal* (he lived at 19 Quai Voltaire), Wagner wrote the words for *Die Meistersinger* (his home was at No. 22), and the eponymous Voltaire died. Closed Sundays, Mondays, and the month of August. No credit cards accepted. Opposite the *Louvre* and near the *Musée d'Orsay*, at 27 Quai Voltaire, 7e (phone: 42-61-17-49).

WINE BARS

Though wine bars are now a Parisian institution, they actually originated among oenophilic Londoners. They vary widely in decor and the types of wines they purvey, but all offer wines by the glass only and a convivial atmosphere; if food is served, it's simple and specially chosen to accompany the wine. While some wine bars offer very expensive wines and edibles, all have some inexpensive wines on their lists. Unless otherwise noted, reservations are unnecessary; however, at lunch hour, if you don't have a reservation and want only a glass of wine, some very busy places may ask you to stand at the bar. The following are some of our favorites among Paris's true wine bars:

L'Ange-Vin This place boasts Paris's best collection of sweet white wines from the Loire Valley (try the Côteaux-du-Layon '89), good *plats du jour* and snacks, and excellent cheeses. There's even a real nonsmoking section—a rarity among Parisian wine bars. Open 11 AM to 8:30 PM (to 2 AM Tuesdays and Thursdays); closed weekends. MasterCard and Visa accepted. 24 Rue Richard-Lenoir, 11e (phone: 43-48-20-20).

Bistrot des Augustins Just across the street from the booksellers on the quays, this old-fashioned café with an excellent *plat du jour* at lunch has fine beaujolais and other wines by the glass. Closed the month of August. No credit cards accepted. 39 Quai des Grands-Augustins, 6e (phone: 43-54-41-65).

Le Bouchon du Marais One of the capital's newer wine bars, it specializes in Loire Valley wines (the owner has a vineyard in Chinon) and simple light snacks. Closed Sundays, the month of August, and daily from 3 to 7 PM. No credit cards accepted. 15 Rue François-Miron, 4e (phone: 48-87-44-13).

Caves Saint-Gilles This Spanish wine bar serves generous tapas (try the *pipérade*, a Basque omelette), rioja and sangria by the glass, and an ample *plat du* *jour.* Closed the month of August. Reservations accepted for a full meal at lunch only. No credit cards accepted. Appropriately located near the *Musée Picasso,* at 4 Rue St-Gilles, 3e (phone: 48-87-22-62).

La Cloche des Halles The dim lighting and dark wood paneling at this cozy establishment add to the pleasure of sampling the wine here. Those with hunger pangs can order the generous cheese platter or try a plate of charcuterie. Closed Saturday evenings, Sundays, and the month of August. No credit cards accepted. 28 Rue Coquillière, 1er (phone: 42-36-93-89).

L'Ecluse This unassuming wine bar overlooking the Seine has fathered several other, more sophisticated places—on the Rue François-Ier, at the *Madeleine,* at the *Opéra* (both the *Palais Garnier* and the *Bastille*), in *Le Forum des Halles,* and in Neuilly. Its red velvet benches and wooden tables—not to mention its bordeaux and the fresh, homemade foie gras and spectacular chocolate cake—remain unchanged. Open daily. Major credit cards accepted. 15 Quai des Grands-Augustins, 6e (phone: 46-33-58-74), and several other locations.

L'Enoteca This wine bar in the Marais features a vast assortment of Italian wines by the glass or bottle, along with Italian fare at lunch. Closed part of August. Major credit cards accepted. 25 Rue Charles-V, 4e (phone: 42-78-91-44).

Espace Hérault Attached to the Hérault *département*'s tourist office, it features wines and simple dishes from Languedoc. Closed Saturday mornings, Sundays, the month of August, and daily between 2 and 7:30 PM. Major credit cards accepted. 8 Rue de la Harpe, 5e (phone: 43-33-00-56).

Au Franc Pinot A restaurant has operated on this spot for 350 years, making this Paris's oldest wine bar. In a lovely setting on the Ile St-Louis, it offers regional wines, many from the Loire, and delicious snacks. Closed Sundays, Mondays, the month of August, and daily from 3 to 7 PM. Major credit cards accepted. 1 Quai Bourbon, 4e (phone: 43-29-46-98).

Jacques Melac An old-fashioned wine bar run by a young, extravagantly mustachioed man from the Auvergne, who bottles and sells his own rustic wines and even stages a harvest celebration in honor of the restaurant's vineyard. Note the sign above the bar that asserts that water should be used only for cooking potatoes. Closed weekends and the month of August. MasterCard and Visa accepted. 42 Rue Léon-Frot, 11e (phone: 43-70-59-27).

Juveniles This friendly spot has excellent wine and top-quality snacks, as well as several fine sherries. The British owners have a loyal British and American following. Closed Sundays. MasterCard and Visa accepted. 47 Rue de Richelieu, 1er (phone: 47-97-46-49).

Millésimes An ideal location next to the renovated St-Germain-des-Prés covered market, plus a wide choice of wines and good *tartines* (open-face sandwiches) and charcuterie platters, have made this one of the most popular wine bars on the Rive Gauche. Open 7 AM to 1 AM; closed Sundays. MasterCard and Visa accepted. 7 Rue Lobineau, 6e (phone: 46-34-21-15).

Le Pain et Le Vin Operated by four top Parisian chefs, including Alain Dutournier of *Le Carré des Feuillants* and *Au Trou Gascon* (see *Eating Out* for both), this place features 40 wines by the glass and daily hot lunch specials. Closed Sundays, the month of August, and daily between 3 and 7 PM. Major credit cards accepted. 1 Rue d'Armaillé, 17e (phone: 47-63-88-29).

Relais Chablisien As the name implies, this wine bar, with its wood-beamed ceilings and warm atmosphere, specializes in chablis. Sandwiches and excellent *plats du jour* also are available. Closed weekends and two weeks in August. Reservations advised for meals. Major credit cards accepted. 4 Rue Bertin-Poirée, 1er (phone: 45-08-53-73).

Le Repaire de Bacchus A tiny wine bar specializing in unusual regional wines, displayed in crowded rows. You can buy wine by the bottle to take home or on a picnic, or sip it at the counter with cheese and charcuterie. Closed Sundays and Mondays. MasterCard and Visa accepted. 13 Rue du Cherche-Midi, 6e (phone: 45-44-01-07).

Le Rouge-Gorge Near the antiques shops of the St-Paul *quartier,* this place has changing, thematic menus that feature the wines and foods of a particular region for two-week periods. Some patrons have complained of indifferent service, however. Closed Sundays and the month of August. No credit cards accepted. 8 Rue St-Paul, 4e (phone: 48-04-75-89).

Le Rubis A tiny corner bar, it has an old-fashioned atmosphere and a selection of about 30 wines. With your glass of wine try the pork *rillettes,* savory meat pies made on the premises. Closed Saturdays after 4 PM, Sundays, and two weeks in August. No credit cards accepted. 10 Rue du Marché-St-Honoré, 1er (phone: 42-61-03-34).

Le Sancerre A hospitable spot featuring nothing but Sancerre wines—red, white, and rosé. Simple lunches of omelettes, charcuterie, apple tarts, and *petits goûters* (snacks) such as goat cheese marinated in olive oil are the perfect accompaniment for the excellent wine. Open 7 AM to 8:30 PM; closed Saturday afternoons and evenings, Sundays, and the month of August. Major credit cards accepted. 22 Av. Rapp, 7e (phone: 45-51-75-91).

Au Sauvignon The couple who run this tiny corner bar seem to be in perpetual motion, pouring the sauvignon blanc (or the white quincy and beaujolais nouveau in November and January) and carving up chunky *tartines* with bread from the famous *Poilâne* bakery not far away. Closed Sundays, two weeks in January, *Easter,* and the month of August. No credit cards accepted. 80 Rue des Sts-Pères, 7e (phone: 45-48-49-02).

La Tartine An old, authentic bistro where Trotsky was once known to sip a glass or two of wine. There's a colorful local clientele and a good selection of mostly inexpensive wines by the glass. Closed Tuesdays, Wednesday mornings, and most of August. No credit cards accepted. 24 Rue de Rivoli, 4e (phone: 42-72-76-85).

Taverne Henri IV A selection of nearly 20 wines is offered by the glass, along with generous servings of simple food such as open-face sandwiches of ham, cheese, sausage, or the more exotic terrine of wild boar. Closed Saturday evenings, Sundays, and most of August. No credit cards accepted. On the Pont Neuf, at 13 Pl. du Pont-Neuf, 1er (phone: 43-54-27-90).

Willi's An enterprising Englishman set up this smart little wine bar, a pleasant walk through the *Palais Royal* gardens from the *Louvre*. The wine selection—a list of 150—is one of the best in Paris, with an emphasis on Côtes du Rhône. The chef creates some appetizing salads as well as *plats du jour*. Closed Sundays. Major credit cards accepted. 13 Rue des Petits-Champs, 1er (phone: 42-61-05-09).

TEAROOMS

Yes, you have crossed the Channel, but even in Paris, taking tea is a revitalizing mid-afternoon break from frantic sightseeing and window shopping. The *salon de thé* originally was the refuge of patrician Parisian ladies, who lingered over ambrosial pastries and fragrant, steaming cups of *cerise* (cherry) tea between social calls. Today, tearooms still lure Parisians and visitors alike to partake of their caloric treats. *L'Arbre à Canelle* (57 Passage des Panoramas, 2e; phone: 45-08-55-87) offers scrumptious chocolate pear and apple tart in a stylish setting. Those with discriminating tea tastes frequent *A La Cour de Rohan* (59-61 Rue St-André-des-Arts, 6e; phone: 43-25-79-67), which offers over 20 varieties described in almost religious detail. You'll find a *plus raffiné* Belle Epoque atmosphere at *Ladurée* (16 Rue Royale, 8e; phone: 42-60-21-79), where it would be a shame to ignore the masterfully decorated petits fours, marrons glacés, and macaroons. Nowhere in Paris is tea taken more seriously than at *Mariage Frères* (30-32 Rue du Bourg-Tibourg, 4e; phone: 42-72-28-11; and 13 Rue des Grands-Augustins, 6e; phone: 40-51-82-50); with a supply of 450 different kinds of tea, it's perhaps wisest to close your eyes and choose a blend at whim. Neoclassical art and classical music contribute to the tranquil ambience at *A Priori Thé* (35-37 *Galerie Vivienne,* 2e; phone: 42-97-48-75), set in one of Paris's lovely *passages* (glass-roofed shopping arcades). In another *passage* is the new *Thé S. F.* (Passage du Grand Cerf, 2e; phone: 40-28-08-76), which features 45 teas, a scrumptious chocolate terrine, scones, and cheesecake; quiches and a cheese platter are also available. The *Tea Caddy* (14 Rue Julien-le-Pauvre, 5e; phone: 43-54-15-56), one of the oldest tea shops in Paris, is very British— from its name to its fine teas and scones. *Tea and Tattered Pages* (24 Rue Mayet, 6e; phone: 40-65-94-35), a combination tearoom and used-English-books store, is a great place to pick up some reading material for a rainy day. And the *Crillon* hotel (see *Checking In*) is one of the city's most elegant spots in which to take very expensive afternoon tea, complete with an assortment of sublime pastries.

AND FOR CHOCOHOLICS

The best hot chocolate in Paris, if not the universe, is served at *Angelina* (226 Rue de Rivoli, 1er, phone: 42-60-82-00; 86 Av. de Longchamp, 16e, phone: 47-04-89-42; 40 Bd. Haussmann, 9e, phone: 42-82-34-56; and in the *Palais des Congrès, Porte Maillot,* 17e, phone: 40-68-22-50). To accompany your cup of sweet ambrosia, order *chocolat l'Africain,* a dessert made with delicious dark chocolate.

Diversions

Exceptional Pleasures
and Treasures

Quintessential Paris

We hear a lot of complaints about Paris these days. Traffic. Pollution. The once harmonious, elegant sweep of Haussmann's boulevards are, say critics, increasingly marred by such modern intrusions as *La Défense,* the futuristic-looking business center that obstructs the skyline to the west, or the Big Mac invasion that also threatens the sanctity of the corner café.

But a century ago the *Eiffel Tower* had its critics, too, and while it may be necessary to look a little harder these days to find the Paris of Proust and Hemingway, happily it still exists. We still encounter with reassuring regularity the Frenchman and his dog on a routine morning stroll to the *pâtisserie.* An organ grinder still plays for Sunday crowds in the Place des Vosges. Piaf sing-alongs occur nightly in Montmartre bistros. And just when we begin to despair that this century has erased the best of the old and to wonder what the next will possibly retain, we happen upon the nonpareil Paris bistro, a perfect little red-awninged gem, hidden away on a tiny, sun-dappled square.

Paris is, after all, still Paris, the quintessential City of Light, and life. Yes, it is more crowded than when Gershwin immortalized it in music. Yes, it becomes more expensive with each passing season. But when the lights rise along the Seine or the *Bois de Boulogne* is filled with the fresh, crisp scent of chestnuts, you really wouldn't want to be anywhere else. The following are other places and experiences that capture the essence of this incomparable city.

ILE ST-LOUIS Joined by a footbridge to the Ile de la Cité, the place where Paris began, this island sits like a medieval oasis between the Rive Gauche and Rive Droite in the middle of the Seine. Once home to the likes of Voltaire, Rousseau, and Baudelaire, the narrow cobblestone lanes that radiate from the island's single lengthwise street, Rue St-Louis-en-l'Ile, are now among the most coveted and expensive pieces of Paris real estate. A narrow one-way lane, Rue St-Louis-en-l'Ile is lined with shops and charming restaurants, some with stone walls and vaulted ceilings, as well as a *fromagerie* (cheese shop) or two. Try the *Montecristo,* a superb, yet inexpensive, Italian trattoria; *Au Franc Pinot,* Paris's oldest wine bar; or the outrageous (and loud) *Brasserie de l'Ile St-Louis,* where the Pont St-Louis footbridge leads from *Notre-Dame.* No trip here would be complete without generous samplings of the island's own *Berthillon* ice cream. Served in two company-owned shops on the island and by several other local *glaciers, Berthillon* has become a legend in its own time—handmade, rich mixtures with inspired combinations of ingredients (the crunchy chocolate nougat will make you swoon!). So confident is *Berthillon* of its reputation that it not only steadfastly refuses to expand off the island (although many cafés elsewhere in Paris also sell the ice cream), but insists on closing altogether during the prime ice cream–consuming month of August.

JARDIN DU LUXEMBOURG (LUXEMBOURG GARDENS) Every day is Sunday in Hemingway's favorite park, where Parisians stroll with babies in prams, children race miniature sailboats in the fountains, and young lovers sit on benches beneath the trees. George Moore may have captured the mood best when he wrote in *Memories of My Dead Life,* "I loitered in the Luxembourg Gardens to watch the birds and the sunlight . . . and began to wonder if there was anything better in the world worth doing than to sit in an alley of clipped limes smoking, thinking of Paris and myself." Enchanting as it is to think of just sitting here enjoying the serenity, there is in fact plenty to do in this 46-acre garden. Requisitioned in 1615 by Marie de Médicis and designed, in part, by Salomon de Brosse, today it's a popular jogging spot; there are six tennis courts (available on a first-come, first-served basis); and for children, there's a puppet theater near the orchards, pony rides, a small carousel, several playgrounds, including one with rubber pavement and elaborate slides, and toy sailboats for rent for cruising around the Médicis fountain. Honey is still produced by the garden's hives, where a beekeeping course is taught in summer by a priest. Clearly, the 20th century hasn't made its mark here yet—as long as you ignore the top of the *Tour Montparnasse,* just visible above the chestnut trees.

CAFÉ SOCIETY If you've ever read a novel, and especially if you've ever thought of writing one, you shouldn't leave Paris without visiting one of its thousands of cafés. Those along the Boulevard St-Germain are as well-known for the inspiration and comfort they have afforded generations of novelists and intellectuals as for the thick, *serré* (strong) coffees they serve.

Among the city's most celebrated hangouts are the *Café Les Deux Magots* (6 Pl. St-Germain-des-Prés; phone: 45-48-55-25), reputed by some to have the world's best hot chocolate (we give the nod to *Angelina's* on Rue de Rivoli), and the place where Sartre drank whiskey while de Beauvoir nursed a Coke. Just next door is the revived *Café de Flore* (172 Bd. St-Germain; phone: 45-48-55-26), an exceptional place to stop for a breakfast of brioches and *oeufs brouillés* (scrambled eggs) before wandering through the bookstores and chic clothing boutiques that line the boulevard. Across the street, the old *Brasserie Lipp* has been a popular *choucroute*-and-conversation spot for actors, writers, and politicians for over a century. And the neighborhood continues to attract a lively arts and tourist crowd. Be warned, though: "Membership" in café society doesn't come cheap—at press time, the price of a cup of coffee in some of the best-known cafés was $5—and service can be excruciatingly slow and indifferent. But then, you never know—the same muse who inspired Sartre may be seated at the table next to yours.

FAUCHON AND PLACE DE LA MADELEINE *Fauchon* is one of the good things about Paris that only keeps getting better. Born in 1886 as a mere pushcart, *Fauchon* (26-30 Pl. de la Madeleine; phone: 47-42-60-11) grew to become such a bastion of the privileged that one of its stores was bombed by radicals back in 1978. With a complex of shops and eating establishments extending from Nos. 26 to 30 on the Place de la Madeleine, the legendary food purveyor stocks some 20,000 items, from Cambodian peppers and African mangoes to New England clam chowder. Here, food is art, and the window displays are the stuff of which dreams (and picnics) are made. (At *Christmas,* the glittering still-life tableau slows traffic to a crawl on this corner, drawing nearly as many gawkers as New York City's *Lord & Taylor* department store's holiday windows.) The first *Fauchon* shop—No. 26—specializes in the most beautiful fruits and vegetables available anywhere, plus pâtés, terrines, and enough other exquisite culinary items to surprise and delight even the most jaded aficionado. The sculptured pâtés are so finely detailed that it's almost a shame to eat them; even grapes are displayed as if they were the crown jewels. There also is a trattoria on the first floor (what we'd call the second floor) that offers a variety of pasta dishes, salads, and other light luncheon food that can be eaten at tables or on stools at counters.

Another member of the *Fauchon* food trilogy—No. 28—carries breads, pastries, and candies. The third incarnation, the grocery (No. 30), is where all of Paris congregates for a variety of delicious reasons. The main floor is stocked with house brand vinegars, olive oils, teas, and coffees, while the rest of the building is given over to an excellent restaurant and a deliciously decadent stand-up snack and dessert spot.

Although discerning shoppers will find several smaller places in the neighborhood with better prices and more patient service, *Fauchon* is still a good place to get a delicious souvenir of your visit or a gift, such as a pound of house blend coffee, a tin of aged sardines from Brittany, or a decanter of peaches soaked in armagnac. We particularly like *Fauchon* vinegar (try the tarragon) and *tchando* (lotus) tea. *Fauchon* also ships anywhere. All branches are closed Sundays.

In Paris, window shopping is called *léche-vitrine,* literally, "window licking." You'll understand why after a walk around the shops fringing the Madeleine. Across the square from *Fauchon,* you'll find *Hédiard,* specialist in exotic fruits; *Maison de la Truffe,* the world's largest truffle retailer; and, in the same building, *Caviar Kaspia,* a retail caviar vendor with a small restaurant upstairs. And then there's *L'Ecluse,* which specializes in fine bordeaux, and Alain Senderens's *Lucas-Carton,* one of Paris's five three-Michelin-star restaurants, just a few steps away across from the *Madeleine.*

PLACE DES VOSGES In the heart of the Marais district, Paris's most beautiful and oldest (1605–12) square remains a most privileged and prestigious address.

Among the 39 houses that grace the red-brick quadrangle are the *Maison de Victor-Hugo* (No. 6) and *L'Ambroisie* (No. 9), one of only five three-Michelin-star restaurants in Paris. With its vaulted arches and arcades, Place des Vosges was the model for the Places Dauphine, Vendôme, and later, de la Concorde. It was previously the site of *l'Hôtel des Tournelles,* where Henri II was killed in a jousting tournament. In 1612, it became known as Place Royale; in 1800 the square was baptized Vosges in honor of the first French *département* to pay all its taxes to the new French Republic.

Today, the square is a garden spot for area residents and tourists alike. The Marais (the name means "marsh," which it was when the city was founded) is to Paris what Greenwich Village is to New York City, with its sense of history, its jumble of interesting shops and restaurants, and its historical architecture. Directly behind the Place des Vosges are synagogues designed by Alexandre-Gustave Eiffel and Art Nouveau architect Hector Guimard. The Marais bristles with art galleries and museums, such as the *Musée Carnavalet* (devoted entirely to the history of the city of Paris, it's the largest municipal museum in the world), *Musée Picasso,* and *Musée de la Chasse et de la Nature.* The area is also home to Paris's largest Jewish population; the colorful Rue des Rosiers is chockablock with restaurants and shops that remind one of a street in Central or Eastern Europe.

PARISIAN MARKETS Paris's markets provide some of its great sensory pleasures, and the lively little sixth-*arrondissement* morning market that begins at the eastern end of Rue de Buci and winds around the corner onto Rue de Seine is a typically tantalizing example. From early morning, the scents of freshly baked bread and creamy Camembert waft above neatly arranged spears of white asparagus, seas of super-slim green beans, carts filled with nothing but wild mushrooms, and an array of fruits worthy of a Gauguin still life. A fishmonger shouts out prices of the day's catch, glistening and fresh *comme l'oeil.* At 81 Rue de Seine is an old-fashioned charcuterie, pleasingly cluttered with hams hanging from ceiling beams, prepared dishes, and pâtés—the makings of divine picnics. Next door (also No. 81) is an excellent cheese shop; try their *fromage frais* and goat cheeses. Around the corner on Rue de Buci (No. 8), foie gras terrines of all sizes glitter like jewels in the windows of *J. Papin,* a sleek, modern *traiteur* (caterer). For cakes, homemade candies, and *fruits glacé* (glazed fruit), try *La Vieille France* (No. 14), one of Paris's oldest pâtisseries (pastry shops), founded in 1834. Continue south on Rue de Seine, cross the Boulevard Saint-Germain, and turn right on tiny Rue Lobineau to the main entrance of the Saint-Germain-des-Prés covered market, recently installed in new quarters after a long renovation project. Less well known than the nearby street market, this is where locals shop. Don't miss the stand offering organic products and produce; other stands sell wine, cheese, fish, meat, and take-out foods from around the globe—Vietnam, Greece, Mexico, and Italy. The market is closed Sunday afternoons and Mondays. Gather up an armful of market goodies and head south to the *Jardin du Luxembourg* for a *déjeuner sur l'herbe*—but you'll have to sit on a bench; the grass is off limits!

BOULEVARD ST-MICHEL In the glitter of street lamps and the evening glow from floodlit *Notre-Dame,* there is a simmering mix of arguing students, strumming guitars, roasting chestnuts, and sizzling street-corner crêpes along the Boul' Mich (as Parisians call it)—a feast that hasn't moved since Hemingway's day. Latin no longer is the lingua franca of this *quartier,* but you'll hear plenty of Greek, Arabic, Farsi, and Wolof, and sharing billboard space in front of the multilingual movie theaters are posters for the latest films from Hollywood to India. The bookstalls along the Seine hold anything from a first edition of Proust to a Simenon whodunit—or a single, illuminated page from a medieval manuscript.

RUE DU FAUBOURG-ST-HONORÉ AND RUE ST-HONORÉ Like the *Grand Bazaar* of Istanbul, the souk of Marrakesh, and the agora of ancient Athens, the mile-long stretch of designer sidewalks between the *Palais de l'Elysée* and the *Palais-Royal* offers one of the world's all-time great shopping experiences. It has the finest names in everything, and an unsurpassed array of specialized retailers of chocolate, leather, and lingerie. Try *Raymond* for gold-plated faucets, *Au Nain Bleu* for a miniature tea set in Limoges porcelain, or *Hermès* for an equestrian-print umbrella. Nearby, on Place de la Madeleine, visit *Fauchon* for plum mustard or a salmon mousse sprinkled with caviar. If you must have something nobody else could have, tour the galleries and antiques dealers, and stop in at that ultimate purveyor of the unique—*Le Louvre des Antiquaires* on the Place du Palais-Royal.

A Few of Our Favorite Things

Paris's nonpareil hotels and restaurants play a large part in making this city the paragon of cosmopolitan sophistication that it is. What follows are some of our top picks—those places that offer the best supping and sleeping in the City of Light. Follow our lead; we promise you won't be disappointed.

Each place listed below is described in detail in THE CITY chapter.

GRAND HOTELS

The following are our special favorites for a stay in Paris. Each offers its own particular combination of impeccable service, proximity to popular sights, plenty of amenities, and luxurious surroundings. Complete information can be found on pages 96 to 98 in THE CITY.

Bristol
Crillon
George V
Lancaster

Lutétia
Plaza-Athénée
Ritz

HAUTE GASTRONOMIE

Not surprisingly, there are myriad dining possibilities in Paris. The places listed below get our vote for providing a peak dining experience—fine service, a rich atmosphere, and of course, the best of haute cuisine. Complete information about our choices can be found on pages 110 to 116 in THE CITY.

L'Ambroisie
Amphyclès
L'Arpège
Guy Savoy
Joël Robuchon
Lasserre
Lucas-Carton
Michel Rostang
Taillevent
La Tour d'Argent
Vivarois

Romantic Hostelries an Hour or Less from Paris

Who doesn't fantasize about staying in a welcoming country inn or a fairy-tale château with a swan-filled moat and acres of gardens and woodlands? The following hostelries, located just outside Paris, offer precisely such an experience. These properties exist in a certain harmony with their settings; they seem to be an integral part of local life. They also have a special warmth, and their staffs make you feel that you count and that they care.

Excellent cuisine often is a feature, though not always. In many of these fine hotels with restaurants, *demi-pension* (breakfast and one other meal added to the room rate at a fixed price) is required in July and August; be sure to verify whether the rates are *demi-pension* when making a reservation. In general, all the establishments listed below feature telephones, TV sets, and private baths. Air conditioning is rarely a feature: the countryside around Paris is generally quite temperate, and a hotel's charm quotient often seems to be in inverse proportion to the number of air conditioned rooms it has. The following are our favorite Parisian getaways, listed alphabetically by town.

HÔTELLERIE DU BAS-BRÉAU, Barbizon Located in the village that gave its name to a school of 19th-century painters including Théodore Rousseau, Corot, and Millet, this is a perfect place to idle away a fall weekend or at least a Sunday afternoon. Fashionable, well-heeled Parisians have frequented this charming, elegant inn since shortly after Robert Louis Stevenson lived and wrote here. A member of the prestigious Relais & Châteaux group, it boasts 12 rooms, eight suites, and a separate villa, all very romantic, furnished with antiques and fine linen, and with modern bathrooms. There's also an intimate bar and a one-Michelin-star restaurant, warmed by a flickering fire during fall and winter (though some have complained of the chilly service). Still, the atmosphere and food are worth the half-hour drive from Paris, even if you don't plan to spend the night. Try the *langouste rôtie au sel de Guérande* (rock lobster roasted in salt) or, in the fall, game dishes such as *noisettes de chevreuil* (medallions of venison) or *pâté chaud de grouse* (warm pâté of grouse). An outdoor pool and clay tennis court round out the amenities. Closed three weeks in January. Information: *Hôtellerie du Bas-Bréau,* 22 Rue Grande, Barbizon 77630 (phone: 60-66-40-05; fax: 60-69-22-89).

LA FORESTIÈRE, St-Germain-en-Laye In a superb garden setting just 20 minutes from Paris, this Relais & Châteaux member is one of the Ile-de-France's best-kept secrets—an agreeable inn with 24 rooms and six suites as well as a fine restaurant, *Cazaudehore,* which features classic and Basque cuisine. Information: *Forestière/Cazaudehore,* 1 Av. Président-Kennedy, St-Germain-en-Laye 78100 (phone: 39-73-36-60, hotel; 34-51-93-80, restaurant; fax: 39-73-73-88).

L'ESCLIMONT, St-Symphorien-le-Château Set on 150 acres of private woodland and landscaped French gardens near Chartres, this 16th-century fairy-tale castle has 47 rooms, plus six romantic circular suites in the turrets. There are two tennis courts and an outdoor pool, and the gardens alone are worth the visit. The restaurant is pricey, but the food is good, if not always memorable. Parisians arrive here by helicopter for Sunday lunch, touching down neatly on the expansive lawn. A Relais & Châteaux member, it's forty-five minutes from *Orly* airport. Information: *L'Esclimont,* St-Symphorien-le-Château, Auneau 28700 (phone: 37-31-15-15; fax: 37-31-57-91).

TRIANON PALACE, Versailles Attached by private gardens to *Versailles,* this renovated palace is one of France's most historic hotels. The vaulted-ceilinged, marble dining room, resembling a great mirrored ballroom, has played host to the likes of Woodrow Wilson, Marcel Proust, Colette, and Marlene Dietrich. Sarah Bernhardt used to arrive in a horse-drawn carriage, wrapped from head to wooden leg in tulle and feathers. When King Edward VIII abdicated the throne of England for the woman he loved, he and the former Wallis Simpson honeymooned here. The 157 rooms and 42 suites are furnished with antiques, and a covered pool and two terraces face the château's park, home to a flock of docile white sheep. Chef Gérard Vié presides over the kitchens of *Les Trois Marches,* which offers perfect service and highly original two-Michelin-star cooking; his foie gras is famous, as are his oysters and wild goose. The wine selection, with especially fine burgundics, is cxccllcnt, too. The beauty salon and spa, an exclusive Givenchy operation, are stocked with the designer's signature cosmetics and perfumes. There's also a conference center as well as shops, two tennis courts, an indoor pool, and underground parking. Information: *Trianon Palace,* 1 Bd. de la Reine, Versailles 78000 (phone: 30-84-38-00, hotel; 39-50-13-21, restaurant; 800-772-3041; fax: 39-51-57-79).

Shopping Spree

For centuries, France has been producing the world's most fashionable clothing, its most delicious food and wine, and its most bewitching perfumes. And all of these benefit from that same Gallic flair and good taste that characterize just about everything to which the French put their hearts and hands. So it's no wonder that shopping in this country—and especially in its capital—is such a delight.

Below is a list of those special things to be found in Paris that any shopper worth his or her salt would be hard-pressed to pass up. For a list of recommended shops, see *Shopping* in THE CITY. For information on getting a refund on the French Value Added Tax (VAT), see GETTING READY TO GO.

BEST BUYS

ART Galleries are concentrated in St-Germain-des-Prés (6e) on the Rive Gauche; and on the Rive Droite, around the *Centre Georges-Pompidou* (4e) and the Place de la Concorde (8e).

CLOTHING The haute couture designers who made Paris the center of the fashion world still are flourishing in the French capital, and still welcoming those able to afford their distinctive and luxurious made-to-order clothing. However, they often sell less expensive clothing of very high quality in couturier boutiques, usually at the same address. Haute couture can be found in the streets around the Champs-Elysées: Avenue George-V, Avenue Montaigne, Rue François-Ier, and Rue du Faubourg-St-Honoré.

Small boutiques that carry the attractive, innovative clothing the French so nicely call *votre bonheur* ("your happiness") are especially numerous on Avenue Victor-Hugo (16e), Rue de Passy (16e), Boulevard des Capucines (2e and 9e), in the St-Germain-des-Prés area (6e), in the neighborhood of the *Opéra* (9e), around the Place des Victoires (1er and 2e), on or near the Rue des Rosiers in the Marais district (4e), and in the shopping centers *Forum des Halles* (Rue Pierre-Lescot and Rue Rambuteau, 1er), *Passy Plaza* (53 Rue de Passy, 16e), and *Carrousel du Louvre* (99 Rue de Rivoli, 1er).

For those in search of high-fashion bargains, discount stores are gradually catching on in France, and new designs from the top couturiers are available a season (sometimes only a few months) later at many outlets. The Rue d'Alésia has several blocks devoted solely to discount fashion shops.

It's true that many Americans living in France buy lingerie in the US, swearing that American products are not only better made and better fitting but even less expensive and prettier than their French counterparts. But the lacy, frilly, silk undergarments sold in France, often covered with polka dots or dripping with ribbons, are the stuff of which fantasies are made, and lingerie makes a delightful souvenir. Department stores carry a wide selection of brands, styles, and sizes and display their wares clearly, making choices simpler than in small shops, where much of the stock may be tucked in boxes behind the counter.

Although men's clothing is not generally considered a good buy (many a male has succumbed to sticker shock in Paris), for some, the blend of classic styling and French flair is irresistible. And for babies and older children, gorgeous hand-smocked and hand-decorated clothing can still be found in Paris, but at painfully high prices. For all but the most indulgent grandparents, the best idea is to head for department stores, which generally display a wide selection of charming clothing for youngsters, often decorated with very French motifs.

CRYSTAL AND CHINA Paris has crystal and china to make the humblest table gleam like a royal banquet hall, and one of the best ways to get an overview of the nation's best is to stroll the length of the Rue de Paradis. The entire street is lined with stores specializing in what merchants here call "the arts of the table." Near the *Gare de l'Est* and the *Gare du Nord,* the neighborhood is less than chic, but it nevertheless yields some sparkling treasures.

FOOD AND WINE At any given point in Paris, it's possible to put together a sumptuous picnic by making four stops: at a charcuterie, a sort of cross between a butcher shop and a deli; at a *fromagerie* (cheese store); at a *marchand de vin* (wine merchant); and at a *boulangerie* (bakery). Usually, such shops will be within a block or two of one another, sometimes right next door.

JEWELRY Most of the world's greatest jewelers have outlets in Paris and several are clustered around the elegant Place Vendôme, a dazzling place to window shop, if not to pick up an heirloom or two.

KITCHENWARE In a country that ranks cooking among the highest of arts, it is not surprising to find an abundance of kitchen items at nearly every turn. Pots and pans that are almost sculptural in their classic beauty are everywhere, as are odd-looking gadgets that perform tasks most cooks never even imagined. Department stores provide an overview of both the most traditional and the latest utensils in the world of French cookery.

LEATHER GOODS It is a pleasure to shop for leather goods in Paris, especially in the best establishments, where every piece of merchandise from key cases to steamer trunks is impeccably designed and perfectly crafted. Bear in mind, however, that lower-quality leather goods are probably more expensive and not as well made as comparable items in the US. Americans also should be aware that some exotic skins sold legally in France—certain species of alligator, crocodile, ostrich, and lizard—are on the Endangered-Species List in the United States and may be seized on arrival back home. The best Parisian stores will steer American shoppers to merchandise that meets US import laws, but it's still wise to check the latest regulations with the *US Fish and Wildlife Service* before leaving home. (For additional information on *US Customs* regulations, see GETTING READY TO GO.)

PERFUME For centuries, the French have been making enticing scents that are synonymous with luxury and romance, and around the world, in all languages, the adjective that springs most quickly to mind to modify the word "perfume" is "French." Consequently, it's not surprising that perfume heads the shopping lists of visitors to Paris more than any other item. But today, with virtually all names and sizes of French perfume available in US stores, is there any reason beyond the mystique to buy French perfume in France?

The answer is yes. Although the current unfavorable exchange rate makes bargains difficult to find, by shopping in the right places and following the rules for getting tax refunds, it's possible to purchase some of France's most expensive and sought-after perfumes at prices as much as 30% lower than in the US.

Do not be taken in by the flashy Tax Free signs sported by perfume stores all over the country. Most shops, the major department stores included, sell basically the same brands and sizes, at rates set by the manufacturers. Regardless of where you shop, the perfume becomes tax free only after you have purchased enough of it at a single store to qualify for the tax refund set up by the government. The exception is airport duty-free shops, which sell without tax even on small bottles of inexpensive perfumes; the selection is more limited than in Paris stores, however.

SHOES Paris is a city for shoe fiends, and it is full of places to buy footwear that is not only stylish but also comfortable, probably because the French walk a good deal and seem to refuse to wear ugly shoes.

MARKETS AND MOVEABLE FEASTS

Going to market is so much a part of Parisian life and culture that it should probably be on every tourist's itinerary. Aside from the rich feast for the eyes—perfectly piled pyramids of oranges, sunbursts of yellow-white endive, and stands of steaming-hot *choucroute*—Paris markets offer enlightening glimpses of the Gallic manner and mentality. Note the brassy produce vendor boasting, "Deal of the century—four avocados for 10 francs," or the rosy-cheeked cheese man serving up a wink with the Camembert. There'll be a buxom matron, basket in hand and dog in tow, huffing indignantly at a skinny chicken. Paris's markets are not only the most brilliantly stocked and colorful in the world, they are ubiquitous. No matter where in the city you are, you're only a short stroll from one of them.

Paris's first market appeared during the 5th century on the Ile de la Cité; it was followed by small markets at the old gates of the city, many specializing in a single food item. Today, there are 70 open-air and covered food markets in Paris, plus about 10 market streets, and the central market— *Les Halles de Rungis* (13e), successor to *Les Halles,* and now the world's largest wholesale market. Most numerous are the open-air roving markets that set up early in the morning two or three days a week on sidewalks or islands of major boulevards, only to tear down again at 1:30 PM. For example, there's the very enjoyable market set up on Wednesday and Saturday mornings on the Avenue du Président-Wilson (16e) between Place d'Iéna and Place de l'Alma, both of which have *Métro* stops. Butchers, bakers, fishmongers, and cheese and flower sellers abound here, and all types of vegetables and fruits are trucked in from farms outside the city. Other good roving markets appear in the Place Monge (5e) on Wednesdays, Fridays, and Sundays, and on the Boulevard Edgar-Quinet (14e) on Wednesdays and Saturdays. But every neighborhood has one, and everyone has his or her personal favorite.

A few tips to the novice: Take along a string bag or basket, since most merchants don't provide bags. Go in the morning, when the produce is freshest and the scene is the liveliest. The general rule is don't touch the merchandise. Vendors take pride in doing the choosing for you. Most markets and market streets are closed Mondays. Below is a small sampling of some of our favorite markets.

MARCHÉ BATIGNOLLES An open-air market existed here, in the 17th *arrondissement* near Place Clichy, for decades before the area was annexed by the city of Paris in 1860. The old covered market built in 1867 came down a decade ago to make way for the current modern structure. *Batignolles* is noteworthy for its reasonable prices—due, no doubt, to its somewhat out-of-the-way location (a bit west of the *Cimetière Montmartre*)—and for the number of stands here (68 in all, more than any other covered market). There's a fine selection, including a cluttered stand with Italian specialties, one featuring exotic fruit (*Godreau*), an Alsatian stand selling *choucroute* and sausages, and a small stand with prepared Asian foods. More food shops line the streets surrounding the market. There's a good charcuterie, *Le Cheneau* (44 Rue des Moines), and *Le Terroir* (40 Rue des Moines), an inviting wine shop. From here, follow Rue Lemercier to Rue Brochant, turn left at the bakery (which makes a wonderful rye bread *ficelle*), and walk to the Square des Batignolles, one of the 20 small garden parks built by a protégé of Haussmann named Alphand. A perfect picnic site, it comes complete with duck pond, tiny waterfall and bridge, and stone sculptures.

RUE MONTORGUEIL This busy, cobblestone market street not far west of the *Centre Georges-Pompidou,* traversing the 1st and 2nd *arrondissements,* is all that remains of "the belly of Paris," the old *Les Halles* wholesale food market, which was relocated south of the city to Rungis more than 20 years ago. Some of Paris's chefs still do their marketing here. The recent restoration of the area's cobblestones and the creation of a pedestrian zone on and around the Rue Montorgueil have made this one of the city's most picturesque markets. Definitely worth a visit is the spruced-up *Pâtisserie Stohrer* (No. 51), allegedly Paris's oldest pastry shop, founded in 1730. The decor is magnificent, particularly the ethereal murals painted on glass in 1865 by Paul Baudry, whose allegorical paintings also adorn the Paris *Opéra/Palais Garnier.* The pastries and prepared foods—including pâtés and individual quiches—of present owner François Duthu are admirable. There are plenty of fruit and vegetable sellers nearby, and farther on is *Ballotin* (No. 41), a tiny, pristine chocolate shop. You can picnic in the park at the end of the street, where a maze of green trellises and stone animals occupies ground on which the old wholesale market once stood. With the magnificent 16th-century *Eglise St-Eustache* on one side and the futuristic shapes and mirrored surfaces of *Le Forum des Halles* (see *Shopping* in THE CITY) on the other, the park offers one of the most arresting views of old and new Paris.

RUE MOUFFETARD Most popular of all Paris market streets, Mouffetard is criticized by locals for its high prices, dubious quality, and circus atmosphere. But this steep, winding street—about halfway between the *Jardin du Luxembourg* and the *Jardin des Plantes* in the 5th *arrondissement,* and invaded in recent decades by ethnic restaurants and tacky clothing shops—retains an old-time flavor and appeal, as well as some very good purveyors. Best known here is *Fachetti* (No. 134), the Italian charcuterie at the bottom of the street, with its appetizing array of hams, pasta, and prepared foods. Farther up the hill, on a small side street, is the African market, where fascinating exotic fruits and vegetables, dried fish, and other curiosities can be found. Off another side street are two shops specializing in hams and sausages of the Auvergne region. There's also a fancy food shop, *l'Epicerie* (46 Rue Daubenton), selling a good foie gras for considerably less than you'd pay in the shops at La Madeleine. Back on Rue Mouffetard, there's a small charcuterie worth a visit (No. 120), and there's no lack of good bread and cheese along the street. A cheese shop at the top of the street, *l'Assiette aux Fromages* (No. 27), has a small garden café in the back where cheese and other items are served. From Place de la Contrescarpe at the top of Rue Mouffetard, follow Rue Lacépède east to the *Jardin des Plantes* (for details on the garden, see *Walk 1: Gardens, Bridges, and Islands* in DIRECTIONS).

GRENELLE This open-air roving market under the elevated *Métro* in the center of Boulevard de Grenelle (15e), though not necessarily the best for bargains, offers excellent, high-quality items. Before strolling through this market, stop in the *Poilâne* bakery (at the corner of Boulevard de Grenelle and Rue Clodion) to sample their famous sourdough bread. Once in the market, you'll find 141 generously stocked stands, among them a stall with huge rustic baskets of loose farm eggs, and one with tables filled with nothing but mushrooms, wild and cultivated. Another offers eight varieties of oysters. Plenty of fresh fruit and cheese is sold here; there also are a handful of stalls with pâtés and other prepared picnic-worthy fare. The market extends to *La Motte–Picquet Métro* stop, only a three-block walk from the *Parc du Champ-de-Mars* in the shadow of the *Eiffel Tower*. If your menu lacks a sweet or pastry (items frequently not found at the roving markets), stop at *La Petite Marquise* (50 Av. de La Motte–Picquet) for one of its butter-rich cakes. They're expensive, but worth every franc.

RASPAIL Paris's only roving street market exclusively devoted to organic foods is held on Sunday mornings on the Boulevard Raspail (6e), between the Rue du Cherche-Midi and the Rue de Rennes. All the meat, vegetables, and fruits sold here are guaranteed to have been produced without chemical fertilizers and additives. The smell of crêpes and freshly baked breads (whole-grain, of course) wafts throughout the market; don't miss the stand where cheese crêpes are cooked to order. There are also stands offering organically produced wine, honey, jam, jelly, and cheese. On Tuesdays and Fridays, a regular market is held here. The nearby *Jardin du Luxembourg* is a great place to savor your purchases.

Antiques Hunting in Paris

The history of France may best be seen in fortresses and châteaux, but it is best felt by holding a fragment of a sculptured choir stall or an Art Deco soup ladle, by touching the satiny surface of a marquetry wedding chest or by slipping on the signet ring that once belonged to a scheming marquise. Such morsels of the nation's past can be savored at some 100-plus Parisian antiques shops and auction houses or at fairs and markets held throughout the city. The following is an overview of the best places to track down antique treasures in Paris.

SHOPS In every neighborhood of Paris you'll stumble across small, often slightly dusty antiques shops. Some are true *antiquaires,* antiques dealers who handle pieces of established value and pedigree. Others are *brocanteurs,* secondhand dealers, whose stock may run the gamut from Second Empire snuffboxes to broken 78-rpm Edith Piaf records. Many dealers belong to either the *Syndicat National des Antiquaires* (National Antiques Dealers' Association) or the *Syndicat National du Commerce de l'Antiquité et de l'Occasion* (National Association of Antiques and Secondhand Businesses), two highly reputable guilds whose members have pledged to be truthful about all items they are selling.

For an important purchase, the wise buyer will request a certificate of authenticity. With furniture, in particular, the dealer should be precise about just which parts have been restored and how; a number of "antiques" are really superbly carpentered composites of partly salvaged pieces, and there is a thriving industry in the recycling of genuinely ancient wood into pieces of "antique" furniture that were actually born yesterday.

A trend of the past decade has been the clustering of individual shops into *villages d'antiquaires,* which are something like shopping centers for antiques, with dozens of dealers housed under a single roof. The prototype is the giant *Louvre des Antiquaires* (2 Pl. du Palais-Royal, 1er; phone: 42-97-27-00; closed Mondays, and Sundays in the summer), whose 250 different shops are in an old department store. Other *villages d'antiquaires* are *La Cour aux Antiquaires* (54 Rue du Faubourg-St-Honoré, 8e; phone: 42-66-38-60; closed Sundays and Monday mornings); *Village Suisse* (78 Av. Suffren, 15e; phone: 43-06-69-90; closed Tuesdays and Wednesdays); *Village St-Honoré* (91 Rue St-Honoré, 1er; phone: 42-36-57-45; closed Sundays); and *Village St-Paul* (entrance on Rue St-Paul just off the Quai des Célestins, 4e; phone: 48-87-91-02). *Le Carré Rive Gauche* (7e), an association of more than 100 antiques shops, is located in the square of streets formed by Quai Voltaire, Rue de l'Université, Rue des Sts-Pères, and Rue du Bac.

Other good hunting grounds include Boulevard St-Germain, Rue Bonaparte, and Rue Jacob on the Rive Gauche, and Rue du Faubourg-St-Antoine, Rue St-Honoré, Rue du Faubourg-St-Honoré, Avenue Victor-Hugo, Rue La Boëtie, and Rue de Miromesnil on the Rive Droite.

The richness and tradition of the French antiques trade have spawned a high degree of specialization, both by genre and by period. Some shops deal exclusively in dolls, maritime instruments, chimneys and mantelpieces, locks and keys, or postcards. Several antiquarians in Paris stock only items from the 1950s. Passionate collectors with a one-track mind should consult the *Guide Emer* (50 Rue/Quai de l'Hôtel-de-Ville, Paris 75004; phone: 42-77-83-44) for information about where in France to indulge their most rarefied whims.

EXPOSITIONS, FAIRS, AND SALONS Paris's most prestigious antiques salon, the *Biennale Internationale des Antiquaires,* is held in September and early October in even-numbered years in the *Grand Palais.* With its stock of the finest pieces available in Europe and a range of exhibitors that includes all the top dealers from France and abroad, the *Biennale* may set the tone of the market for the following two years.

The *Foire Nationale à la Brocante et aux Jambons* (National Flea Market and Regional Food Products Fair) is a curious event that takes place twice a year, usually in March and September, and mixes antiques, handicrafts, and regional foods from all over France; fairgoers do lots of wine tasting, cheese nibbling, and bric-a-brac browsing. This party is held on Ile de

Chatou, an island in the Seine west of Paris, accessible by the *RER* suburban train. For information contact *SNCAO (Syndicat Nationale du Commerce de l'Antiquité et de l'Occasion;* 18 Rue de Provence, Paris 75009; phone: 46-71-66-14; fax: 48-01-09-81).

In Ivry-sur-Seine, the *Foire Internationale Brocante Antiquité (FIBA)* attracts over 1,000 exhibitors every March, June, and September. The *Foire à la Ferraille et aux Jambons* (literally "iron and ham fair," meaning that both imperishables and edibles are sold) is held every spring and fall in the *Parc Floral* of the *Bois de Vincennes.*

Less impressive, but nonetheless worth a visit if you happen to be in Paris in late November or early December, is the *Salon des Antiquaires,* held in various locations annually. Contact the Paris tourist office (see *Tourist Information* in THE CITY) for more details on these and other antiques-related events.

FLEA MARKETS The best-known and largest of Paris's *marchés aux puces*—literally, "markets with fleas"—is the *Marché aux Puces de St-Ouen* (better known as *Puces de Clignancourt*), located at the Porte de Clignancourt (18e). This incredible collection of some 3,000 stalls is actually a maze of different submarkets, including *Biron, Paul Bert, Vernaison,* and *Serpette,* all sprawled over a vast area and encompassing everything from rather elegant little shops to ramshackle lean-tos and rickety tables or blankets spread on the curbstone. It's easy to get lost here, so stay close to your companions or give each other a precise time and place at which to rendezvous. There are several cafés and even a little restaurant (*Chez Louisette,* in the *Marché Vernaison*) where a Piaf sing-alike croons on Sunday afternoons. The Paris tourist office sells an official guide to this market (*Guide Officiel & Pratique des Puces*), and a map is sold at the market itself. It's open weekends and Mondays from 9 or 10 AM (some stands open as early as 8 AM) to around sundown (in summer, this can be as late as 8 PM).

Lesser known and lower brow are the *Puces de la Porte de Montreuil* (11e), held on weekends and Mondays at the Porte de Montreuil; and *Les Puces de la Porte de Vanves* (14e), held on weekends near the Porte de Vanves on Rue Didot. Both run from early morning to sunset, or later. Both also consist mostly of *brocanteurs,* dealers in secondhand items. *Vanves* sprawls along the sidewalk and around a corner for several blocks; you have to venture well along the street before you begin to see items that are better than junk. But there are some treasures to be found, including a lot of Art Deco items and old French linen; some of the items offered here turn up later in the *Puces de St-Ouen* with higher price tags attached. The *Montreuil* is even more lowbrow than *Vanves,* crowded with peddlers selling everything from an old espresso machine and African beads (in the same stall) to spare automobile parts. Though there are not many great antiques to be found here, the occasional bargain does turn up, especially in used clothing and furniture. Those in the market for a 19th-century armoire will find a good selection here, and many pieces can be dismantled for shipment.

AUCTIONS Once something of a professional club for dealers only, auctions—known in French as *ventes aux enchères*—have become the favorite indoor sport of the *haute bourgeoisie* in the last few years, and in the *salles des ventes* (salerooms) of France, there are fewer bargains around than there used to be. However, those who know their market may still save as much as a third of the retail price; and even for those who don't, auctions are hard to beat for pure theater. The auction situation in France is different than in the US, for all sales take place under the aegis of a government-authorized auctioneer known as the *commissaire-priseur*. Paris's venerable auction house, the *Hôtel des Ventes Drouot-Richelieu*, is basically a cooperative managed by a guild of *commissaires-priseurs*, and it is their reputations for probity and expertise that are on the line, not those of specific salerooms or companies. By law, French auctioneers are responsible for the authenticity of any item they sell for 30 years after the sale.

The *Hôtel Drouot* (9e), on the Rive Droite not far from Boulevard Montmartre, is the center of the auction world in Paris. Some 600,000 lots go through its 16 salerooms every year, and the activity is frantic. If you find yourself in a room full of plumbers' fittings or vintage cognacs when what you really wanted was antiques, just go up to the next floor. It's closed Sundays. For information contact the *Hôtel des Ventes Drouot-Richelieu* (9 Rue Drouot, Paris 75009; phone: 48-00-20-20; fax: 48-00-20-33). Sales also are held at the *Drouot-Montaigne* (15 Av. Montaigne, Paris 75008; phone: 48-00-20-80).

The weekly *Gazette de l'Hôtel Drouot* (10 Rue du Faubourg-Montmartre, Paris 75009; phone: 47-70-93-00), available at newsstands, prints a calendar of auction sales throughout France and a running tally of the results.

A bidding-free variation on the auction theme is the *dépot-vente*, a saleroom where private sellers leave lots on consignment with a dealer who sets the price and takes a commission. These generally are well patronized by bargain-hunting professionals. The largest is the immense *Dépot-Vente de Paris* (81 Rue de Lagny, Paris, 75020; phone: 43-72-13-91).

RULES OF THE ROAD FOR AN ODYSSEY OF THE OLD

Buy for sheer pleasure and not for investment. Forget about the carrot of supposed resale values that French dealers habitually dangle in front of amateur clients. If you love something, it probably will ornament your home until the next Revolution.

Don't be afraid to haggle. This is true even in the most awesomely elegant boutique on the Rue du Faubourg-St-Honoré. Everything is negotiable, and the higher the price, the harder (and farther) it falls.

Buy the finest example you can afford of any item, in as close to mint condition as possible. Chipped or broken "bargains" will haunt you later with their shabbiness.

Train your eye in museums. These probably are the best schools for the acquisitive senses, particularly as you begin to develop special passions. Collections like those of tapestries at Aubusson, of porcelain at Limoges, and of furniture in the *Louvre* will set the standards against which to measure purchases.

Peruse French art and antiques magazines. French newsstands abound in them. The best include *Connaissance des Arts, L'Estampille, Beaux-Arts,* and *L'Oeil. Trouvailles* deals with bric-a-brac and flea markets.

Get advice from a specialist when contemplating a major acquisition. Members of the various national guilds of antiques experts are well distributed throughout the country. For more information, contact the *Chambre Nationale des Experts Spécialistes en Antiquités* (4 Rue Longchamp, Nice 06000; phone: 93-82-21-40) or the *Syndicat Français des Experts Professionnels en Oeuvres d'Art* (81 Rue St-Dominique, Paris 75007; phone: 47-05-50-26).

Casinos Royale

Forbidden by Napoleonic decree within 100 kilometers (about 60 miles) of Paris, there are only two "legitimate" gaming houses within easy reach of the city. These establishments draw a crowd that is a heady mixture of Parisian chic and Arab sheik, while the scenario is pure Hollywood. But behind all the glitter is a system of tight surveillance by the *Brigade des Jeux,* France's gaming police, and a gambling code that regulates everything from the odds on the slot machines to the dinner jacket on the croupier—which has, by law, no pockets. The result is an almost totally aboveboard industry, though internecine squabbles among operators occasionally evoke memories of 1920s Chicago. As in any casino, however, players are fairly certain to lose their money according to the inexorable laws of mathematics.

Passports are required for admission, which is limited to those 18 and older. Though marathon games of chemin de fer are allowed to continue until the players drop, most French casinos open daily in mid-afternoon and close at 3 or 4 AM. Dress has become far more casual in recent years, but there still are many casinos where jacket and tie are de rigueur for gentlemen; in any case, it's always better to err on the side of decorum. A number of the larger casinos have glamorous, first-rate restaurants right on the gaming room floor; their waiters discreetly reheat the food of those kept away from their meal by a winning streak.

The staples of the French casino diet are roulette, baccarat, and *boule;* craps and blackjack increasingly are in evidence, the result of creeping Americanization. If you're not familiar with the rules or the vocabulary, many casinos will provide an explanatory booklet. And still others have roving *chefs de partie* (game chiefs), who will be more than happy to help a player who doesn't mind looking like a greenhorn in the midst of all that savoir faire.

CASINO D'ENGHIEN, Enghien-les-Bains, Val d'Oise Though inside Napoleon's 100-km zone, this lakeside establishment—part of Lucien Barrière's glittering gaming empire—has all the prerequisites of a world class casino. A recent face-lift has restored its Art Deco elegance. Gaming begins daily at 3 PM and continues well into the night. A rather steep entry fee and hefty minimum betting requirements discourage dilettantes; the gambling here is serious and the crowd is relatively chic. The small café in the gaming room offers light meals and afternoon tea. Arrive from Paris by taxi (a 20-minute to one-hour ride north, depending on traffic) and the management will exchange your cab receipt for its equivalent in chips. (The casino also is easily reached from the *Gare du Nord.*) In addition, there are three meeting and conference rooms here (for 35 to 600 guests), and a theater seating 700. A chip's throw away is the *Grand* hotel (85 Rue Général-de-Gaulle; phone: 34-12-80-00) and the *Etablissement Thermal* (Thermal Bath), somewhat dated monuments to the turn-of-the-century elegance of this resort town. Information: *Casino d'Enghien,* 3 Av. de Ceinture, Enghien-les-Bains 95880 (phone: 34-12-90-00; fax: 34-12-41-70).

CASINO DE FORGES, Forges-les-Eaux, Seine-Maritime Just outside Napoleon's roulette-free zone, Forges attracts all the capital's players who don't want to risk the wheels at the city's various *clandés,* as its clandestine gaming dives are called. Those who can't face the predawn drive back to Paris can stay at the *Continental* hotel, right in the casino complex—and those who lose enough in the course of the evening are guests of the management. Information: *Casino de Forges,* Av. des Sources, Forges-les-Eaux 76440 (phone: 35-09-80-12).

Learning the Culinary Arts: Cooking Schools

What better place to perfect your culinary skills than in the capital of gourmet cooking? Visitors to Paris can study with famous chefs such as Gaston Lenôtre, or they can gain hands-on experience at such world-renowned cooking schools as *Le Cordon Bleu* and *L'Ecole de Gastronomie Française Ritz-Escoffier.* A wide variety of cooking courses are offered in the city. There are programs that last weeks or even months, as well as workshops for those who have only an afternoon or two to devote to the pursuit of better cooking skills. Programs tend to be casual and are geared to novices and experts alike. Each course is limited only by one's vision and by one's command of French (knowing the language goes a long way toward making the experience meaningful, even though translators are usually available). The point is to go with an open mind and a willing spirit, ready to acquire a few additional culinary skills and authentic French experiences—and have a good time besides.

ECOLE FERRANDI This *Centre de Formation Technique* is the only Paris cooking school to offer professionally motivated foreigners preparatory courses for a *CAP,* the French government's culinary certification. Though its basic course runs for nine months (five days a week) and is recommended only for the most serious students, shorter programs—including biannual week-long pastry and cuisine courses—also are offered. Owned by the *Chambre de Commerce de Paris* (Paris Chamber of Commerce), the *Ferrandi* school has been endorsed by such famous French chefs as Joël Robuchon and Pierre Troisgros. Information: *CFT Ferrandi,* 11 Rue Jean Ferrandi, Paris 75006 (phone: 49-54-29-03).

LE CORDON BLEU This famous school has been instructing an international group of students in French cooking and pastry making since 1895. During the summer, special four-week courses are offered in cooking and pastry, while 10-week sessions are available throughout the year. Intensive one-week "gourmet" sessions on such subjects as bistro cuisine, bread making, and *cuisine légère* also are offered. All of these programs give credits toward certificates and diplomas. Visitors may reserve a few days ahead for one-day workshops or afternoon demonstrations. Most of the one-day, one-week, and four-week courses, as well as the 10-week pastry and basic cuisine programs, are translated into English. Students are responsible for their own lodging, but the school can help with referrals. Information: *Le Cordon Bleu,* 8 Rue Léon-Delhomme, Paris 75015 (phone: 48-56-06-06; 800-457-2433; 914-741-0606 in New York City; fax: 48-56-03-96).

ECOLE DE GASTRONOMIE FRANÇAISE RITZ-ESCOFFIER Escoffier was to food what Daimler was to automobiles. Today, the *Ritz* hotel, where the legendary chef made his debut in the last century, houses the ultimate cooking school. Courses last one to six weeks and involve 25 hours of instruction weekly. There also is a course in *pâtisserie*—the art of cake, ice cream, chocolate, and candy making—and a 12-week program for professionals. Instruction is in French and English. Information: *Ecole de Gastronomie Française Ritz-Escoffier,* 38 Rue Cambon, Paris 75001 (phone: 42-60-38-30; fax: 40-15-07-65).

ECOLE LENÔTRE Working in groups of up to a dozen under France's best-known and most respected pastry chef, Gaston Lenôtre, professionals and serious amateurs study French pastry, chocolate, bread, ice cream, charcuterie, and catering in the huge, modern, and spotless Lenôtre laboratory in the suburb of Plaisir, about 17 miles (28 km) outside Paris. Courses, which are conducted in French, generally last five days and include breakfast and lunch (though students are responsible for their own lodging and transportation). Reserve at least one month in advance. Information: *Ecole Lenôtre,* 40 Rue Pierre-Curie, Plaisir 78370 (phone: 30-81-46-46; fax: 30-54-73-70).

PRINCESS ERE 2001 The outgoing, enthusiastic Princess Marie-Blanche de Broglie teaches small groups of students in classes that last one, three, five, 10, or 20 days. These include demonstration courses that deal with cooking professionally, the harmony of wines and foods, pastry, the art of entertaining, and French regional cooking. Courses may be arranged in English. Programs run year-round, except August; students are responsible for their own lodging. Reserve at least one month in advance. Information: Marie-Blanche de Broglie, *Princess Ere 2001,* 18 Av. de La Motte-Picquet, Paris 75007 (phone: 45-51-36-34; fax: 43-47-38-68).

Celebrated Cathedrals and Châteaux Within an Hour of Paris

For half a millennium, the Gothic cathedral and the Renaissance château reigned as the most sublime reflections of the French spirit. These structures were the statements of the power, both religious and secular, that was France, and their massive stone structures overshadowed the life of the towns and surrounding countryside.

The Gothic mode took shape during the middle of the 12th century and then spread throughout Western Europe. With its vaults and spires straining heavenward and its pointed arch, which the sculptor Rodin called "a pair of hands in prayer," the cathedral was a celebration of both God and engineering. Searching for ever greater elevation and ever more light, its architects replaced the massive walls of earlier styles with airy windows and raised the vaults higher and higher like stakes in some Olympian poker game. The result was a whole new system of stress and support, characterized most obviously by the famous *arc boutant,* or flying buttress.

The onset of the Hundred Years' War in 1338 put an end to the golden age of Gothic cathedral building. But the end of the conflict in the middle of the 15th century marked the beginning of the château-building years, when new generations of royalty subjected Paris and its surrounding countryside to an orgy of regal real estate development. As decoration replaced defense as a prime architectural motivation, the once stolid and brooding medieval fortress gave way to the fanciful wonder that is the Renaissance château.

Paris's most famous architectural monuments, the *Cathédrale de Notre-Dame* and the *Louvre,* are described in detail in *Special Places* in THE CITY. Here are other noteworthy cathedrals and châteaux within a short drive of Paris. Entries are arranged alphabetically by town.

CHÂTEAU DE FONTAINEBLEAU, Fontainebleau, Seine-et-Marne Set in the midst of a verdant forest 40 miles (65 km) south of Paris, *Fontainebleau* was built, expanded, redecorated, or otherwise touched by all the greats of French royalty. In the early 16th century, François I—with the help of some of Italy's most talented artists—transformed what had been a 12th-century hunting lodge into a Renaissance palace. Henri IV created its lakes and carp-filled pond, Louis XIII was born here, Louis XIV signed the Revocation of the Edict of Nantes here in 1685, and Louis XV was married here. Napoleon lived here for most of his reign. During World War II, after three years of German occupation, the château was used as Allied headquarters. Some people find *Fontainebleau* more beautiful than *Versailles,* though it is far more austere. Don't miss the *Cour des Adieux* (Court of Farewells), also called the *Cour du Cheval Blanc* (Court of the White Horse), named for the site of Napoleon's farewell to his Old Guard on April 20, 1814, and for the equestrian statue of Marcus Aurelius that formerly stood here. The splendid *Salle de Bal* (Ballroom), designed by Philibert Delorme, includes mythological paintings conceived by Primaticcio and painted by Dell'Abate. The medieval château's original chapel was consecrated by Thomas à Becket in 1169; its replacement, the *Chapelle de la Sainte-Trinité* (Chapel of the Holy Trinity), is to the left of the vestibule. Another creation of Delorme, it was the site of the marriage of Louis XV and Marie Leczinska in 1725. Also be sure to visit the *Galerie de François I.* Dating from the 1530s, the long gallery includes the original works of such Italian masters as Rosso and Scibec de Capri. The *Appàrtements Royaux* (Royal Apartments) comprise several rooms, including the *Salon Louis XIII;* the *Appartements de la Reine* (Queen's Apartments), decorated by Marie-Antoinette; and the *Salle de Trône* (Throne Room), which served as the king's bedroom from the reigns of Henri IV to Louis XVI. Also worth exploring are the *Salle du Conseil* (Council Chamber), the *Appartements de l'Empereur* (Apartments of the Emperor, including Napoleon's bedchamber and the room where he abdicated), and the *Appartements des Reines Mères et du Pape* (Apartments of the Queen Mother and of the Pope). Before leaving, visit the *Musée Napoléon* and the extensive and beautiful gardens, particularly the *Jardin de Diane,* created for Catherine de Médicis. Closed during lunch hours and Tuesdays. Admission charge. Information: *Office du Tourisme,* 31 Pl. Napoléon-Bonaparte, Fontainebleau 77300 (phone: 64-22-25-68), or *Château de Fontainebleau,* Fontainebleau, Seine-et-Marne 77300 (phone: 64-22-27-40).

DOMAINE DE VAUX-LE-VICOMTE, Melun, Seine-et-Marne On the evening of August 17, 1661, Louis XIV's superintendent of finance, Nicolas Fouquet, proudly invited his 23-year-old king to see the new castle on whose construction Fouquet had just spent his entire personal fortune. Special serenades composed by the renowned Lully, a new stage production by Molière, a fabulous five-course banquet, and a fireworks display all heralded the occasion. Three weeks later, the jealous Louis XIV had Fouquet clapped into jail for life on trumped-up charges and hired his former superintendent's architect, painter, and landscaper to whip him up a pied-à-terre called

Versailles. Vaux-le-Vicomte, Fouquet's castle, is today the largest private property in France; its magical, stylized gardens alone cover more than 125 acres. It is full of lovely fountains, placid pools, sculptured lawns, and fields of flowers that look like giant illuminated medieval manuscripts. The *Vaux-aux-Chandelles* (Vaux-by-Candlelight) tours show off all of the château's splendors at their most dramatic. The tours take place on the second and last Saturdays of each month. Admission charge. Information: *Service Touristique,* Domaine de Vaux-le-Vicomte, Maincy 77950 (phone: 64-14-41-90).

BASILIQUE DE ST-DENIS, St-Denis, Seine-St-Denis Located north of Paris (off the A1 highway, less than 2 miles/3 km north of Porte de la Chapelle), this is one of the great—albeit one of the least visited—of the city's ecclesiastical monuments.Considered the cradle of French Gothic style, the basilica is noteworthy not only as an architectural milestone, but also for its magnificent tombs. Among those who were buried here are Clovis, the first King of the Franks; Dagobert; Charles Martel; and Pepin the Short. Elaborate Renaissance structures, many of them created by the sculptor Germain Pilon, represent Catherine de Médicis and Henri II, Louis XII and Anne de Bretagne, and most moving of all, Louis XVI and Marie-Antoinette. Most of the tombs now are empty—the royal remains were exhumed during the Revolution and heaped into a nearby communal grave. Regular guided tours of the transept are available for a fee. Visitors may also rent headphones with commentary in any of several languages. Closed Sunday mornings. Information: *Office de Tourisme de St-Denis,* 1 Rue de la République, St-Denis 93200 (phone: 42-43-33-55).

CHÂTEAU DE VERSAILLES, Versailles, Yvelines Many consider Versailles the most magnificent of all the French châteaux, but its beginnings were modest enough: In 1624, Louis XIII had a hunting lodge built on a hill above the small village of Versailles. It became a favorite retreat of the young Louis XIV, who began enlarging it during the 1660s. By 1682, he had created a palace whose splendor would help him earn the title the "Sun King," and the town and château of Versailles became the French court's new home. Besides a nucleus of a thousand nobles, Louis XIV's retinue consisted of some 9,000 men-at-arms and an equal number of servants. At any given moment between 5,000 and 6,000 people were living here, which only begins to suggest the scale of this royal commune.Before crossing the wide avenue that passes in front of the château, notice the king's stables and carriage house, constructed by Jules Hardouin-Mansart. Past the Louis XVIII gates, three successive courtyards—the *Cour de Ministre* (Minister's Courtyard) and the *Cour Royale* (Royal Courtyard), separated by a bronze statue of Louis XIV on horseback, and the internal *Cour de Marbre* (Marble Courtyard)—lead to the visitors' entrance. The main entrance to the right of the *Cour Royale* leads to a vestibule and ticket booth through which some four million visitors pass annually.

Visitors first encounter the chapel, built between 1699 and 1710 by Mansart and dedicated to St. Louis. It's a masterpiece of white stone and multicolored marble, punctuated by great gilded doors and bas-reliefs by such masters as Puget and Vasse. Note the elaborate ceiling paintings dedicated to the Holy Trinity and the magnificent gilded organ loft. Some of the château's most extraordinary rooms, the *Grands Appartements*, are in the first floor wing. Start at the *Salon d'Hercule*, named for François Lemoine's ceiling painting, the *Apotheosis of Hercules*. Next is the *Salon de l'Abondance*, which marks the beginning of the king's state apartments (many recently renovated). Each of the following five rooms was dedicated to a Greek god: the *Salon de Vénus* and the *Salon de Diane*, with their Italianate marble decors; the *Salon de Mars*, with an early Gobelins tapestry depicting the life of the king; the *Salon de Mercure*, where Louis XIV lay in state for eight days after his death; and the *Salon d'Apollon*, the former throne room. The famous *Galerie des Glaces* (Hall of Mirrors), flanked on either side by the *Salon de la Guerre* (Salon of War) and the *Salon de la Paix* (Salon of Peace), is perhaps the most memorable of all of *Versailles*'s rooms. Extending along the west façade of the château, it measures 240 feet long, 33 feet wide, and 40 feet high. Seventeen tall, arched windows facing east are reflected in 17 sparkling mirrors on the opposite wall, each separated by red marble and bronze pilasters. Scrolls and cherubs, ornate candlesticks, crystal chandeliers, and a celebrated ceiling painting by Le Brun add to the pomp and splendor of this hall, once the scene of magnificent balls and the Sun King's venue for holding court with ambassadors from Persia, Siam, and other distant lands. The *Treaty of Versailles* was signed in this gallery on June 28, 1919, putting an official end to World War I.

The *Appartements de la Reine* (Queen's Apartments)—a bedchamber, private suite, antechamber, and guardroom—were created for Marie Thérèse, first wife of Louis XIV. Most outstanding is the sumptuous bedchamber. The elaborate floral motifs amid rococo ornamentation reflect the queen's love of flowers; it is said that royal gardeners replanted the garden outside these windows daily so that the queen would see a new assortment of blossoms each morning. Nineteen royal children were born in this room, including Louis XV and Philippe V of Spain. The king's state and private chambers comprise some 15 rooms arranged in a "U" around the *Cour de Marbre*, on the east façade of the palace. Completed in 1701, these rooms clearly illustrate the evolution of the Louis XIV decorative style. Louis-Philippe converted the palace's south wing into a museum of French history, whose centerpiece is the *Galerie des Batailles* (Hall of Battles) where busts, bronze plaques, and huge paintings present a survey of French history from the 17th to the 19th century (Thackeray once called these among the "worst paintings that eye ever looked on"). The museum also includes 16th- through 19th-century rooms, including many royal apartments that are open to the public. Louis XV commissioned the *Opéra*, a dazzling display of colorfully painted imitation marble and glittering crystal, in honor of the marriage of his grandchildren, in particular that of the dauphin to Marie-Antoinette on May 16, 1770. Built in just 21 months, it was designed by Gabriel with decorative motifs by Pajou. It was stripped during the Revolution, used for *Assemblée* (Assembly) and *Sénat* (Senate) meetings from 1870 to 1875, and restored in the 1950s.

Le Nôtre created the *Versailles* gardens between 1661 and 1668, with assistance for the fountains from Mansart and magnificent sculpture by Le Brun. Spread over 1,800 acres, the gardens represent the pinnacle of French formal landscaping. An in-depth visit, which requires nearly as much time as a tour of the château, can uncover a multitude of delightful surprises. On summer Sundays, the fountains dance to a son-et-lumière presentation.

Apparently not content with the size of the domain encompassed by *Versailles,* Louis XIV also bought the small village of Trianon, located at the edge of his gardens, and had his architects construct a pavilion for casual gatherings and rustic fetes. The resulting *Trianon de Porcelaine* (House of Porcelain), completed in 1670, was covered with blue and white Delft tiles. It proved too small and quaint for the king, however, so to replace it, he commissioned the glamorous marble palace—the *Grand Trianon*—that remains today. Nearby is the *Petit Trianon,* a small masterpiece by Gabriel set in the midst of a botanical garden, commissioned by Louis XV in 1761. After the king's death, his son gave the *Petit Trianon* to Marie-Antoinette, who went there frequently in an effort to escape the hustle and bustle of Versailles. Several other structures are grouped in this area, including *Le Hameau,* a model village and farm emulating Chantilly.

Between May and September, on specified afternoons, the 600 jets of water in the 50-odd fountains and pools in the gardens are all turned on; it's a spectacular sight. *Versailles* is accessible by public transportation from downtown Paris. Closed Mondays; guided tours in English are available from 10 AM to 3:30 PM. The *Grand Trianon* and the *Petit Trianon* are closed Mondays, and from October through April during lunch hours on weekdays. There is an admission charge for the château, but not the gardens. Information: *Office du Tourisme,* two branches at 7 Rue des Réservoirs, Versailles 78000 (phone: 39-50-36-22; fax: 39-50-68-07) or Av. Général-de-Gaulle, Versailles 78000 (phone: 39-53-32-11; fax: 39-53-31-63).

Euro Disneyland: An American in Paris

Just 20 miles (32 km) east of Paris (35 minutes by train; an hour by car)—yet light-years away from some of the magnificent châteaux described above—this French version of the altogether American attraction is worth a detour for some. To aficionados of the Disney properties in the US—*Walt Disney World* and *Disneyland*—this is a place to touch base with all of your favorite characters, and perhaps to wish upon an *étoile* before returning to Paris.

At press time, the park was experiencing serious financial difficulties, and although it was recently saved from ruin by the sale of most of its shares to a single investor, its future remains uncertain. In spite of such controversy, more than 11 million visitors passed through the $4.5 billion European home-away-from-home of Mickey, Minnie, Donald, et al., in its first year alone (though attendance figures still failed to live up to Disney's expectations). Familiar Disney attractions include *Main Street USA, Frontierland, Adventureland, Fantasyland,* and *Discoveryland* (known as *Tomorrowland* in the US parks), although there are some French additions, such as a fire-breathing dragon at Sleeping Beauty's castle and a theater that features videos and live entertainment (it turns into a disco at night). Disney-philes can enjoy such facilities as six theme hotels, a campground, restaurants, shops, an 18-hole golf course, and *Festival Disney,* an entertainment center and the site of the terrific *Buffalo Bill Wild West Show.* The food available in the park is pricey and mediocre; it's a good idea to pack a picnic lunch and take advantage of the picnic areas adjoining the park. The park is open daily. The site can be reached by a 35-minute *RER* (regional express train) ride from Paris; passengers disembark at *Euro Disneyland*'s entrance. A combined *RER-Disneyland* entrance ticket is available in Paris's main *Métro* stations, where you can also purchase a special, reduced-price "Star Nights" admission ticket for adults who enter the park after 5 PM. In addition, a shuttle service provides transportation from the *Charles de Gaulle* and *Orly* airports (the park site is located between the two) to the Disney hotels. The *TGV (train à grande vitesse)* may serve the park from Paris sometime this year.

Note: This *Disney* park and its hotels are much pricier than their US counterparts. All rooms accommodate up to four people, and the log cabins at *Camp Davy Crockett* can sleep six. At *Euro Disneyland,* expect to pay from $150 to as much as $350 per night for a double room. Information: *Euro Disneyland,* Marne-la-Vallée 77777 (phone: 64-74-30-00, general information; 60-30-60-53, hotel reservations, ask for an English-speaking operator if necessary; 407-W-DISNEY in the US; fax: 60-30-60-65).

Great Golf Nearby

Food, wine, castles, and cathedrals are what first come to mind when thinking about France—not golf. But golf has been a tradition in Gaul since 1856, when the first course was laid out in Pau (in the Pyrénées). Since that time, the game has attained enormous popularity here. By the end of 1993, there were 482 courses around the country, and 25 more are expected to be completed by the end of this year. In fact, except for England, France has more courses than any other country in Europe, including Scotland!

The countryside around Paris offers several opportunities for a round of golf. The five courses below, listed alphabetically by town, are open to visitors.

URBAN CÉLY GOLF CLUB, Cély-en-Bière This perfectly manicured and landscaped course (18 holes, 6,500 yards, par 72) has a beautiful clubhouse that resembles a medieval castle. Electric carts are available. Close to Fontainebleau, Barbizon, and Milly-la-Forêt. Information: *Urban Cély Golf Club,* Le Château, Rte. de St-Germain, Cély-en-Bière (phone: 64-38-03-07; fax: 64-38-08-78).

GOLF CLUB DE CHANTILLY, Chantilly Known for its lace, Chantilly is also famous for the *Château de Chantilly,* one of France's royal palaces, and this elegant club, only five minutes from the historic castle. With Old World charm and aristocratic ambience, the two British-designed, 18-hole courses (each 6,820 yards) wind through an impressive forest just 25 miles (41 km) north of Paris. In July and August, non-members may play every day except Thursdays; the rest of the year non-members may play on weekdays except Thursdays. Information: *Golf Club de Chantilly,* Vineuil–St-Firmin, Chantilly 60500 (phone: 44-57-04-43).

GOLF NATIONAL, Guyancourt Owned and operated by the *Fédération Française de Golf,* this huge public golf complex is in St-Quentin-en-Yvelines, 19 miles (30 km) southwest of Paris. The first of its three courses, the 18-hole, 7,400-yard stadium course *Albatros* (designed by Hubert Chesneau and Bob Von Hagge) is host to the *French Open.* Water hazards abound. Information: *Golf National,* 2 Av. du Golf, Guyancourt 78280 (phone: 30-43-36-00).

EURO DISNEYLAND, Marne-la-Vallée This 18-hole competition-level course in Marne-la-Vallée, just 20 miles (32 km) east of Paris, is part of Disney's "megaresort" project (which, when complete, will be nearly one-fifth the size of Paris). The Ron Fream design is laid out around a lush landscape including manmade lakes with stepped tees and characteristic mouse-ear–shaped sand bunkers. Information: *Euro Disneyland,* Marne-la-Vallée 77777 (phone: 64-74-30-00).

GOLF DES YVELINES, La Queue-lès-Yvelines Set in a protected park, here are an 18-hole, par-72 forest course and a nine-hole course, 28 miles (45 km) southwest of Paris. Its clubhouse is in a château. Information: *Golf des Yvelines,* La Queue-lès-Yvelines 78940 (phone: 34-86-48-89).

Game, Set, and Match:
Tennis Around Paris

As in the United States, interest in tennis as a sport for spectators and participants alike has increased enormously in France over the past 20 years. The surface of choice here is red clay, although there are a fair number of all-weather and hard courts in the countryside around Paris. It can be hard to get court time in the city itself; conditions are far less crowded outside the capital. For more information on tennis courts in Paris, see *Tennis* in THE CITY.

_____

TENNIS CLUBS

The many tennis clubs in France—of which the most famous by far is Paris's *Racing Club,* unquestionably one of the greats among the world's athletic clubs—are organized by *département* or league. Most require annual membership, and virtually all are closed to outsiders who aren't personally acquainted with a member. However, some are less exclusive than others, and occasionally it's possible for business associates to provide an entrée. The clubs below are located close to the capital and allow non-members.

TENNIS CLUB DE LONGCHAMP, Boulogne-Billancourt, Hauts-de-Seine This club is in the *Bois de Boulogne* on the western outskirts of Paris, down the road from *Stade Roland-Garros.* Weekly instruction sessions are available in English on the club's 20 courts. The club also can arrange a match with a player at the same level of skill. Call a day in advance to reserve a court or arrange lessons. Information: *Tennis Club de Longchamp,* 19 Bd. Anatole-France, Boulogne-Billancourt 92100 (phone: 46-03-84-49).

TENNIS CLUB VITIS, La Défense-Puteaux, Hauts-de-Seine Lessons are available in English at this club, which has seven outdoor and four indoor courts. Call at least a day in advance to reserve a court or arrange lessons. Information: *Tennis Club Vitis,* 159 Rue de la République, La Défense-Puteaux 92521 (phone: 47-73-04-01).

TENNIS FOREST HILL, Aubervilliers, Seine-St-Denis Six miles (9 km) from Paris, this club offers instruction, in French only, on its eight indoor courts. Closed August. Information: *Tennis Forest Hill,* 111 Av. Victor-Hugo, Aubervilliers 93300 (phone: 47-29-91-91).

TENNIS DE VILLEPINTE, Villepinte, Seine-St-Denis Fourteen miles (22 km) from Paris, this club has two outdoor and five indoor courts. Weekend and extended courses in English are available. Information: *Tennis de Villepinte,* Rue du Manège, Villepinte 93420 (phone: 43-83-23-31).

UNION DE CENTRES DE PLEIN AIR, Bois-le-Roi, Seine-et-Marne With 14 outdoor courts (two covered), the *UCPA* offers a seven-hour weekend instruction program (though it's not always available in English). Call a day in advance to reserve a court or arrange lessons. Information: *UCPA,* Rue de Tournezy, *Bois-le-Roi* 77590 (phone: 64-87-83-00).

TOURNAMENT TENNIS

The *French Open,* formally called the *Championnats Internationaux de France* and locally known as the *Roland Garros* after its home stadium in the 16th *arrondissement,* takes place during the last week in May and the first week in June in Paris. The world's premier red-clay-court tournament and one of the four *Grand Slam* events (the other three are *Wimbledon, the US Open,* and the *Australian Open*), it attracts most of the top international players. Tickets for early-round matches generally are easy to obtain as late as early May at the box office or by mail through the *Fédération Française de Tennis* (Service Reservation, *Stade Roland-Garros,* 2 Av. Gordon-Bennett, BP 33316, Paris 75767; phone: 47-43-48-00); tickets for the semifinals and finals must be reserved up to a year in advance.

Cruising Paris's Waterways

The Seine cuts through the heart of the French capital, dividing the right and left banks and harboring the two islands where the city began. Among our favorite ways to pass a soft summer afternoon or evening is cruising on one of its many glass-domed tourist boats or canal cruisers.

Everyone knows about the *bateaux-mouches* that parade from morning to evening along the Seine between the Pont de l'Alma and the Pont de Sully at the eastern end of Ile St-Louis; they look horribly touristy from afar, but once you're on board you'll gain an entirely new perspective on Paris. Less well known, but perhaps even more charming, are the morning and afternoon cruises along the Canal St-Martin, between the *Jaurès* and *Bastille Métro* stops, and the full-day excursions on the Canal de l'Ourcq, which take in some lovely green areas starting at the Bassin de la Villette near the *Jaurès Métro* stop. For information on these cruises, contact the *Office du Tourisme* (127 Champs-Elysées, Paris 75008; phone: 49-52-53-54).

Daily from mid-April through September 26, the *Batobus*—a small cruise barge, more like a miniature *bateau-mouche*—travels up and down the Seine from near the *Eiffel Tower* to the *Hôtel de Ville,* making several stops which are marked by signs on the quays. Contact *Batobus/Bateaux Parisiens* (Pont d'Iéna, Port de la Bourdonnais, Paris 75007; phone: 44-11-33-44) for details.

Two companies, *Paris Canal* (19-21 Quai de la Loire, Bassin de la Villette, Paris 75019; phone: 42-40-96-97) and *Canauxrama* (13 Quai de la Loire, Bassin de la Villette, Paris 75019; phone: 46-07-13-13), offer three-hour barge trips starting on the Seine and traveling to and through Paris's old canal networks, which once served as supply routes to Paris from the provinces. An interesting commentary is given in both English and French, though *Canauxrama* only offers descriptive brochures in English when there aren't enough English-speaking passengers. *Paris Canal* offers two trips daily on weekdays, the first departing at 9:30 AM from the *Musée d'Orsay* (7e) and the second from the Bassin de la Villette at the *Parc de la Villette* at 2:30 PM; on weekends two additional trips are scheduled, departing from the Bassin de la Villette at 10 AM and the *Musée d'Orsay* at 2:25 PM. *Canauxrama* offers four trips daily (except *Christmas* and *New Year*'s *Day*).

They depart from the Bassin de la Villette at 9:30 AM and 2:45 PM, and from the Port de l'Arsenal at 9:45 AM and 2:30 PM; reservations are recommended. *Paris Canal* also offers a full-day excursion on the Marne; boats leave from the *Musée d'Orsay* every Sunday in July and August at 9:30 AM and return at 5:30 PM; reservations are necessary.

Yachts de Paris (Port de Javel-Hunt, Paris 75015; phone: 44-37-10-20) offers dinner cruises, which, unlike other such operations, serve excellent food, with menus devised by a two-Michelin-star chef, Gérard Besson. Romantic panoramas of Paris accompany your meal. There are two cruises nightly from May through September, one per night the rest of the year. Reservations are necessary, and jacket and tie are recommended.

A Shutterbug's Paris

The historic corners and *places* of Paris, its gardens and regal buildings, the serene Seine—all afford shutterbugs myriad photo opportunities. Even a beginner can achieve remarkable results with a surprisingly basic set of lenses and filters. Equipment is, in fact, only as valuable as the imagination that puts it to use.

LANDSCAPES The Paris architecture is so varied and picturesque that it is often the photographer's primary focus. Be sure to frame your subject appropriately, however.

Although a standard 50mm to 55mm lens may work well in some landscape situations, most will benefit from a 20mm to 28mm wide-angle. *Sacré-Coeur* and the Place de la Concorde offer just two of the panoramas that fit beautifully into a wide-angle format, allowing not only the overview, but the opportunity to include people or other points of interest in the foreground.

PEOPLE As with taking pictures of people anywhere, there are going to be times in Paris when a camera is an intrusion. People are often sensitive to having a camera suddenly pointed at them, and a polite request, while getting you a share of refusals, will also provide a chance to shoot some wonderful portraits that capture the spirit of the city as surely as the scenery does. For candid shots, an excellent lens is a zoom telephoto in the 70mm to 210mm range; it allows you to remain unobtrusive while the telephoto lens draws the subject closer. And for portraits, a telephoto can be used effectively as close as two or three feet.

For authenticity and variety, select a place likely to produce interesting subjects. The courtyard of the *Louvre* and its glass pyramids is an obvious spot for visitors, but if it's local color you're after, visit the Marais, Montmartre, or the Ile St-Louis. Or capture a picture of chic and outrageously clad commuters hopping the *Métro* at rush hour or rushing home with a baguette or a bunch of flowers. Aim for shots that tell what's different about Paris. In portraiture, there are several factors to keep in mind. Morning or afternoon light will add richness to skin tones. To avoid the harsh facial shadows cast by direct sunlight, shoot in the shade or in an area where the light is diffused.

NIGHT If you think that picture possibilities end at sunset, you're presuming that night photography is the exclusive domain of the professional. If you've got a tripod, all you'll need is a cable release to attach to your camera to assure a steady exposure (which is often timed in minutes rather than fractions of a second).

For situations such as evening strolls along the Seine or a moonlight ride on a *bateau-mouche,* a flash usually does the trick, but beware: Flash units are often used improperly. You can't take a picture of *Notre-Dame* from the Ile St-Louis with a flash. It may reach out as far as 30 feet, but that's it. On the other hand, a flash used too close to your subject may result in overexposure, resulting in a "blown out" effect. With most cameras, strobes will work with a maximum shutter speed of 1/125 or 1/250 of a second. If you set the exposure properly and shoot within range, you should come up with pretty sharp results.

CLOSE-UPS Whether of people or of objects, close-ups can add another dimension to your photography. There are a number of shooting options, one of which is to use a 70mm or a 210mm lens at its closest focusable distance. Unless you're working in bright sunlight, a tripod will be worthwhile. If you are very near your subject and there is a good deal of reflective light, it may pay to underexpose a bit in relation to the meter reading.

If you do not have a telephoto lens, you can still shoot close-ups using a set of magnification filters. Filter packs of one-, two-, and three-time magnification are available, converting your lens into a close-up lens. Even better is a special macro lens designed for close-up photography.

A SHORT PHOTOGRAPHIC TOUR

Here are some of Paris's picture-perfect places.

ARC DE TRIOMPHE A daytime shot of this massive structure at the head of the Champs-Elysées at the Place Charles-de-Gaulle can be appealing, but a more memorable picture can be taken at dusk. If you stand on the Champs-Elysées, you can get a side-angle shot of the arch as it glitters against the deepening colors of the sky.

CENTRE GEORGES-POMPIDOU From the brightly colored blue and yellow tubes that wrap around it to the amusing papier-mâché sculptures in the interior garden (we especially like the pair of Parisian-red lips that spout water), every photo taken here is a keeper. In the summertime, you can snap a shot of street entertainers who perform such feats as juggling and fire-eating. A massive renovation project gets under way this year, however, and construction may mar some vantage points.

EIFFEL TOWER Some may feel that this well-known symbol of France has been photographed ad nauseam, and perhaps so. The challenge for the innovative shutterbug is to try looking at the same old thing from a different angle. If you walk down the steps of the *Palais de Chaillot* and frame your picture horizontally, you'll capture the lean, minimalist curves in an almost dizzying perspective. And if your plans call for a climb up the tower (and they should), stop at the second level and have someone take a corny but how-can-you-leave-Paris-without-it picture of you with a section of the black steel erector-set structure and all of Paris in the background.

FAUCHON Mouth-watering displays of meat, poultry, baked goods, spices, and exotic produce from every corner of the world tempt the eye as well as the palate. Everything is artistically arranged to dazzle. Be sure to use a flash when shooting indoors, and try including customers as well as store staff in your photos—shots of shoppers selecting mustards and attendants cutting choice wheels of cheese for Sunday brunch exemplify Paris every bit as much as its splendid monuments.

JARDIN DU LUXEMBOURG This is the perfect place to get a shot of children frolicking in the grass, office workers basking in the noonday sun, and couples embracing, blissfully oblivious to the rest of the world. And nowhere else in the city will you find as many species of animals to photograph—cats, dogs, and birds alike seem to enjoy a daily outing here almost as much as their owners.

CATHÉDRALE DE NOTRE-DAME The spectacular cathedral where Napoleon and Henri IV were crowned is among the most popular photo spots for tourists and locals alike. Unfortunately for current visitors, however, this beautiful symbol of Paris will be obstructed by scaffolding at least through this year, while the cathedral undergoes a major renovation. The stained glass windows are especially beautiful when photographed at sunset, with the last rays casting shadows across the nave of the church. Interior shots generally require a flash, unless the camera's shutter speed is very slow and the lens is open wide.

PÈRE-LACHAISE A jaunt to a cemetery just to capture a few headstones and mausoleums on film may sound a trifle morbid, but one visit to this unique site will change your mind. Cobblestone paths, flowering trees, a weeping willow or two, and cavalries of cats form the backdrop for the thousands of gravesites in this, the final resting place of such luminaries as Chopin, Oscar Wilde, and Sarah Bernhardt, among other famous and infamous folk.

PLACE DE LA CONCORDE This extraordinary square, bordered by eight impressive statues that represent the regions of France, is crowned by its magnum opus, *l'Obélisque de Louqsor* (Obelisk of Luxor). Use a wide-angle lens to best capture the square's formidable grandeur. The corner where Avenue Gabriel meets the Rue de Rivoli affords an incomparable vista. Try to ignore the hundreds of cars whizzing by—or better yet, come back at dusk, when the streetlamps begin to glow and the City of Light puts on its best face.

PLACE DES VOSGES If there were a competition for Most Beautiful Square in the World, Place des Vosges could vie for the title. Lined with picturesque homes (including Victor Hugo's), it is a delightfully serene oasis of beauty. Once the site of the *Hôtel des Tournelles,* the royal palace of Henri IV, the courtyard now houses many upscale shops. If you enter the square from the *Hôtel de Sully,* you will be able to get a good shot of a section of it. Then point your camera upward and zoom in on the lovely architecture: red-brick façades, gables, and windows, some of them stained glass.

SEINE Almost any shot of the Seine makes a lovely photo and, with pictures of the *bâteaux-mouches* chugging along, you can't go wrong. Snap from almost any bridge, anchoring the shot with the slender trees and distinctive buildings that line the river. An especially fine view is from the Ile St-Louis—aim your camera toward *Notre-Dame* and shoot.

Directions

Introduction

Paris is a city for walkers. With 20 distinct *quartiers* and *arrondissements,* each revealing a different aspect of Parisian life, the most often described city on earth still manages to defy the clichés it has engendered. Even for those who think they have seen it all, there will always be an unexpected discovery, whether it is one of the less celebrated of the nearly 150 museums that grace the city, a surprising side street off a major thoroughfare, or perhaps one of the hundreds of unassuming—but wonderful—neighborhood cafés.

The mood of the city changes with the seasons. Paris under the slate gray skies of winter, with bare chestnut trees gracing an elegant boulevard is quite different from Paris in the full bloom of spring, when its numerous parks and well-tended gardens burst into glorious color. (Be aware, however, that this riot of blossoms normally comes far later in the season than the composer of "April in Paris" would have you believe.)

From the circuit of famous monuments that loom like stage sets, to the continual joie de vivre of the city's fluid street life, to the unassuming little cafés on the Rive Gauche, there are constant reminders that beauty is paramount here. Paris is the spectacle of the Place Charles-de-Gaulle, with its 12 lanes of traffic defying each other in a daily test of wits and will. It is children sailing their miniature boats in the *Jardin du Luxembourg.* And it is a busy afternoon in the *Tuileries,* where, if you squint your eyes, you can almost see an Impressionist painting by Renoir. Even the city's cemeteries, where homage is regularly paid to painters, poets, musicians (including an American rock star), and philosophers, have an evocative eloquence.

Paris is arranged in a kind of spiral, which was part of the brilliant master plan of Baron Haussmann, the visionary architect/city planner appointed by Napoleon III in 1853 to transform the layout of the city. The result, a uniform classical elegance surrounded by graceful parks and promenades, has gained it the almost uncontested title as the most beautiful city in the world.

To assist you in your explorations of this grande dame of European capitals, here are seven walks that encompass some of the most interesting and accessible *arrondissements,* each offering a different perspective on the city. The first meanders through the botanical gardens and along the quays of the Seine, before exploring the city islands, Ile de la Cité and Ile St-Louis, and *Notre-Dame.* The next walk takes in Place Pigalle, with its long-standing reputation as Paris's "sin street," as well as other vestiges of the lively, bohemian history of the 18th *arrondissement,* crowned by *Sacré-Coeur* at the summit of Montmartre. Our third walk includes the Rive Gauche's most dazzling monuments, including the *Eiffel Tower,* the

Hôtel des Invalides, and the surrounding areas, before ending in the equally grand neighborhood of the *Palais de Chaillot* on the Rive Droite. Some of the Rive Droite's more famous sights are covered next, with a walk that encompasses Baron Haussmann's magnificent, 19th-century design for a Paris that deserved its reputation as Europe's cultural capital. Our fifth walk provides a closer look at the grandeur of the *Louvre* and the *Tuileries,* then moves on to the contrast of the quaint, narrow streets and atmospheric cafés of St-Germain-des-Prés and the Quartier Latin, ending up in the Rive Gauche's answer to the *Tuileries,* the beautiful *Jardin du Luxembourg.* Our next walk begins at the thoroughly modern *Centre Georges-Pompidou,* then returns to an earlier era with a stroll through the former market district of *Les Halles* and a visit to the historic *Hôtel de Ville.* Finally, we visit the 4th *arrondissement,* site of the Marais district, where you'll find the lively Jewish quarter of the city as well as the subdued elegance of the Place des Vosges.

Though some of the terrain will no doubt be familiar to repeat visitors, the point of these walks is to serve as a framework for your explorations. Using our tours as your guide, you can find other special spots, little-known shops, and as-yet-undiscovered eateries. In short, you can make Paris your own.

Walk 1: Gardens, Bridges, and Islands

At the turn of the century, the most pleasant way to arrive at the *Jardin des Plantes* (Botanical Gardens) was by steamboat, gliding up the Seine past the *Louvre* and *Notre-Dame;* these days one must settle for a local bus or the *Métro* to the *Gare d'Austerlitz.* The magnificent 46-acre gardens are in the 5th *arrondissement* on Paris's Rive Gauche, and they border the Quartier Latin and the Seine. Originally founded by Louis XIII in 1626 as a royal garden of medicinal herbs, they met with such hostility from the medical community that for years the land lay fallow. Later, the gardens were revived and enlarged to include—in addition to medicinal herbs—live animals, minerals, research laboratories, and a library. During the 19th century, the complex grew to include a museum of natural history; today, the vast range of academic facilities here enjoys a worldwide reputation for teaching and research.

The gardens boast a varied collection of plants and trees from all over the world. There is an alpine garden, an ecological park, and a tropical plant complex, as well as examples of French and English garden landscape design. Some of the oldest trees in Paris can be found here, including a 200-year-old American sequoia, a ginkgo from China, an iron tree from Persia, and a cedar of Lebanon, 40 feet in circumference, that was supposedly brought from Syria as a seedling in 1735. After wandering up the main promenade and the winding paths, cross over to the Quai St-Bernard. Along the river are the *Jardin Tino Rossi* (Tino Rossi Gardens), with an open-air sculpture museum boasting several impressive works, including Zadkine's *Development of Form.* Parisians come here to stroll and to walk their dogs; students from the university (across the boulevard) come to relax between lectures. From here one can also enjoy a spectacular view of the Ile St-Louis, one of two important islands in the middle of Paris. Take a seat on a bench for a moment and watch the barges floating by and the light shifting over the bridges.

Continue along the path bordering the quay and walk toward *Notre-Dame.* The tall, modern glass-and-aluminum building on the left is the *Institut du Monde Arabe* (Institute of the Arab World), which houses a museum, a library, a cultural center, and a rooftop café offering excellent cappuccino and splendid city views. The institute was created by France and 20 Arab countries as a means of encouraging French-Arab cooperation and a better understanding of Arab culture. The building itself is a good example of Paris's modern architecture. Designed by Jean Nouvel, it has a spectacular façade of 240 light-sensitive geometric panels that auto-

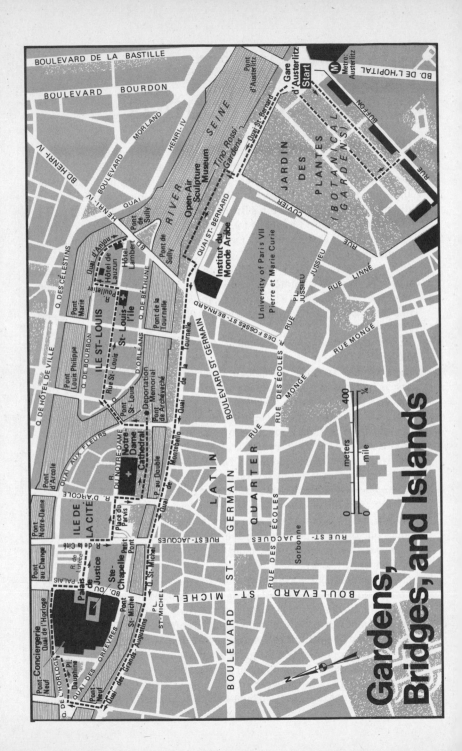

Gardens, Bridges, and Islands

BOULEVARD DE LA BASTILLE

BOULEVARD BOURDON

BD. DE L'HOPITAL

Metro: Austerlitz

Gare d'Austerlitz **Start**

RIVER SEINE

BOULEVARD HENRI-IV

Pont d'Austerlitz

Quai St-Bernard

Quai St-Bernard

Tino Rossi Gardens

BUFFON

JARDIN DES PLANTES (BOTANICAL GARDENS)

MORLAND

BD. HENRI-IV

QUAI

Q. DES CÉLESTINS

Pont de Sully

Open-Air Sculpture Museum

CUVIER

Quai d'Anjou

Pont Marie

Hôtel de Lauzun

Pont de Sully

RUE LINNÉ

Hôtel Lambert

Quai St-Bernard

Institut du Monde Arabe

University of Paris VII Pierre et Marie Curie

PL. JUSSIEU

JUSSIEU

RUE

Q. DE HÔTEL DE VILLE

Pont Louis Philippe

Q. DE BOURBON

Poulletier

Rue St-Louis

ÎLE ST-LOUIS

St-Louis l'Île

Q. DE BÉTHUNE

Q. D'ORLÉANS

Q. de la Tournelle

Quai de la Tournelle

R. DES FOSSÉS ST-BERNARD

RUE MONGE

Pont St-Louis

Déportation Memorial

Pont de l'Archevêché

BOULEVARD ST-GERMAIN

RUE DES ÉCOLES

RUE MONGE

Pont d'Arcole

QUAI AUX FLEURS

R. D'ARCOLE

Notre-Dame Cathedral

RUE DU NOTRE-DAME

Quai au Double

Quai de Montebello

LATIN QUARTER

RUE

RUE DES ÉCOLES

Pont Notre-Dame

ÎLE DE LA CITÉ

Place du Parvis

Pont au Double

RUE ST-JACQUES

RUE DES ÉCOLES

Pont au Change

Conciergerie

Quai de l'Horloge

Quai de la Cité

Palais de Justice

Ste-Chapelle

Pont St-Michel

BD. ST-MICHEL

Sorbonne

RUE ST-

Pont Neuf

Pont-Neuf

PL. DE L'HORLOGE

Quai des Orfèvres

PL. Dauphine

Pont Neuf

Quai des Grands-Augustins

U. St-Michel

PL. ST-MICHEL

BOULEVARD ST-MICHEL

BOULEVARD ST-GERMAIN

meters 0 400

mile 0 ¼

N

matically filter the sunlight. Across the street along Quai de la Tournelle, at No. 15, is *La Tour d'Argent;* after *Maxim's* it is Paris's best-known restaurant (for details see *Eating Out* in THE CITY).

Continue along the riverside quays, whose names change at practically every intersection (for example, Quai de Montebello becomes Quai St-Michel, then Quai des Grands-Augustins, and so on). In all, there are more than 40 quays that run for several miles alongside the Seine. Many date from the Middle Ages, when boats were the quickest, safest, and most efficient way to bring goods into the city. The quays were divided into separate docking areas for wine, coal, grain, and other items. Nowadays, some 30 bridges cross the Seine, while numerous *Métro* tunnels go under the river.

While walking along the Seine, with *Notre-Dame* on the right, browse among some of the green, box-like bookstalls that line both sides of the river. These *bouquinistes* (booksellers) are a Paris institution. It's still possible to find bargains among the volumes, and many dealers also purvey cheap postcards, some of them vintage versions in pastel tints. The stalls have no fixed hours, so you may find shops that seem closed or look deserted; probably the owner has just walked next door to have a coffee with a colleague.

Walk farther along the Rive Gauche to the hubbub of the Place St-Michel intersection, with its raucous mix of milling students from the nearby *Sorbonne,* bustling bookstores, sidewalk cafés, and Middle Eastern snack bars that typify Paris's Quartier Latin. A stop into 5 Place St-Michel, a branch of a *Gibert Jeune* bookshop, may yield, among other things, some interesting cookbooks. Continue along the Seine on the Quai des Grands-Augustins, then turn right onto the next bridge, the Pont-Neuf, said to be the oldest span in Paris. Dating from 1578, its construction began during the reign of Henri III and was completed by Henri IV. Before the Revolution, the Pont-Neuf was the greatest thoroughfare in Paris, attracting beggars, vaudeville acts, medicine shows, and other assorted entertainments. Here it was possible to do almost anything—from having a tooth extracted to getting a poodle trimmed. And if you were looking for someone, native or foreign, you would eventually run across him or her here.

The Pont-Neuf intersects the Ile de la Cité at its western tip. This island in the middle of Paris is a major historic site, with the *Palais de Justice* (law courts), *Sainte-Chapelle,* the *Conciergerie* (a former prison, today the police headquarters), and the magnificent *Cathédrale de Notre-Dame de Paris* all located here. Turn right off Pont-Neuf and stroll through the Place Dauphine. Dating from 1607, this charming square was named after Louis XIII when he was the dauphin. It was one of Henri IV's three urbanization projects; there is a splendid statue of this very popular king on the Pont-Neuf, overlooking the Seine. The original statue was erected by his widow, Marie de Médicis, but was melted down during the Revolution and converted into cannon. By way of retaliation, Louis XVIII ordered a statue of Napoleon and one of General Desaix to be melted down in order to provide material for the new statue of the king. But the sculptor commissioned by Louis XVIII, an ardent Bonapartist, had the last laugh: He stashed a small statuette of Napoleon and various documents honoring the emperor inside his finished sculpture.

Make a note to have a meal at *Paul* (15 Pl. Dauphine; phone: 43-54-21-48), an unassuming restaurant on the square with family-style seating and friendly service. Try the roast duck with cherries and roasted apples. Just across the way is *Fanny Tea* (20 Pl. Dauphine; phone: 43-25-83-67), as intimate and cozy as your grandmother's parlor, but with definite Gallic touches. It is the perfect place to have a pot of tea and one (or several) of the delicious warm apple tarts. Also on the Place Dauphine is *Henri IV* (25 Pl. Dauphine; phone: 43-54-44-53), one of Paris's most popular inexpensive, no-frills hotels, beloved of students and eternal bohemians. To give you some idea of how many students and/or eternal bohemians there are in the world today, it is necessary to book a room here at least three months in advance.

Head east from the Place Dauphine along Quai de l'Horloge and walk around the *Conciergerie,* the former prison (now police headquarters) that housed Marie-Antoinette and many others before they were taken to the guillotine.

The entrance to the *Palais de Justice* is around the corner, on the Boulevard du Palais. Now home to the law courts, it was originally the seat of the Roman military government, then the headquarters of the early French kings. Inside one of its courtyards, to the left after entering, is one of the jewels of Paris, the 13th-century *Sainte-Chapelle* of King Louis IX (St. Louis). The chapel, built to house the Sacred Crown of Thorns and other holy relics (many of which now are in *Notre-Dame*), has 15 splendid stained glass windows—with practically no walls in between—and a rose window, all under a 247-foot spire. *Sainte-Chapelle* is especially impressive in sunny weather. (For additional details on the *Conciergerie,* the *Palais de Justice,* and *Sainte-Chapelle,* see *Special Places* in THE CITY.)

Walk east along Rue de Lutèce, a pleasant pedestrian mall, whose benches afford a welcome respite for foot-sore explorers; a plant market is held here daily except Sundays, when a bird market takes its place. Turn right on the Rue de la Cité to reach *Notre-Dame,* the magnificent cathedral (begun in 1163) that has become, to the world's imagination, the quintessence of Gothic architecture. Its steeple rises 285 feet above the ground, and the entire structure is supported by a series of flying buttresses that were, at the time of their construction, considered an architectural marvel. Note the exquisite stained glass windows, the 37 chapels, the archaeological crypt, and the organ, which dates from 1730. It was here that Napoleon was crowned, and where Victor Hugo's famous hunchback lived.

The views from the church's tower, reached by climbing 397 steps, are still the finest in the city; a popular tourist spot, they rarely offer any solitude. Its great 16-ton bell is one of the largest in existence—though not quite as large as the one at *Sacré-Coeur*. After viewing the church, walk through the park on the riverfront to the easternmost tip of the island. Cross the street to the Square de l'Ile de France and the *Mémorial de la Déportation*. The entrance to this unusual installation is below street level and easy to miss because of the dozens of *Notre-Dame* tour buses parked outside. Worth seeking out, the memorial is a moving tribute to the 200,000 French citizens who were exterminated in concentration camps during World War II. Sometimes a survivor of one of the camps unofficially acts as a volunteer guide, giving a short tour in several languages. Though he does not demand a fee, it is customary to give him a few francs. (For additional details on *Notre-Dame*, see *Special Places* in THE CITY; for more on the *Mémorial de la Déportation*, see *Museums* in THE CITY.)

Retrace your steps toward *Notre-Dame* and cross Pont St-Louis to the neighboring Ile St-Louis. Until the beginning of Louis XIII's reign, this island was still uninhabited pastureland and was composed of two islets: a small one called Ile aux Vaches (Isle of Cows) and a larger one, known as Ile de Notre-Dame. In an ambitious engineering project—begun in 1614 and completed in 1664—the isles were joined, equipped with streets, and surrounded with stone quays. Described by Anatole France almost a century ago as "a pleasantly quiet and elegant backwater of Paris life," these days it is considered a desirable (albeit exclusive) place to dwell, accessible to the heart of the city, yet apart from it. Still quaint and serene, it is a fine place to ramble. In addition to its classic 17th-century architecture, it offers several refreshing views of Paris. For a special treat, indulge in an ice cream at *Berthillon* (see *Shopping* in THE CITY), worthy of its reputation as the best in the city, if not the world. During the summer, there always is a line stretching around the corner. Since it is closed during August, as well as on Mondays, Tuesdays, and school holidays, a more dependable place to get your Berthillon fix might be *Le Flore en l'Ile*, a tea house/café at the foot of the Pont St-Louis (42 Quai d'Orléans). Enjoy the cozy ambience inside, or buy a cone from the outdoor vendor and enjoy it while taking a leisurely stroll around the island.

Ile St-Louis is small enough to walk in its entirety from quay to quay, and offers a relaxing place to sit by the riverside, write a postcard alongside a fisherman hauling in his catch, or sip a coffee with businesspeople reading *Le Figaro* during their lunch hour. Rue St-Louis-en-l'Ile is the main street, which runs down the middle of the island and is the site of several small hotels, restaurants, and quaint shops. Seasoned travelers will enjoy the *Ulysse* bookstore (No. 26), which specializes in travel books, with an extensive inventory of both new and used volumes. Owner Catherine Domain speaks English and is very helpful in providing information. At No. 21 is the *Eglise St-Louis-en-l'Ile,* built between 1664 and 1726, and distinguished by its unusual iron clock. The church's ornate interior is in the 17th-century Grand Siècle style, adorned with wood, gilt, and marble (it's closed

Sunday afternoons and Mondays). The great political caricaturist Honoré Daumier lived at No. 9 for a time. Turn left at Rue Poulletier, then right onto the Quai d'Anjou, on the north side of the island. Along the quay are several old mansions of note: No. 17, for example, is the *Hôtel de Lauzun*, built in 1657. Its typically austere 17th-century façade belies the excessiveness of its interior, with its cut-velvet walls, golden nymphs, and elaborate ceilings. Its original owner was an army caterer, but during the 1800s many poets and writers lived here, among them Baudelaire, Rilke, and Théophile Gautier. More recently it has been used by the city of Paris for official receptions, but is currently closed to the public for an extensive restoration project (phone: 43-54-27-14). No. 7 is still the site of the *Syndicat des Maîtres Boulangers de Paris* (Paris Pastry and Bakery Syndicate), founded in 1801 and headquartered here since 1843.

The walk concludes outside the *Hôtel Lambert* (2 Rue St-Louis-en-l'Ile), near the Pont de Sully. It was built in 1640 by Le Vau, principal architect to Louis XIV, who also did the early work on the *Eglise St-Louis* and many of the other buildings on the island. No expense was spared in creating this magnificent home for Nicholas Lambert de Thorigny, who was known as Lambert the Rich. In 1742, Voltaire completed his *Henriade* while visiting here; during the next couple of centuries it served as a girls' school, and later a depot for military stores, before returning again to private ownership.

Walk 2: Montmartre

Until it officially became part of the city of Paris at the turn of the century, Montmartre, in the 18th *arrondissement,* was a secluded, picturesque village. Set on the tree-lined Butte Montmartre, the highest of Paris's seven hills, it had no more than 1,000 inhabitants living amidst a charming landscape of windmills, vineyards, and pleasant country houses. Construction of the *Basilique du Sacré-Coeur*—which began in 1875—heralded a brighter future after the devastating defeat in the Franco-Prussian War of 1870–71, and gave the remote village new prominence. Ironically, the church wasn't completed until 1914, on the verge of the fresh destruction of World War I, and had to wait to be consecrated until 1919, following the war.

Located on the site of the ancient abbey of Montmartre, the enormous, grandiose basilica is visible for many miles around Paris. While some marvel at its beauty, there are many who think its Roman-Byzantine–influenced design is definitely mediocre from an architectural point of view; some critics have gone so far as to describe it as a giant salt or pepper shaker.

Sacré-Coeur was built at a cost of about 36 million francs—pretty expensive considering the 6-million-franc price tag for the *Eiffel Tower.* Monies were raised mostly by subscriptions and government subsidies. The foundations alone cost 3½ million francs, since the 83 masonry columns that support the structure had to be sunk over 100 feet into the soft soil of the butte to bear their weight. The foundations are so strong that it has been said that even if the hill were taken away, the church would remain intact. The 19-ton *Sacré-Coeur* bells, purported to be the heaviest in the world, can be heard at least 20 miles away.

During the 19th century, Parisians came to Montmartre to wander at leisure through the steep footpaths along the butte. These days, crowds of tourists from all over the world make that same trek, trying to recapture a glimpse of "Gay Paree." For those who can't manage the climb, there is a sleek funicular railway at the bottom of the hill on Rue Foyatier. There's also a tourist train, the *Petit Train de Montmartre* (phone: 42-62-21-21), that starts at Place Pigalle and weaves up through the surrounding streets, passing points of interest along the way; there are also stops at Place Blanche, Place Pigalle, and *Sacré-Coeur.*

Some historians believe that the name Montmartre is derived from "Mon Mars," the name of the temple dedicated to the god of war. Other scholars argue that the area was named for another temple dedicated to Mercury. Still others contend that Montmartre comes from *"mons martyrium,"* because (legend has it) St. Denis and his companions were martyred on the site of what is today an old convent at No. 9 Rue Yvonne-Le-Tac. (The legend goes on to say that St. Denis, decapitated, carried his head to a spot about 4 miles north where he was buried and where the *Basilique de St-Denis* now

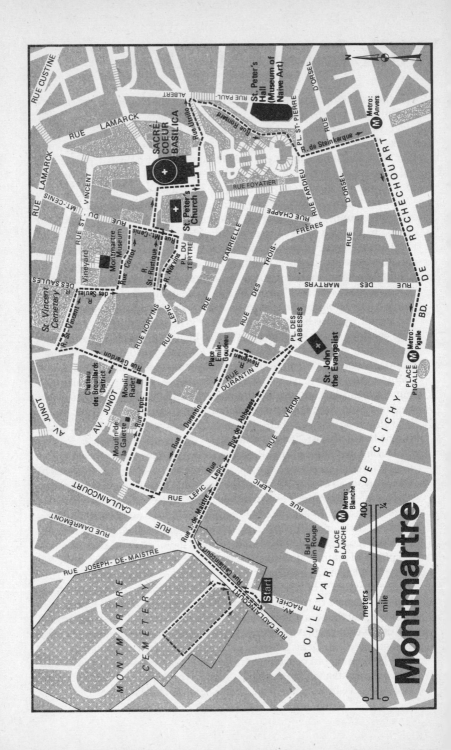

Montmartre

stands.) The battle over Montmartre's name is somewhat fitting, as this naturally fortified area is no stranger to conflict. For centuries it served as a refuge for armies fighting off invaders bent on capturing Paris.

From the mid-1800s into the early part of this century, Montmartre was home to many aspiring artists; they chose the area partly because of its good light and, more importantly, its inexpensive lodgings. Braque, van Gogh, Renoir, Toulouse-Lautrec, and Utrillo all made their homes here at one time; in fact, many of their paintings of street scenes were inspired by this neighborhood. Following World War II, the erection of many taller, modern buildings caused Montmartre to lose its sleepy village quality.

The area was once known for its charming windmills, but, sadly, only two or three remain. Despite its name and design, Montmartre's famous nightclub *Le Moulin Rouge* (The Red Windmill), immortalized in many a canvas by Toulouse-Lautrec, was never actually the real thing. But according to local lore, one of the surviving authentic windmills should be credited with making Montmartre the center of nightlife in Paris. In 1833 (the story goes), the *Moulin de la Galette* was the place villagers came to get fresh cow's milk and tasty rolls. Père Debray, the proprietor, was also fond of dancing and began selling dance lessons to his customers in addition to bread and milk. Supposedly, this is how the dance hall called the *Moulin de la Galette* came into being. Over the next 20 years it became quite the nightspot, doubling in size, and (so it's said) its popularity inspired the opening of other dance halls and clubs in the neighborhood.

This walk begins in the southwest corner of the *arrondissement* at the *Cimetière Montmartre* (Montmartre Cemetery), which dates from the 17th century, when it served as a parish graveyard. Although smaller than the *Père Lachaise* and *Montparnasse* cemeteries, it is the final resting place of many illustrious people, and is equally rich in monuments and statuary. Among those who were buried here are Emile Zola (whose remains were later transferred to the *Panthéon* in 1908), Edgar Degas, Vaslav Nijinsky, François Truffaut, Heinrich Heine, and Hector Berlioz. (The composer is buried between his first and second wives. He arranged this by having one wife exhumed from a prior burial place and taken to Montmartre to wait for him.)

The cemetery grounds are entered by descending the steps from Rue Caulaincourt and passing under a busy, low-hanging overpass. Until 1888, the cemetery blocked direct access into Paris, necessitating the construction of a bridge that would link the Boulevard de Clichy with Rue Caulaincourt. Unfortunately, the span was built directly over some of the older monuments, nearly grazing their tops.

Up a few steps at the Carrefour du Croix, a tall column marks the burial spot of the victims of the coup d'état of 1851. There are several tombs of interest: The red granite tomb of Zola has a bust by Solari; nearby, the tomb of Castagnary features a fine bust by Rodin. Turn around and walk under the bridge and up the stairs; turn left to find the grave of Dalida, the popular French singer of the 1960s, who shocked her fans by taking poison. Fresh bouquets are still left here year-round. On the right, just before reaching the singer's grave, there is an unusual statue. The property of Dr. Guy Pitchal, Dalida's psychiatrist, it is a headless bust holding a pipe, with a life-like death mask behind it whose eyes appear to follow you as you pass by.

Walk out the main entrance again, up the steps to the right and cross the bridge. Look for the *Terrasse* hotel (12 Rue Joseph-de-Maistre) and turn right on Rue Joseph-de-Maistre. Walk down this street toward the busy Rue Lepic, a good venue for observing typical Parisian life. Continue along Rue Joseph-de-Maistre to Rue des Abbesses and the Place des Abbesses. On the right is the *Eglise St-Jean-l'Evangéliste* (Church of St. John the Evangelist), a distinctive brick structure built in 1904. It is the first church in Paris to be built with reinforced concrete, a forerunner of the modern style of architecture represented in many of the city's newer buildings. En route, take a break at one of the pâtisserie/tearooms, or buy a slice of quiche to eat along the way. From the Place des Abbesses, walk up the steep Rue Ravignan, an ancient street that was once part of the only road that led from Paris to the abbey above. A few steps from here is the Place Emile-Goudeau, site of the *Bateau-Lavoir,* the famous artists' colony where Picasso, Braque, and other modern artists painted in adjoining studios. These simple, wooden dwellings later earned the moniker "the Villa Médici of Modern Art." After Picasso and his group moved on, the equally impressive *Ruche* (beehive) took root, with such fledgling artists as Léger, Modigliani, and Soutine seeking inexpensive studios in which to live and work. Unfortunately, these famous shanties burned down in 1970, but many were rebuilt (at No. 13) as artists' studios and apartments. Even for those not artistically inclined, this is a good place to pause and watch the Parisian street scene. When leaving the square, turn right at Rue Garreau (which becomes Rue Durantin); after a few blocks turn right again into the upper end of Rue Lepic. To the left, at the top of a small incline, is a view of the *Moulin de la Galette,* which has topped the butte for more than six centuries (it is no longer accessible to the public). Walk to the corner of Rue Girardon where stands the *Moulin Radet,* another of the area's surviving windmills, now an Italian restaurant. Turn left, following Rue Girardon. You can take an enjoyable detour through the neighborhood around the *Château des Brouillards,* an interesting example of 18th-century architecture, to the left off Rue Girardon; this area was home to many French celebrities. Continue along Rue Giraudon; at the bottom of a descending stairway turn right on Rue St-Vincent, where, enclosed by high walls, is the cemetery of the same name. Ahead, at the crossing of Rue des Saules and Rue St-Vincent is *Au Lapin Agile* (22 Rue des Saules; phone: 46-06-85-87). Formerly an inn where crowds assembled at the turn of the century to hear local poets read from their work, and later frequented by Picasso and other painters of the time, it remains a popular cabaret attracting an international crowd who love a good French sing-along. Originally called the *Cabaret des Assassins,* it takes its present name from the artist A. Gill, who painted a rabbit on a signboard advertising *"poèmes et chansons"* (poems and songs).

Across the street is a modest vineyard, owned by the community and still in use today. It is here that a festive grape harvest takes place on the first Saturday in October. About 500 bottles of a red wine (Clos Montmartre) that makes no pretense of being exceptional are produced here. The wine is sold to the public on weekdays at the *Mairie du 18e Arrondissement* (Montmartre Town Hall; 1 Pl. Jules-Joffrin; phone: 42-52-42-00); it's also sold at private fundraising auctions throughout the year.

Turn south on Rue des Saules to Rue Cortot and turn left to find the *Musée de Montmartre* (12 Rue Cortot; phone: 46-06-61-11). This simple, rustic-looking building, dating from the 17th century, houses a rich collection of paintings, drawings, and documents depicting life in the quarter. The museum is closed Mondays. At No. 6 is the house where the composer Erik Satie lived. At the eastern end of Rue Cortot, look to the left down the descending walkway for a magnificent view of the northern suburbs of Paris. Turn right and go to Place du Tertre, which unfortunately has become a tourist trap; the many souvenir stalls make it all but impossible to really appreciate the charming 18th-century houses surrounding the square. While art is a tradition in this area, the plethora of portrait artists who now hawk their wares here have become a matter of controversy, as the government is now deciding whether to regulate the number of licenses issued to them. And speaking of tourist traps, be sure to check the prices at the local cafés carefully; many of them shamelessly take advantage of visitors.

From the Place du Tertre, wander past the shops along Rue Norvins; turn right at Rue Lepic and immediately right again onto the narrow and often deserted Rue St-Rustique, a good place for a leisurely stroll before encountering the crowds at *Sacré-Coeur*.

At the end of the street, note the *Eglise St-Pierre* (St. Peter's Church). One of the oldest churches in Paris, it was begun by Louis VI in 1134, and completed during that century. It has been added to, rebuilt, and revived so many times since then that there is a real contrast in architectural styles— though a few sections of its original Gothic roots remain. It is interesting to note the sharp contrast of this simple church with the massive proportions of *Sacré-Coeur.* Just to the back of *St-Pierre,* on the site of the ancient cemetery, is the *Jardin du Calvaire* (Calvary Garden), which is no longer open to the public. For a magnificent view of the city (especially on a clear day), bear left and walk a short distance toward the *Sacré-Coeur* terrace. Unfortunately, the vendors who clog the steps of *Sacré-Coeur* are often an unwelcome distraction from the vista.

At *Sacré-Coeur,* it is possible to make the very steep ascent into the dome for a view that is about equal to that from the top level of the *Eiffel Tower.* A stroll through the vast interior of this famous church, with its capacity of 8,000, is an experience not to be missed. For additional information about the basilica, see *Special Places* in THE CITY.

When leaving *Sacré-Coeur*'s grounds, avoid the busy stairs directly in front and descend instead via the scenic steps called Rue Maurice-Utrillo at the east of the *Sacré-Coeur* terrace. (If a break from the crowds is in order at this point of the tour, turn right for a stroll through the church's terraced gardens.) At the bottom of the steps, turn right and head down another set of steps called Rue Paul-Albert and follow Rue Ronsard south, noting on the left *Halle St-Pierre* (St. Peter's Hall; 2 Rue Ronsard; phone: 42-58-72-89), a fine 19th-century iron structure that houses a children's museum *(Musée en Herbe)* on the ground floor and the *Musée d'Art Naïf Max Fourny* (Max Fourny Museum of Naive Art) on the first floor. Both museums are open daily and have an admission charge. At Place St-Pierre, turn right to view the Montmartre carousel; turn left and head down Rue de Steinkerque, the heart of Paris's fabric district, recognizable by the abundance of yard goods and trimming supply stores, and the crowds of needle-and-thread aficionados. Farther down Rue de Steinkerque is Boulevard de Rochechouart, a wide shopping street with a large *Métro* station to the left, where it seems all of the immigrant population of Paris comes to buy clothes at bargain prices, mostly at the stretch of *Tati* shops (a chain of clothing boutiques).

It is important to realize that there is an upper Montmartre and a lower Montmartre, and nothing depicts lower Montmartre better than Place Pigalle, with its dubious strip of entertainment spots lining the edge of Boulevard de Clichy, the western continuation of Boulevard de Rochechouart. It earned its original image as "sin street" with the first burlesque cabaret, *Chat Noir,* founded in 1884, which once stood at No. 84 Boulevard de Rochechouart. The American author Henry Miller immortalized the street in several of his books during the late 1930s and early 1940s. These days, Boulevard de Clichy and its tacky neon surroundings have become more of a cliché. If planning a visit here, remember that Place Pigalle comes to life only at night.

Walk 3:
The Grandeur of Paris

This walk begins just off the Champs-Elysées, on Avenue Winston-Churchill, site of the *Petit Palais* and the *Grand Palais*. The *Grand Palais,* a magnificent building with an Ionic colonnade, mosaic frieze, and three porches built from the designs of three different architects, has long been used for a variety of annual trade exhibitions and shows, and now houses a cultural center, the *Galeries Nationales,* where such temporary exhibitions as the *Paris Book Fair* are held. (Note that parts of it will be closed for structural repairs throughout this year.) The back of the *Grand Palais* is the science museum and planetarium, called the *Palais de la Découverte* (on Av. Franklin-D.-Roosevelt). The *Galeries Nationales* are closed Tuesdays; the *Palais de la Découverte* is closed Mondays. There's an admission charge for both (phone: 44-13-17-17).

The *Petit Palais,* now a museum of fine arts, is architecturally notable for its ornamental flat glass dome. It's closed Mondays and holidays; there's an admission charge (phone: 42-65-12-73). Both palaces were built for the *1900 World Exposition,* replacing the former *Palais de l'Industrie* (for additional details on both, see *Special Places* in THE CITY).

Walk to the Seine and across the Pont Alexandre-III, which was built at the same time as the palaces. This single-span bridge, with its numerous gilded statues, is a fine example of the ornate style of popular 19th-century steel architecture. Walk down the busy Avenue du Maréchal-Galliéni along the vast tree-lined *Esplanade des Invalides* toward the *Hôtel des Invalides* (Av. de Tourville, Pl. Vauban, 7e; phone: 45-55-37-70). Built by Louis XIV in the 1670s as a refuge for disabled soldiers, *Les Invalides* is a vast classical structure designed by Libéral Bruant. The royal *Eglise du Dôme* (Church of the Dome), a masterpiece of 17th-century architecture topped by a 19th-century golden dome by Mansart, is the site of the tomb of Emperor Napoleon I. *Les Invalides* is open daily; there's an admission charge. If time allows, visit the nearby *Musée Rodin* (77 Rue de Varenne, 7e; phone: 47-05-01-34). It's closed Mondays; admission charge. For more information on *Les Invalides* and *Musée Rodin,* see *Special Places* in THE CITY.

From *Les Invalides,* walk north toward the Seine along the pleasant Rue Fabert. Turn left at Rue St-Dominique, with its lineup of cafés, greengrocers, wine shops, pâtisseries, *boucheries,* and *boulangeries.* Neighborhood folk casually go about their business, ignoring the fact that the magnificent *Eiffel Tower* is right in their own backyard. If you're ready to rest and sample some Parisian sweets, stop at *Pâtisserie G.-Millet* (103 Rue St-

The Grandeur of Paris

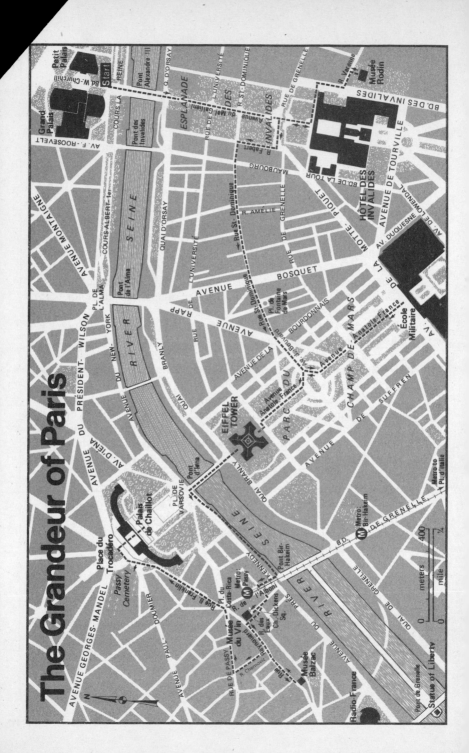

Dominique), a neighborhood institution for 30 years. Winners of a recent contest for the best croissant in Paris, they also make a luscious mille-feuille (puff pastry layered with creamy filling) and the *Sully,* a mousse of fruits and sauternes. Here there is also a choice of two restaurants at which to lunch, depending on your mood—and the availability of a table. The small (only four tables) *L'Auberge Normande* (No. 127) specializes in *produits du terroir,* or rural cuisine. Next door, *La Fontaine de Mars* (No. 129; see *Eating Out* in THE CITY) is a family bistro that serves southwestern French cooking in a friendly atmosphere. Continue on Rue St-Dominique and note how the neighborhood shifts from a French ambience to an Italian one, as you pass the heavy-arched Place de la Fontaine de Mars with its adjacent fountain.

Cross the busy intersection of Avenue de la Bourdonnais and Place du Général-Gouraud and walk ahead to Avenue Joseph-Bouvard, which leads directly to the extensive grounds of the *Parc du Champ-de-Mars.* In 1793 a guillotine was erected at its northeast corner. Stroll to the southern end of the park to view the *Ecole Militaire* (French Military Academy), the impressive complex to the left. Originally built to accommodate 500 soldiers-to-be, it has been through many transitions over the centuries—alternately used as a barracks, then headquarters of the Imperial Guard, and back to a training school once again. It is one of the finest examples of 18th-century French architecture, with its two-story Corinthian columns and handsome gilded dome. Not long after it opened in 1752, Napoleon I was among its many students. It's closed to the public except by special arrangement.

The *Champ-de-Mars* was the scene of a battle in 888 between the Parisians and the Normans, who were ultimately defeated. From 1770 to 1900, the area was the place for both military reviews and the great *Paris World Expositions* of 1867, 1878, 1889, and 1900. In 1908, it was transformed into a park to be more in keeping with the high class residences of the surrounding neighborhood.

Of all the great expositions held here, it was perhaps the one held in 1889, commemorating the centenary of the French Revolution, that was most memorable. This was the occasion of the unveiling of the *Eiffel Tower.* During the exposition, more than 25 million people visited the unusual tower, which at 984 feet was then the tallest structure in the world. Even with the addition in 1957 of television antennae that increased its height to its current 1,051 feet, the tower had long since given up the title, first relinquishing it in 1930 to the 1,284-foot-high Empire State Building in New York City. Controversial and despised by many, it was nearly torn down in 1909 when its first 20-year lease expired, only to be saved when the invention of the wireless gave it a new lease on life—as a radio transmitter. Beneath the tower's north pillar is a statue by Antoine Bourdelle of Alexandre-Gustave Eiffel, its architect and engineer.

Having ceremoniously celebrated its 100th anniversary in 1989, the *Eiffel Tower* continues to make its glorious presence known at the northwestern end of the *Champ-de-Mars,* facing the *Palais de Chaillot* on the opposite bank of the Seine. Try to view the tower from as many perspectives as possible. Walk down the middle of the *Champ-de-Mars,* with its tree-lined paths and children's park; from there note the graceful lines and impressive craftsmanship of Eiffel's work, even more fascinating as one climbs the stairs to the second level to take an elevator to the top. On an exceptionally clear day, it is possible to see about 50 miles. There are shops and three restaurants within the tower, which is open daily; admission charge (phone: 45-50-34-56; also see *Special Places* in THE CITY).

After leaving the tower, walk across the bridge facing it, the Pont d'Iéna, which leads to the Place du Trocadéro and the *Palais de Chaillot* (both of which can be visited at the end of this walk). After crossing the bridge, don't take the easy route straight ahead, but turn left and walk along the footpath bordering the Seine, avoiding the noise and traffic of the upper level of the Avenue du Président-Kennedy. This route offers yet another look at the *Eiffel Tower,* as well as a view of the high-rise buildings to the west, a skyline that looks something like Paris confronting Manhattan.

The walk along the river ends at Pont de Bir-Hakeim. Follow the steps up to the right, where there is a pedestrian tunnel and another bridge across noisy Avenue du Président-Kennedy leading to Rue de l'Alboni.

Walk up Rue de l'Alboni; before the steps to the *Passy Métro* stop, turn left at Square Alboni and right on Rue des Eaux. At Square Charles-Dickens is the *Musée Du Vin* (Wine Museum; 5-7 Sq. Charles-Dickens, 16e; phone: 45-25-63-26). Located in the cellar of the former *Abbaye de Passy* (Abbey of Passy), which was built during the second half of the 14th century by St. Francis of Paule, the museum couldn't be better situated. During that time, many of the hills around Paris were vineyards and several, operated by local monks, produced very good wine, which the monks of Passy stored here. Between 1650 and 1720, mineral water sources were discovered on this spot, which explains the name Rue des Eaux (Street of Waters). Passy became a very famous thermal site and was visited by such luminaries as Benjamin Franklin and Jean-Jacques Rousseau. The abbey was destroyed after the Revolution, but during the 1960s the foundations were rediscovered by a Parisian restaurateur, who restored the space as wine cellars to supply the restaurants of the *Eiffel Tower.* The museum, which opened in 1981, also hosts the wine brotherhood *(Conseil des Echansons de France),* an order dedicated to the promotion of high-quality French wines.

Within its *cave*-like environment, the museum displays interesting scenes depicting the history of wine—from harvesting to bottling—as well as examples of vintage pressing equipment, casks, corkscrews, and labels, that give the visitor a good overview of oenology. One can also buy wines, champagnes, and spirits at prices lower than those at many wine shops, or visit the tasting room to enjoy a simple lunch served with a selection of wines by the glass or bottle. (A free glass of wine is included in the admission price.) Private parties, complete with traditional wine tasting ceremonies, also can be arranged. Even for those familiar with Paris, a visit to this museum is a unique experience. It's closed mornings; admission charge.

For an interesting detour, take a round trip from the *Passy Métro* stop to the *Pasteur Métro* stop (toward *Nation*). This is one of the city's most scenic rides, beginning in *le seizième* (the 16th *arrondissement*), one of Paris's richest, most elegant neighborhoods. The main part of the ride goes aboveground for several stops, crossing over the Seine and affording a great view of the *Eiffel Tower*. The ride along the Boulevards de Grenelle and Garibaldi at second-story level provides a refreshing perspective of Parisian life. To get to the *Passy Métro* after leaving the *Musée Du Vin,* go back down Rue des Eaux to the first corner and turn left.

Those who decide against the *Métro* excursion should walk up the steps through the narrow passageway (on the right side of the square as you leave the museum) and make a left onto Rue Raynouard to the *Maison de Balzac* (No. 47; phone: 42-24-56-38). The plain exterior of the house belies the flamboyant excesses of its renowned inhabitant; the treasures in art and antiques he once accumulated are no longer to be found here, as they were sacrificed to creditors during his colorful life. However, this unassuming house is a testament to his hard work, evidenced by the manuscripts and memorabilia on display in the museum/library. It's closed Mondays and holidays.

From Balzac's house, turn right on the Rue Raynouard and then left on the Rue Chernoviz, which will take you to the bustling Rue de Passy, the neighborhood's chic commercial street. At No. 53 is *Passy Plaza,* a new luxury shopping mall (see *Shopping* in THE CITY); at No. 67 is one of Paris's most famous pâtisseries, *Coquelin Aîné* (phone: 45-24-44-00), which has been pampering *tout Paris* with fine pastries since 1900. Sit on the lovely terrace and have a light lunch topped off by one of their famous macaroons.

As you ramble around this well-tended neighborhood, complete with discreet doormen and private roads, remember that the Passy quarter is the city home to Paris's wealthiest class. For a change of scene, walk east past the Place du Costa-Rica and up Rue Benjamin-Franklin (he was the US Ambassador to France from 1776 to 1785); note the *Café Franklin* on the corner. On the left above Place du Trocadéro is the terraced *Cimetière de Passy,* enclosed by high walls. Among the prominent people buried here are artists Edouard Manet and Berthe Morisot, composers Claude Debussy and Gabriel Fauré, and the actor Fernandel. Proceed to the large open space of Trocadéro to fully appreciate still another view of the *Eiffel Tower* and the Rive Gauche, as well as the elegance of the stunning, white-stone *Palais de Chaillot.* Its dazzling twin pavilions and sweeping horizontal lines contrast nicely with the verticality of the *Eiffel Tower.* Housed in the palace complex are the national theater, the *Cinémathèque,* and several museums: the *Musée des Monuments Français* (Museum of French Monuments), the

Musée de l'Homme (Museum of Anthropology), the *Musée de la Marine* (Maritime Museum), and the *Musée du Cinéma*. The gardens are a nice place in which to stroll and unwind, and at night, the verdant area takes on a dramatically different look when its powerful fountains are illuminated. The museums are closed Tuesdays and major holidays; also see *Special Places* in THE CITY.

Walk 4: Haussmann's Master Plan

In the middle of the 19th century, Napoleon III gave his urban planner, Baron Georges-Eugène Haussmann, an order: Clean up Paris. The emperor wanted to eliminate the city's warren of narrow streets, which had become the scenes of riots by rambunctious crowds. Haussmann proceeded to tear down much of the capital to make way for broad, tree-lined boulevards, but rather than destroying the city, he created a unique urban unity. His best work is on the Rive Droite, where the avenues spread out from the rococo *Opéra/Palais Garnier.*

This walk begins at the *Opéra,* an imposing rococo edifice designed by Charles Garnier and completed in 1875. Its magnificent interior (don't miss the spectacular ceiling decorated by Marc Chagall) and special exhibitions are open to the public; closed the month of August and on days when there are special performances. There's an admission charge (phone: 47-42-53-71; for additional details see *Special Places* in THE CITY). The Place de l'Opéra is intersected by the Boulevard des Capucines and five other main avenues that lead to many of the city's—and the world's—most elegant shops.

Just behind the *Opéra,* on Boulevard Haussmann, are two of Paris's major department stores, or *grands magasins: Printemps* (No. 64; phone: 42-82-50-00) and *Galeries Lafayette* (No. 40; phone: 42-82-34-56). Shoppers can spend hours wandering from one cosmetic counter to another on the store's main floors before entering any one of a number of elegant galleries carrying high-fashion designs with sky-high prices. The *Galeries Lafayette*'s gourmet food supermarket has edibles from all over the world, and there's a counter serving quick lunches. Both stores are closed Sundays. Just outside these department stores are rows of sidewalk displays with clothing and various products for sale. Shop carefully, as these are operated by private vendors who are not affiliated with the stores.

From the Place de l'Opéra, walk southwest along the Boulevard des Capucines toward *La Madeleine.* At the corner of Rue Scribe is the monumental 19th-century *Grand* hotel (2 Rue Scribe), which houses the famous *Café de la Paix* (you can also enter at 12 Bd. des Capucines), where generations have come to watch the diverse parade of passersby (also see *Cafés* in THE CITY). Just next door was the equally popular (but no longer standing) *Grand Café.* It was here, on December 28, 1895, that the first public showing of a motion picture was held. In 1990s parlance, it was a bomb; only 33 people (the house held 100), paying 1 franc each, attended the program of 10 short films.

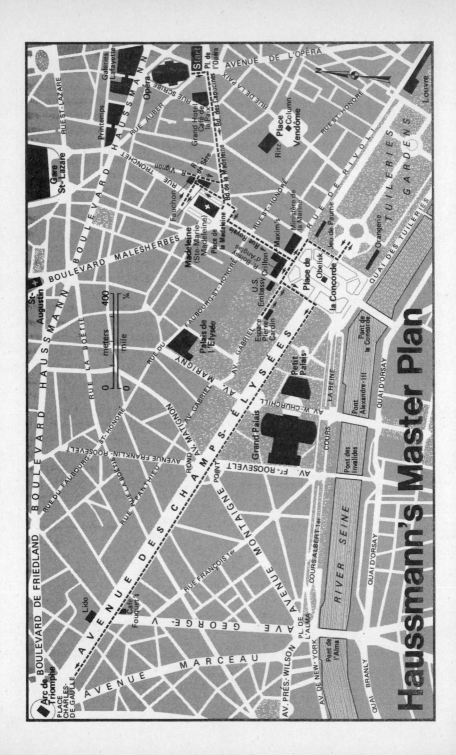

Haussmann's Master Plan

Past the Rue Scribe on the right, where the grand boulevards come to an end, is the *Eglise Ste-Marie-Madeleine* (Church of St. Mary Magdalene), or *La Madeleine*. This late-Roman–style adaptation of a Greek temple, begun in 1764 and not completed until 1842, is surrounded by an imposing group of massive Corinthian columns. In 1806, Napoleon Bonaparte had it redesigned (its plans had already been through two previous incarnations) and consecrated as a "Temple of Glory" honoring his armies. (Also see *Special Places* in THE CITY.)

While other neighborhoods pay homage to haute couture, the Madeleine quarter pays homage to *haute gastronomie*. Near this temple of worship are several culinary "temples" that cater to their own following of culinary aficionados. Just opposite the small flower market next to the *Madeleine Métro* station—and also in another building across the street—is *Fauchon* (26-30 Pl. de la Madeleine), with its distinctive chocolate-brown logo emblazoned on the walls and canopies of its complex of shops. Whether you choose just to look or to partake, this is the ultimate moveable feast. For a detailed description of this gastronomic landmark, see *Quintessential Paris* in DIVERSIONS and *Eating Out* in THE CITY.

Also on Place de la Madeleine (across Rue Tronchet) is *Hédiard* (21 Pl. de la Madeleine; phone: 42-66-44-36), another gastronomic emporium on a smaller scale, with exotic fruits and spices, flavored vinegars and oils, and at least 30 varieties of tea. The wine cellar offers an extensive selection (sorry, no bargains). Within *Hédiard* is *Créplet-Brussol,* regarded as one of the city's best cheese purveyors. Although the windows are filled with a lot of fancy packaged cheeses, their renowned collection of aged brie, fine raw milk camembert, and other classic cheeses is inside. Both stores are closed Sundays.

Even more fancy fare is found at *Maison de la Truffe* (19 Pl. de la Madeleine; phone: 42-65-53-22), where the city's best fresh truffles are sold from November through February. Otherwise, there are preserved truffles, and rich foie gras, exotic fruit, and a variety of charcuterie. It's closed Sundays. In the same building is *Caviar Kaspia* (phone: 42-65-33-52), a simple, straightforward store that specializes in (what else?) caviar. Choose from a selection of well-priced pressed caviar, excellent smoked salmon, and tasty fresh blinis. If you like, go upstairs to their elegant, informal restaurant and sample a few dishes along with a frosty glass of vodka.

Cross back to *Fauchon* at the corner of Rue de Sèze. Enter Rue de Sèze and turn left on Rue Vignon. Not far from the corner is *La Maison du Miel* (House of Honey; 24 Rue Vignon; phone: 47-42-26-70), which has been operated by the Galland family at this location since 1908. Devoted totally to honey and honey products, it produces about one-fourth of the 53 tons of honey sold here each year. There are many varieties from which to choose and sample tastings are available. It's closed Sundays. Just across the street is *La Ferme Saint-Hubert* (No. 21; phone: 47-42-79-20), a compact little shop that has extraordinary varieties of cheese and a friendly staff to advise you. They have one of the best selections of Roquefort, dozens of *chèvres* (goat cheeses), and a fine assortment of reasonably priced house wines, as well as bread from the famous *Poilâne* bakery. For a unique experience, visit their adjoining lunchroom/restaurant; in the evening, it serves special *dégustation* (sampler) plates of cheese and raclette, a melted cheese dish from Switzerland served with boiled potatoes, pickled onions, and *cornichons* (small sour gherkins). It's closed Sundays and Mondays.

Walk back to Rue de Sèze and cross it, continuing along Rue Vignon. Turn right on Boulevard de la Madeleine and then left on Rue Royale. Walk down Rue Royale, past the chic shopping street of Rue du Faubourg-St-Honoré (see *Quintessential Paris* in DIVERSIONS). If you decide to take a detour along it, check out the window displays at *Hermès* (No. 24; phone: 40-17-47-17), to the right on the corner of Rue Boissy d'Anglas, which offer just a sampling of the fabulous merchandise to be found on this street. Directly ahead on Rue Royale is *Maxim's* (No. 3); long a legend for its Belle Epoque decor and atmosphere, it remains a landmark, although the quality of the food has ceased to merit the high prices (see *Eating Out* in THE CITY).

At the corner of Rue Royale and Place de la Concorde are two stately mansions designed by Gabriel, with colonnades similar to those at the *Louvre.* The pavilion across the street on the left is the *Ministère de la Marine,* now headquarters of the French navy. The pavilion at the right is shared by the *Automobile-Club de France* (French Automobile Club) and the *Crillon* hotel, with its discreet sign and elegant gold C's on the door (see *Checking In* in THE CITY). Directly in front is Place de la Concorde, considered to be one of the finest public squares in the world. Dominated by its famous obelisk, the square has eight massive statues designed by Gabriel, representing provincial capitals in France, and two bronze fountains. It's bounded on the east by the *Jardin des Tuileries,* on the south by the Seine and the Pont de la Concorde (Concord Bridge), and on the west by the Avenue des Champs-Elysées. Looking in any direction at this point will bring you face to face with one of the major monuments of Paris.

The central monument of the square is *l'Obélisque de Louqsor* (Obelisk of Luxor). At 75 feet high and weighing more than 220 tons, it is similar to its London counterpart, *Cleopatra's Needle.* The obelisk was presented by the government of Egypt to the government of Louis-Philippe and was erected on its present site between 1834 and 1836. It had quite an ambitious journey: It was removed from the *Temple of Luxor* and brought to the Nile; it was then shipped 600 miles to Alexandria, where it crossed the Mediterranean and traveled north on the Atlantic to Cherbourg, and was finally transported by road through Normandy to Paris. In 1793, where the obelisk now stands, a guillotine was erected that took the lives of some 3,000 victims of the Reign of Terror, including King Louis XVI, his queen, Marie-Antoinette, and other members of the royal family. The site was originally called Place Louis-XV, and, afterward, the Place de la Révolution.

It was then renamed Place de la Concorde, then Place Louis-XVI; in 1830 its present name was restored. The square was given the name *Concorde* ("peace") to erase the memory of the deeds performed here.

Across the street is the *Tuileries,* a lovely park framed at its western end by two small museums, the *Jeu de Paume* and the *Orangerie,* flanking a large pond that's usually surrounded by children and young couples. At the eastern end of the *Tuileries* is the *Louvre,* one of the world's greatest museums (see *Special Places* in THE CITY for details on the park and all three museums).

Cross the Place de la Concorde—carefully, and preferably not directly across the heavily trafficked square—to the park-like, tree-lined street which is the eastern end of the Champs-Elysées, the most famous thoroughfare in Paris. It was first called the Grand Allée du Roule and then the Avenue des Tuileries. The *American Embassy* is on the right at 2 Avenue Gabriel. At No. 1 is *L'Espace Cardin,* a theater complex and restaurant owned by fashion designer Pierre Cardin, who also owns *Maxim's.* You might want to return here to see a theatrical or musical performance, or else sample the buffet at the restaurant, with its amusingly funky decor (phone: 42-66-11-70).

As you continue down the Champs-Elysées, note the *Palais de l'Elysée,* set in a large garden off to the right. A magnificent structure that dates from 1718, it has been the residence of the French president since 1873. Just ahead is the Rond-Point des Champs-Elysées, a large, circular, flower-filled *place* at the intersection of Avenues Matignon, Franklin-D.-Roosevelt, and Montaigne.

It was only after Haussmann's changes in the mid-19th century that the Champs-Elysées came to be considered one of the world's great promenades. Once lined by hotels and mansions, over the years landmark buildings such as the *Grand Palais* and *Petit Palais* were constructed for the *1900 World Exposition* (they are just to the left; see *Special Places* in THE CITY for details). Later, the area grew to include banks, corporate headquarters, luxury shops, and a number of automobile dealers; during the last few decades, many large cinemas with attached shopping complexes were built on both sides of the broad street, as were more restaurants and cafés to accommodate the growing number of visitors. Even more recently, fast-food franchises have intruded on the ambience of this high-rent neighborhood. Still, quintessentially French institutions hold sway: *Café Fouquet's* (pronounced Foo-*kett*) is on the left (99 Champs-Elysées, at the corner of Av. George-V; phone: 47-23-70-60). It is perhaps the most famous café along the route, for decades the place for *tout* Paris to see and be seen.

Directly ahead is the *Arc de Triomphe* and Place Charles-de-Gaulle (also known as Place de l'Etoile). The large, circular traffic hub from which 12 avenues radiate is the centerpiece of Baron Haussmann's inspired master plan. The famous arch—as synonymous with Paris as the *Eiffel Tower*—crowns the long vista of the Champs-Elysées. Conceived by Napoleon I to commemorate his victories of 1805–6 and later dedicated to the memory of the Unknown Soldier, it features an impressive frieze and 10 monumental sculptures. Climb or take the elevator to the platform at the top of the monument for a memorable view of the city. A small museum under the platform contains souvenirs relating to Napoleon I, the *Arc de Triomphe,* and both world wars. The arch is open daily; admission charge (phone: 43-80-31-31). For additional details, see *Special Places* in THE CITY.

For a relaxing break after your explorations, walk downhill on the Avenue Carnot to *Le Pain et le Vin,* just ahead at No. 1 Rue de l'Armaillé (phone: 47-63-88-29). This is one of Paris's best wine bars, with an excellent selection of 40 wines from which to choose (but note that it's closed in the afternoons between 3 and 7 PM, as well as Sundays and the month of August).

For a special perspective on the *Arc de Triomphe,* take the *Métro* (line No. 1) at the *Place Charles-de-Gaulle–Etoile* stop to the *Grande Arche de la Défense* (the end of the line). Built in 1989, this massive contemporary arch houses a library, a bookstore, and the offices of a research foundation dedicated to peace and brotherhood, the *Fondation des Droits de l'Homme.* Take the elevator up for a stunning view, but even from the ground-floor terrace you can see the *Arc de Triomphe* and, in the distance, the obelisk in the Place de la Concorde, framing either end of the Champs-Elysées. The arch is open daily; admission charge (phone: 49-07-27-57).

Walk 5: From the Louvre to the Luxembourg

Begin this walk on the Rive Droite, at the main entrance to the *Jardin des Tuileries,* at the east side of the Place de la Concorde. The main path of the gardens bisects the park and leads straight to the *Louvre.* The *Tuileries* were originally commissioned in 1563 by Catherine de Médicis, the queen mother, who wanted an Italianate park next to the palace (now the *Louvre*) that she shared with King Henri II. These were to be no ordinary gardens; they would include fountains, a maze, a grotto, and a menagerie. A century later, in 1664, Le Nôtre, Louis XIV's celebrated landscape gardener, redesigned the park to become what is said to be the epitome of formal French design. Years later, sensual sculptures by Maillol were placed on the lawns, as were busts of prominent figures and statues of mythical deities, like Mercury, the messenger of the gods, who sits here atop his winged horse.

The *Tuileries* were enlarged in 1889 with more garden space created on the site of the former *Palais des Tuileries* (Tuileries Palace), which was destroyed by the Communards in 1871. Today the park remains the most popular promenade in Paris, most likely because of its central location. Nannies stroll with baby carriages; lovers embrace on benches; mimes entertain among groves of trees; lines of schoolchildren wait for ice cream cones at a kiosk; and in a nearby pond, charming miniature sailboats complete this idyllic Parisian scene. Currently, the gardens are undergoing extensive renovations, which will continue into 1997.

As you enter, on the immediate left is the *Jeu de Paume,* and on the right, the *Orangerie.* Each of these elegant pavilions was built during the Second Empire and has served as an art gallery since the turn of the 20th century. Before the main works of the collection were moved to the *Musée d'Orsay,* the *Jeu de Paume* was known for its Impressionist exhibitions; now it contains a collection of contemporary art. The *Orangerie* holds temporary exhibitions, in addition to housing the prestigious *Walter-Guillaume Collection,* which includes works by Picasso, Matisse, Cézanne, Modigliani, Renoir, Monet, and others. The museums in the *Tuileries* are closed on Tuesdays; there's an admission charge for both (phone: 47-03-12-50, *Jeu de Paume;* 42-97-48-16, *Orangerie*). For additional details, see *Special Places* in THE CITY.

To the left outside the *Tuileries* is Rue de Rivoli, with its uniformly designed 19th-century arcades of bookstores, cafés, hotels, and boutiques. To the far right are the quays bordering the Seine. Walk a while, look back, and enjoy the panoramic view, impressive despite the renovations currently taking place around the *Louvre* complex (which should be completed by 1997). The *Louvre* enjoys the distinction of being the largest museum in

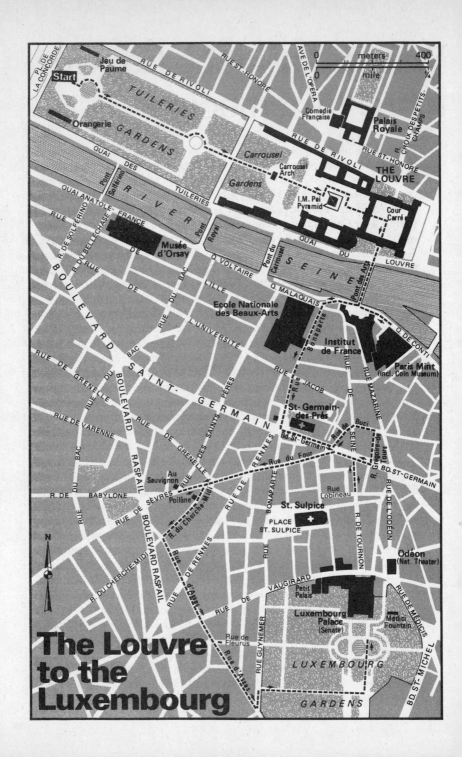

Start

Jeu de Paume

Orangerie

RUE DE RIVOLI
RUE ST-HONORÉ
AVE DE L'OPÉRA

PL. DE LA CONCORDE

meters 400
0 ¼ mile

TUILERIES GARDENS

QUAI DES TUILERIES

Pont Solférino

RIVER

QUAI ANATOLE FRANCE

RUE DE SOLFÉRINO

R. DE BELLECHASE

Musée d'Orsay

DE

RUE

DE

L'UNIVERSITÉ

RUE DU BAC

RUE DE LILLE

Comedie Française

Palais Royale

CROIX DES PETITS CHAMPS

RUE DE RIVOLI
RUE ST-HONORÉ

THE LOUVRE

Carrousel

Carrousel Arch

Gardens

I.M. Pei Pyramid

Cour Carré

Pont du Carrousel

Pont Royal

QUAI DU LOUVRE

Q. VOLTAIRE

Q. MALAQUAIS

SEINE

Pont des Arts

Ecole Nationale des Beaux-Arts

RUE Bonaparte

Institut de France

RUE DE

RUE MAZARINE

Q. DE CONTI

Paris Mint (incl. Coin Museum)

BOULEVARD

SAINT-

GERMAIN

RUE DU BAC

RUE DE GRENELLE

RUE DE VARENNE

RUE DE GRENELLE

BOULEVARD RASPAIL

RUE DES SAINTS-PÈRES

RUE DE RENNES

RUE Jacob

St- Germain-des-Prés

Bd. St-Germain

Rue de Buci

Rue de SEINE

R. G.

BD. ST-GERMAIN

RUE DE

BABYLONE

RUE DE SÈVRES

Au Sauvignon

Poilâne

RUE DU CHERCHE-MIDI

Rue du Four

RUE BONAPARTE

St. Sulpice

PLACE ST. SULPICE

Rue Lobineau

RUE DE L'ODÉON

Odéon (Nat. Theater)

R. DE

R. DU CHERCHE-MIDI

BOULEVARD RASPAIL

Rue DE PLAISSE

RUE DE RENNES

RUE DE TOURNON

VAUGIRARD

Petit Palais

Luxembourg Palace (Senate)

Médici Fountain

RUE GUYNEMER

Rue de Fleurus

RUE D'ASSAS

LUXEMBOURG

GARDENS

RUE DE MÉDICIS

BD. ST-MICHEL

N

The Louvre to the Luxembourg

the world, and when the renovation is completed—including an ambitious plan for a new bridge and pedestrian pathway linking the *Musée d'Orsay* and the *Palais-Royal*—that distinction will surely be unrivaled (for more on the *Louvre,* see *Special Places* in THE CITY).

Stroll around the glass pyramid, designed by I. M. Pei, for an entirely updated perspective of the former palace. Some (like us) believe that the Egyptian-inspired design is out of place here, although it fits more comfortably into the surroundings now that the nearby exterior walls of the *Louvre,* grimy for decades, have been restored to their light-reflecting, creamy hue. Overlooking the pyramid on the north are the tall windows of the *Louvre*'s new *Richelieu Wing,* inaugurated last year in honor of the museum's 200th anniversary. Continue straight ahead to the last building, the *Cour Carrée* (Square Court), considered to be the most impressive of the old *Louvre* buildings. Walk through the elegant courtyard and out the door to the right toward the Seine. Enjoy the impressive view across the Pont des Arts (Bridge of Arts), taking in the domed complex of the *Institut de France* across the river on the Rive Gauche.

Cross the Pont des Arts to the institute, which encompasses five prestigious academies, including the *Academie Française.* Designed by Le Vau and opened in 1688, it seemed rather mediocre compared to his more illustrious monument across the Seine, the *Louvre.* Even though the buildings were meant to complement one another, the institute was actually considered one of the prominent architect's failures. The institute has had an interesting history and is notorious for its former exclusion of women and for the notable male candidates it has refused. Among the rejects were Descartes, Pascal, Molière, Proust, Balzac, and Zola. Today, it accepts women members; author Marguerite Yourcenar was the first to be admitted (in 1980).

To the left of this rarefied intellectual complex is the *Hôtel des Monnaies* (Paris Mint), a fine, unpretentious building by Antoine, who lived here until his death in 1801. The *Musée de la Monnaie,* with its wonderful collection of coins and exhibitions on the art of engraving, is on the premises. It's closed mornings, Mondays, and holidays (phone: 40-46-55-33). Walk west along the Quai de Conti and then the Quai Malaquais to the *Ecole Nationale des Beaux-Arts* (National School of Fine Arts) at the corner of Rue Bonaparte. This former monastery was founded in 1608 and closed down in 1791, during the Revolution. In 1795, it became the *Musée des Monuments Français* (Museum of French Monuments), displaying treasures—such as the tombs of the early French kings from the *Basilique de St-Denis*—that its meticulous curator, Alexandre Lenoir, had managed to save from destruction by overzealous revolutionaries. The school was created in 1816 by the union of the national painting and sculpture academy and the national architecture school. That same year the museum was permanently closed, although some of the monuments remain in the courtyard where, in the early days of the school, they helped inspire the Romantic movement, with its fascination for all things medieval. Entrance to the courtyard is at 14 Rue Bonaparte; the school itself is closed to the public except by special arrangement (phone: 42-60-34-57).

Turn up Rue Bonaparte to see rows of exclusive and pricey antiques shops and art galleries. This narrow street dates to 1250, and today it can barely accommodate the steady flow of city traffic crossing from the Rive Gauche to the Rive Droite. Walk a bit farther to the Boulevard St-Germain. On the left is the *Eglise St-Germain-des-Prés* (Church of St. Germain-in-the-Fields) to the right is the *Café Les Deux Magots* (6 Pl. St-Germain-des-Prés; phone: 45-48-55-25), said to be the birthplace of surrealism. Just next door is *Café de Flore* (172 Bd. St-Germain; phone: 45-48-55-26), the existentialist hangout where Jean-Paul Sartre and Simone de Beauvoir held court over *café espresso*. Each is worth a visit, depending on where your loyalties lie, and if you don't mind paying inflated prices to watch people watching people, which is basically what happens here. On weekend nights, this stretch of boulevard is the place to get a front-row seat to watch the lively stream of street entertainers—from mimes to fire-eaters to acrobats. *Café de Flore* is closed in July; *Café Les Deux Magots* is closed in August.

Across the street at *Brasserie Lipp* (No. 151; phone: 45-48-53-91), politicians rub well-tailored elbows with the fashion and publishing crowds who work in the surrounding quarter. It is so crowded that one's only chance of sampling the house specialty, *choucroute,* is in the Siberia section in the upper dining room. This Alsatian combination plate of sausages, smoked meat, and sauerkraut found its way into the French capital during the middle of the 19th century, when there was a wave of immigration from the Alsace region. Many Alsatians opened brasseries (beer halls distinguished by their brass dispensers). These days, even some *Lipp* regulars say the food has lost some of its charm, so why not just settle for a glass of Alsatian beer and take in the atmosphere. It's closed in July and August.

Cross the street once again and visit the unassuming *Eglise St-Germain-des-Prés,* the oldest church in Paris. It was built around 543 by Childebert I, on the advice of St. Germain, the Bishop of Paris, who is buried here. During the Middle Ages it became the center of a powerful Benedictine abbey, known by contemporaries as the "Ville St-Germain," literally a city in its own right.

After leaving the church, turn left down Boulevard St-Germain, taking a left at Rue de Buci. This is where one of Paris's most expensive, and usually most jam-packed, market streets begins. Each morning this area is a jumble of fruit, vegetable, and *fromage* vendors alongside fishmongers, bread sellers, and meat merchants. If you don't want to grab a bite here— or would like to sit at a table—why not go where many of the market vendors themselves go: *Orestia's* Greek taverna (4 Rue Grégoire-de-Tours; phone: 43-54-62-01), off Rue de Buci to the right. Here you will squeeze into rickety chairs and sit at a long table with tourists and locals from all walks of life. Founded in 1929, this place is as busy and noisy as it is welcoming and friendly. Try the mixed appetizer plate, and if you want to please the waiter, order retsina, the unique resin-flavored wine affectionately known as the "Blood of the Gods."

Walk south on Rue Grégoire-de-Tours and turn right at Boulevard St-Germain and then left a block up at Rue de Seine. At the corner of Rue de Seine and tiny Rue Lobineau is the entrance to the Saint-Germain-des-Prés covered market, recently installed in renovated quarters that include a day-care center, a pool, and other facilities. The market is much quieter than the more visible Rue de Buci street market and has an excellent array of products, including many possibilities for take-out meals, from Vietnamese chicken with coriander to organic breads and goat cheese. It's closed Sunday afternoons and Mondays. For more details on the markets, see *Quintessential Paris* in DIVERSIONS.

For a delightful shoppers' detour, head back to Boulevard Saint-Germain, take a left, then take another left on Rue du Four. Continue into Rue de Sèvres, or turn left a few blocks down on Rue de Rennes; either way, this area has boutique after fashionable boutique, such as *Guerlain* (29 Rue de Sèvres; phone: 42-22-46-60); *Dorothée Bis* (33 Rue de Sèvres; phone: 42-22-02-90); and *Sonia Rykiel* (175 Bd. St-Germain; phone: 49-54-60-60). Or stop for a bite at *Au Sauvignon* (80 Rue des Sts-Pères, at the corner of Rue de Sèvres; see *Eating Out* in THE CITY).

The delicious bread served at *Au Sauvignon* is made at the *Poilâne* bakery shop (8 Rue du Cherche-Midi; phone: 45-48-42-59), not far from the café (take a right back at the busy intersection of Carrefour de la Croix-Rouge). There probably will be lines of customers waiting to buy the trademark flour-dusted sourdough loaves. The bread is sold by the ounce, so you can buy a slice or two. The apple tarts also are well worth tasting. If the place is not too hectic, visit the basement and watch the bread being mixed, kneaded, and baked in ancient wood-burning ovens.

Walk past *Poilâne* and turn left at the upcoming street, Rue d'Assas, which will lead to a side entrance of the *Jardin du Luxembourg* and the adjacent palace. Along the way, there are interesting shops, galleries, and old bookstores through which to browse. *J-C & C* (16 Rue d'Assas) is an aromatic tea shop with a good selection of tea and coffee, as well as some unusual tea-flavored honeys and jams.

Continuing down Rue d'Assas, briefly turn left onto Rue de Fleurus. Gertrude Stein once resided with Alice B. Toklas at No. 27, where they held spirited salons with the likes of Picasso and Hemingway sparring for attention.

Continue down Rue d'Assas and enter through the gate of the *Jardin du Luxembourg* on Rue Guynemer. These surrounding streets were originally part of the garden complex, developed after 1870. The *Jardin du Luxembourg* was built in 1613 on the site of an ancient Roman encampment and a 13th-century convent. When the convent was demolished in 1790, the surrounding gardens were enlarged and remodeled. There are several entrances to this park: Boulevard St-Michel, Rue de Vaugirard near the historic *Odéon* theater, Rue Guynemer, and Rue Auguste-Comte.

The impressive *Palais du Luxembourg* at Rue de Vaugirard was originally built between 1615 and 1620 for Marie de Médicis, mother of Louis XIII. It was inhabited by successive generations of the royal family until the time of Louis XVI. During the dark days of World War II, it served as German Air Force headquarters. It now houses the French *Sénat* (Senate). Guided tours of the palace are conducted on the first Sunday of the month; for information, contact the *Caisse Nationale des Monuments Historiques et des Sites.* There's an admission charge (phone: 44-61-21-69/70).

The *Petit Palais* next door is now the home of the President of the Senate, and it includes the original *Hôtel de Luxembourg* that Marie de Médicis presented to Cardinal Richelieu as a residence.

These gardens are, after the *Tuileries,* a favorite Parisian promenade, particularly during the summer when many outdoor concerts are held here. Each section of the park is different, with tennis courts, pony rides, a carousel, a puppet theater, a large fountain with toy sailboats gliding by, and several play areas for children. A bas-relief of Leda and the Swan is one of the more original examples of the statuary; located near the Médicis fountain, it is worth seeing. In addition to the ubiquitous park benches, there are hundreds of chairs that can be moved to a spot of your choice. Many travelers will find this tranquil setting the perfect place in which to conclude this tour of the Rive Gauche.

But those sightseers who wish to see more can cross the Boulevard St-Michel and walk toward the Seine (about a block). Here is the center of Parisian student life, the Quartier Latin (Latin Quarter)—so named because classes used to be conducted in Latin—an area rife with cafés that welcome scholars (very few of whom speak Latin these days) and visitors alike. The boulevard opens up onto a square, dominated by the *Eglise de la Sorbonne* (Church of the Sorbonne) with university buildings surrounding it. Founded in 1256, the *Sorbonne* is the oldest university in Paris; although it still has a certain cachet, it has fallen far behind the *Grandes Ecoles* in prestige. Many of the most famous institutions of French intellectual life, including the *Collège de France, Ecole Polytechnique,* and *Lycée Louis-le-Grand,* where Molière, Voltaire, and Robespierre studied, also are located in this neighborhood.

Behind the *Sorbonne,* the Rue St-Jacques leads south to Rue Soufflot, named in honor of Germain Soufflot, the original architect of the vast, domed *Panthéon,* down the street to the left. Commissioned by Louis XV in 1744 and finished only in 1789, the church is of interest mainly because it houses the remains of Voltaire, Zola, and Rousseau. The *Panthéon* is closed some holidays; there's an admission charge (phone: 43-54-34-51; also see *Special Places* in THE CITY). It was here that Socialist François Mitterrand held his first large rally after winning the presidency in 1981. The intellectual, book-loving Mitterrand makes his home in this neighborhood on nearby Rue de Bièvre.

Walk 6: Beaubourg, Les Halles, and the Hôtel de Ville

The *Centre Georges-Pompidou* and the surrounding Beaubourg neighborhood, with its street entertainers, have become a center for international youth of all ages. One either loves it or detests it; there is no middle ground. The *Centre Georges-Pompidou* was built on the initiative of former President Georges Pompidou to create a multipurpose cultural center that would revive the area following the demise of the old *Les Halles* market. Today the hustle and bustle, scents and sights of Paris's colorful wholesale market have been replaced with not only the vibrant cultural scene at the *Centre*, but also a new "market," the underground *Forum des Halles* complex, with shops, museums, and theaters that continue the area's tradition of lively commerce.

Begin the walk by exploring the Quartier de l'Horloge, just north of the *Centre Georges-Pompidou,* between Rue Beaubourg and Rue St-Martin. This is a pedestrian area with many shops, and, with the neighborhood still in transition, it is a dynamic melting pot with a real sense of street life. The landmark *horloge* (clock), off the entrance to the quarter at Rue Rambuteau, is an unusual construction of brass and steel that is electronically operated by a life-size figure, known as "the defender of time." Not far to the east, at the end of the Impasse Berthaud off Rue Beaubourg, is the *Musée de la Musique Méchanique,* with a collection that includes over 100 mechanical reproducers of music dating from the late 19th century. It's open afternoons on weekends and holidays.

The *Centre Georges-Pompidou* is a futuristic concoction of steel, glass, and brightly colored piping that resembles a surrealistic refinery. What you first notice are the oversize see-through escalators, which look like giant caterpillars transporting a constant flux of people into the building. The piazza, which is directly in front of the main entrance, is swarming with spectators and the ubiquitous fire-eaters, jugglers, musicians, and mimes. (Be wary of pickpockets here.)

Take time to visit the center, which houses the *Musée National d'Art Moderne* (National Museum of Modern Art), the *Centre de Création Industrielle* (Industrial Design Center), a public information library, and the *Institut de Recherches et de Coordination Acoustique/Musique* (Institute for Acoustic and Musical Research). The art museum's permanent collection traces modern art's roots back to Fauvism and Cubism. There is some-

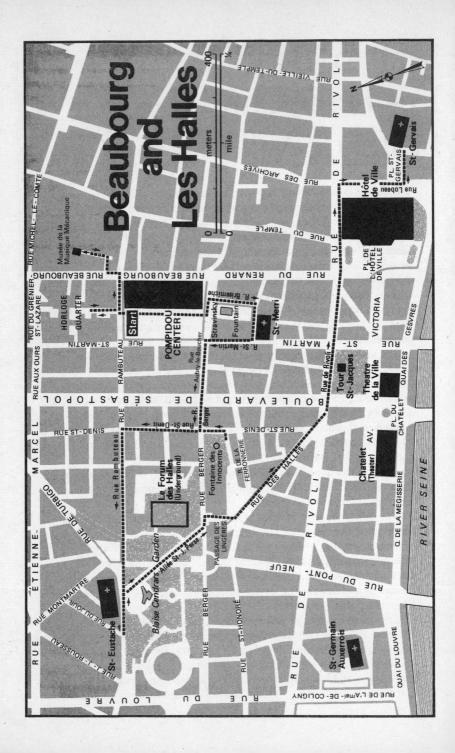

thing for every taste, from Picasso and Matisse to Mondrian, Rauschenberg, and Warhol. The temporary exhibitions are always quite spectacular, and the bookstore and poster shop are also worth a visit. Go up the escalator to the fifth floor and step outside for a view of Paris's distinctive rooftops. The café here is a nice place to relax before moving on, or stay awhile for one of the classic films shown at the center's *Salle Garance* cinema. The center is closed Tuesdays, weekday mornings, and May 1. There's an admission charge (except Sundays) only for the art museum and special exhibitions (phone: 42-77-12-33). A $100-million renovation and repair project begins this year with work on the exterior of the center and on adjoining areas and buildings. Note that sections may close for renovation, but the center as a whole will remain open.

Leave the *Centre Georges-Pompidou* and walk to the left for a pleasant and peaceful diversion. Place Igor-Stravinsky is the site of a delightful pool-size fountain, the product of a collaboration between the playful artists Nikki de Saint-Phalle and Jean Tinguely. In homage to the works of the great composer of *The Firebird* and *The Rite of Spring,* colorful Saint-Phalle creations, including water-spouting lips, twirling female torsos, and a dancing skeleton, all happily interact with Tinguely's animated black steel sculptures.

Walk gingerly, taking care not to be sprayed by the fountain, which can be seen as a little satire on the monumental fountains that have long graced Paris's boulevards. You are now in the St-Merri quarter of Beaubourg, the name of the old village that stood on this site in the 12th century. At the southern end of the Place Igor-Stravinsky is the *Eglise St-Merri* (St. Merri Church); "Merri" is a corruption of "Mederic," the name of the saintly monk who was buried on this spot around AD 700. The church was completed in 1612, but most of it was built in its unusual Gothic style during the reign of François I, around 1520.

After circling the Stravinsky fountain, follow the crowds on the pedestrian road west on Rue Aubry-le-Boucher, cross the Boulevard de Sébastopol into Rue Berger, and enjoy the active street life around the *Fontaine des Innocents.* The fountain itself is a Renaissance work by Pierre Lescot—much altered and restored—that once adorned the old *Marché des Innocents,* which preceded the *Halles* market, which in turn replaced a cemetery, the *Cimetière des Saints-Innocents,* dating back to Gallo-Roman times.

There are several cafés along this pedestrian area, which borders *Le Forum des Halles* shopping complex. One of the more popular ones is *Café Costes* (4-6 Rue Berger; phone: 45-08-54-38/9), a postmodern–looking place designed by French wunderkind Philippe Starck. Prices are high, and even more so at one of the sought-after outdoor tables. (Keep in mind that there is a three-level price structure—for dining outdoors, sitting indoors, and standing at the bar. When you sit on a terrace on a lovely day with a good vantage point, you are literally "renting" your chair.) But this eatery is worth a visit just for the contrast in design compared to other more typical French cafés.

After leaving the café, follow Rue St-Denis north; turn left on Rue Rambuteau and continue to *Eglise St-Eustache* (St. Eustache Church), considered to be one of Paris's most beautiful churches after *Notre-Dame*. A mixture of late-Gothic and Renaissance architecture, it mostly was constructed between 1532 and 1637. The front portion of the church, with its Ionic and Doric columns, was added in 1778. The church is especially known for its organ, one of the finest and largest in the city; it is here that Berlioz and Liszt composed some of their finest works. The white marble altar, with its sculptured canopy, is also remarkable. The church's collection of 16th- and 17th-century paintings, sculpture, and painted glass is definitely worth noting. Beneath the spacious gardens adjacent to the church is the underground *Forum des Halles* complex of shops, restaurants, theaters, and museums (phone: 44-76-96-56). The gigantic *FNAC* store here sells everything from stereos and cameras to books and records at discount prices (phone: 40-41-40-00). In the gardens are several children's play areas and a stunning 19th-century carousel, one of the two oldest still operating in Paris. (It was once steam-powered.) On tiny Rue du Jour, which begins in front of *Saint-Eustache,* are several trendy boutiques, reflecting the contemporary face of *Les Halles*.

After passing through the gardens, cross Rue Berger and go through Passage des Lingères (toward the eastern end of the gardens) to get to Rue des Halles. Our favorite shop in the neighborhood is *Papeterie Moderne* (12 Rue de la Ferronnerie; phone: 42-36-21-72), to the left off Rue des Halles, which for decades has been the source of many of the city's signs. You can choose from among hundreds of typical Parisian signs or have your own made to order: everything from the ordinary *"défense de fumer"* (no smoking) to an 18th-century saying outside a cemetery: *"De par le roi, défense à Dieu, de faire miracle en ce lieu"* (By order of the king, even God isn't allowed to work any miracles here).

For a change of scenery, walk down Rue des Halles to Rue de Rivoli. Turn left at Rue de Rivoli and continue to the *Hôtel de Ville* (Town Hall); it's about a five-minute walk. On the way, notice the 16th-century *Tour St-Jacques,* the former belfry of a church torn down in 1802. A statue of the scientist-philosopher Blaise Pascal stands in the tower. The Place de l'Hôtel de Ville, known as the Place du Grève until 1830, was the scene of many important historical events. From 1310 until 1832, public executions took place here, and it was here that Dr. Guillotin's machine was first put into action on humans on April 25, 1792, before being moved to the Place de la Concorde. Foulon, one of the first victims of the Revolution, was hanged here by a mob whom he had enraged by saying that "the hungry should eat grass."

During the late 1800s this was a place where men lined up for jobs, specifically those in the building trade. On some mornings as many as 4,000 men were assembled, with only a few gendarmes on duty to keep the road clear. The Place du Grève was thus the origin of the French term for being on strike, "en grève." Originally built between 1533 and 1628, the *Hôtel de Ville* has always been considered one of the city's most splendid buildings. The design of the present building is French Renaissance, with distinctive mansard windows and sculpture-adorned columns. Statues grace the courtyard and gilded figures decorate the roof. It was rebuilt between 1878 and 1882, with alterations and enlargements very much along the lines of the original *Hôtel de Ville,* which was burned down during the fierce street fights in the days ending the Commune in 1871.

Just east of the *Hôtel de Ville* is the *Eglise St-Gervais–St-Protais,* built between 1616 and 1621, the first example of the imposing neoclassical style in Paris. The interior maintains the 17th-century theme with its finely carved stalls. The organ, said to be the oldest in Paris, was built in 1601 and was once played by the Couperins, father and son. François Couperin composed his two masses on it in 1685. An elm tree that stood in the Place St-Gervais in medieval times was, according to custom, the place where people came to pay their taxes. Naturally, some of them failed to show up, and the cynical expression "Wait for me under the elm tree" was born. The elm that stands here today was planted in 1912 to commemorate this ancient tradition, but now there's nothing unpleasant beneath it—just a few Parisian squirrels.

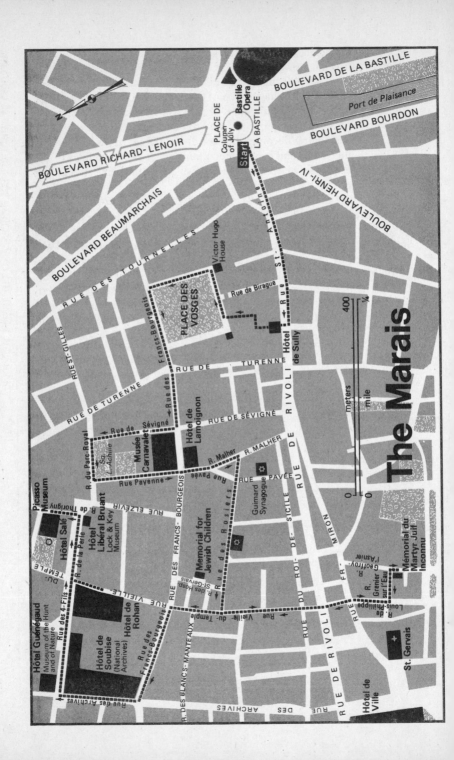

The Marais

Start

Bastille Opera

Column of July

LA BASTILLE

BOULEVARD DE LA BASTILLE

Port de Plaisance

BOULEVARD BOURDON

BOULEVARD RICHARD-LENOIR

BOULEVARD BEAUMARCHAIS

BOULEVARD HENRI-IV

RUE DES TOURNELLES

PLACE DES VOSGES

Victor Hugo House

Rue de Birague

Rue St- Antoine

Hôtel de Sully

RUE DE TURENNE

RUE DE RIVOLI

RUE D'EST-GILLES

Rue des Francs-Bourgeois

Rue de Sévigné

Hôtel de Lamoignon

RUE DE SÉVIGNÉ

R. du Parc-Royal

Sq. L'Achille

Musée Carnavalet

Rue Payenne

R. Malher

R. MALHER

Rue Pavée

RUE PAVÉE

RUE DE SICILE

Guimard Synagogue

Picasso Museum

Hôtel Salé

Rue de Thorigny

RUE DU TEMPLE

R. de la Perle

Hôtel Liberal Bruant

Lock & Key Museum

RUE ELZEVIR

RUE DES FRANCS- BOURGEOIS

Rue des Rosiers

Memorial for Jewish Children

RUE DU ROI-DE- SICILE

R. MIRON

R. Geoffroy- l'Asnier

Mémorial du Martyr Juif Inconnu

Hôtel Guénégaud

Museum of the Hunt and of Nature

Rue des 4-Fils

Hôtel de Rohan

R. Vieille-

RUE DES FRANCS-ST-GERVAIS

R. des Hosp

Rue Vieille- du- Temple

R. Grenier sur l'Eau

St. Gervais

Hôtel de Soubise

(National Archives)

Rue des Francs-Bourgeois

RUE DES BLANCS- MANTEAUX

Rue du

Rue Louis-

R. de Louis-Philippe

RUE DE RIVOLI

Hôtel de Ville

RUE DES ARCHIVES

Rue des Archives

0   meters   400

0   mile   ¼

Walk 7: The Marais

This route begins at the Place de la Bastille, a historic intersection of several important thoroughfares connecting the 4th, 11th, and 12th *arrondissements,* where many events of the 1789 Revolution took place. Until the end of the 18th century, the formidable *Bastille* stood here. Originally built in 1369 by Charles V as a castle to defend Paris against the English, it later became the infamous, dreaded state prison. For some inmates, conditions were not as horrendous as one would imagine, however; it is rumored that some prisoners had the privilege of inviting guests over for multi-course banquets. But then, there are as many myths as truths associated with the *Bastille.*

Among the detainees in the *Bastille* was the so-called Man in the Iron Mask (his mask was actually black velvet), immortalized by Alexandre Dumas *père.* Imprisoned by Louis XIV, the mysterious inmate was rumored to be the twin brother of the king. The writer Voltaire, who was locked up on two different occasions for writing inflammatory pamphlets (in 1717 and 1726), is said to have spread the rumor himself. Even though the *Bastille* gradually fell out of use, it remained such a powerful symbol of the arbitrary power of the king to imprison whomever he pleased summarily, without trial, that it was ordered destroyed when the Revolution erupted on July 14, 1789, an event celebrated annually as *Bastille Day.* A thousand workmen were employed to raze the prison, and trumpets proclaimed the news at all the crossroads of the city. The contractor of the demolition sold some of the stones as souvenirs, but others were used to build the Pont de la Concorde (Concord Bridge). Today, on the former site of the *Bastille* is the controversial opera house designed by Carlos Ott, which opened in 1989. The 2,700-seat auditorium presents lyric and contemporary opera and could be mistaken for a modern version of its namesake (for details see *Special Places* in THE CITY).

In the center of the Place de la Bastille is the *Colonne de Juillet* (Column of July), a handsome, 154-foot-tall pillar that was built in 1840. The column, which rests on a white marble base, bears the name of the 615 combatants who struggled for liberty in July of 1830 and 1848 and who are interred beneath it.

Cross the large intersection near the *Colonne de Juillet* (opposite the opera complex) and walk down fashionable Rue St-Antoine. Look to the right down the Rue de Birague. At the end of this narrow street is the façade of the *Pavillon du Roi* (King's Pavilion) and the Place des Vosges, a spot of unique historical interest. But first proceed on Rue St-Antoine to the *Hôtel de Sully* (No. 62), one of the most beautiful old houses in Paris. It was built in 1624 by a Monsieur Gallet, a rich financier and gambler. In 1634, Gallet lost his house in a game of cards to Count Sully, a minister of Henri

IV. Enter the *Hôtel de Sully*'s first courtyard, which is filled with sculptured wall reliefs that depict allegories of the changing seasons. Take the small passageway into the garden, where you face a former *orangerie* (orange grove). Continue through the narrow door on the far right to the southwestern corner of the Place des Vosges. If this door could speak, it would recount the adventures of Madame Sully, the young wife of Count Sully, who was told by her much older husband to divide her monthly household allowance into three equal parts—"for the house, yourself, and your lovers. Just be discreet and have them use the back door."

The Place des Vosges, once known as the Place Royale (it was the courtyard of a royal palace), is the site where Henri II accidentally met his death in a tournament in 1559. When the court was removed to the *Louvre* after that tragedy, the deserted courtyard became a horse market, and was also used as a dueling ground. In an attempt to beautify Paris in 1605, Henri IV had the Place des Vosges constructed as it is today; soon it became the fashionable address of more celebrities than any other residential area in Paris— among them Richelieu, Madame de Sévigné, Prince de Condé, and Molière. This was the center of Parisian social life, the place where some of the sophisticated residents held *ruelles,* intimate gatherings at which the elegant guests attempted to one-up each other in witty repartee. These rituals, which preceded the popular salons of the 18th century, were parodied by Molière in his play *Précieuses Ridicules.*

The fashionable neighborhood was named after the French *département* of Vosges after Lucien Bonaparte (the minister of finance and Napoleon's brother) announced in 1800 that the first *département* to pay all its taxes on time would be given the honor of having a street named after it. Vosges was the first to pay its full contribution, and was duly rewarded.

Enter the Place des Vosges from the *Hôtel de Sully;* follow the arcades to the right to the next corner, passing the hallway of the *Pavillon du Roi,* the largest of the original 36 buildings constructed at the order of Henri IV and balanced on the opposite side of the square by the *Pavillon de la Reine* (Queen's Pavilion). At the corner, at No. 6, is the former home of Victor Hugo, now a museum. The objects of interest here include illustrations of the great writer's work by many well-known artists, as well as sketches by Hugo himself, who was quite a fine draftsman. Among the collection of ink stands and pens belonging to Hugo and his peers—Dumas, Lamartine, and George Sand—is his chest-high writing table (he wrote standing up) and the bed on which he died. The museum is closed Mondays and holidays; admission charge (phone: 42-72-10-16).

As you leave the *Maison de Victor-Hugo,* stroll on through the arcades of the Place des Vosges. Today they are occupied by expensive shops, a popular corner café, and one of Paris's most exclusive restaurants, *L'Ambroisie* (No. 9). Enter the park, where couples stroll, children play, and busy city life seems to be suspended, and have a drink or snack at *Ma Bourgogne* (No. 19; 2-78-44-64), a popular meeting place since 1920 for tourists and locals alike. (See *Eating Out* in THE CITY for details on both restaurants.)

Upon leaving the square, turn left on Rue des Francs-Bourgeois and walk directly into the historic Marais quarter. Turn right at Rue de Sévigné; at No. 23 is the *Musée Carnavalet,* once the residence of Madame de Sévigné, a noted 17th-century writer, and now a museum. The collection includes mementos of Madame de Sévigné, as well as exhibitions on the history of Paris from the era of François I to the turn of the century. The museum is closed Mondays; there's no admission charge on Sundays (phone: 42-72-21-13). For additional details, see *Special Places* in THE CITY.

Leave the *Musée Carnavalet* and walk left up Rue de Sévigné to the end. Turn left into the Rue du Parc-Royal. At the Square Léopold-Achille on the corner, the visitor is literally surrounded by elegant *hôtels.* (Note that the term "hôtel" originally referred to the large and elegant city residences of the nobility, not the French equivalent of a *Holiday Inn.*) Turn left down Rue Payenne; at the corner of Rue des Francs-Bourgeois is *Marais Plus* (20 Rue des Francs-Bourgeois; phone: 48-87-01-40), a delightful bookstore, gift shop, and tea salon. Still on Rue Payenne, bear left to Rue Malher, with the post office on the right and the *Hôtel de Lamoignon* on the left. This *hôtel* was originally built in 1585 by Robert de Beauvais, the comptroller-general of the city of Paris. It was bought in 1658 by Lamoignon, the president of the French Parliament, and was the setting for many dazzling soirees.

During the 18th century, the Marais started to lose its fashionable cachet as the aristocracy and their social activities moved on to the area around the Place de la Concorde and the Rue du Faubourg St Honoré. Many of the superb palaces were divided into apartments or turned over to trade. The entire area became industrialized and was a center of small businesses and crafts shops well into the early part of the 20th century. After the Second World War, the trend reversed again as Parisians who had settled in the distant suburbs sought to live in the heart of the city. But centuries of neglect had seen the destruction of many of the area's beautiful buildings by long use as industrial or commercial spaces and by the carelessness of government officials, who allowed many to be razed or modified beyond recognition. Renewal of the Marais district began after 1972, and there was no lack of people who wanted to live here—especially, at first, with its reasonable rents. In recent years, however, with the proliferation of chic shops that have spread through the quarter, it once again has a fashionable image and is no longer a low-rent district.

Walk ahead on Rue Malher and turn right into the narrow Rue des Rosiers, the heart of Paris's Jewish quarter. It was here that Jews came, first at the end of the 19th century when they fled the pogroms of Eastern Europe, and again to escape the Nazis in Germany. (This is also the street that the Nazis marched down as they led 75,000 French Jews to concentration camps.) After the French exodus from Algeria, a third wave of Jews settled in the Marais. Like New York City's Lower East Side, this is a hectic neighborhood, whose streets are the scene of an ongoing ballet of bicycles, motorcycle couriers, and assorted French automobiles competing for the right of way.

Walk along the Rue des Rosiers and its surrounding streets with their small neighborhood synagogues, kosher meat markets (with signs that say *strictement cachère*), and shops that sell Jewish artifacts, and you will see a totally different side of Paris. (Be aware that most shops here are closed on Saturdays and open Sundays.) Walk to Rue Pavée, a tiny street off Rue des Rosiers and near Rue Malher. At 10 Rue Pavée is the synagogue built in 1913 by Hector Guimard, the famous Art Nouveau architect of the *Métro*. The design recalls the shape of the tablets of the Ten Commandments. If it's a Saturday morning, the doors will be open.

Back on Rue des Rosiers, stop in at *Le Loir dans la Théière* (The Dormouse in the Teapot; No. 3; phone: 42-72-90-61), a cozy tearoom in a loft-like space with long wooden tables and comfortable chairs. At the counter, choose from a display of delicious homemade pastries. Relax in the Alice-in-Wonderland ambience, then take a look at the shop's art and photo gallery. Or stop for lunch at *Jo Goldenberg* (No. 7; see *Eating Out* in THE CITY), a traditional Jewish delicatessen with very Parisian prices. Farther up the road on the left is *Café des Psaumes* (No. 14; phone: 48-04-74-77), which serves kosher specialties. A number of Judaica shops, stocked with gifts and artwork, are in the area; a good place to browse (or buy) is *Diasporama* (No. 20; phone: 42-78-30-50). Don't miss the bakery/take-out shop *Finkelsztajn* at No. 27 Rue des Rosiers (phone: 42-72-78-91) or No. 24 Rue des Ecouffes (phone: 48-87-92-85), to the left off Rue des Rosiers; their *challah, tarama* (fish-roe spread), and cream cheese tart called *vatrouschka* shouldn't be missed. For a culinary experience on the move, try a falafel on pita while wandering these narrow streets. This Middle Eastern treat of mashed chick-peas deep-fried and served with roasted eggplant, carrots, and a tasty yogurt sauce is healthy fuel and a bargain besides. There are several stands along the road: *L'As du Falafel* (No. 34; phone: 48-87-63-60) is one of the most popular. A bit farther, at the corner of Rue des Rosiers and Rue des Hospitalières-St-Gervais, is *Chez Marianne* (No. 2; phone: 42-72-18-86), a restaurant and falafel stand that is one of our favorites. The tables both upstairs and downstairs always seem to be full, but it's worth the wait for the tasty buffet. Otherwise, buy a falafel from their take-out window and continue walking.

Turn right onto Rue des Hospitalières-St-Gervais and notice a school with a placard that is a memorial to hundreds of Jewish children who were sent to concentration camps during the war. There is a bench here for a moment of quiet reflection. Also worth a visit is the *Mémorial du Martyr Juif Inconnu* (Memorial to the Unknown Jewish Martyr) at 17 Rue Geoffroy-l'Asnier. To get there, turn left from Rue des Rosiers down Rue Vieille-du-Temple, and, a few blocks down, left again on Rue Grenier-sur-l'Eau.

Dedicated to Jews killed in the Holocaust, it has an impressive crypt with a torch burning on the lower level; upstairs is a museum that documents the Holocaust. The memorial is closed Saturdays and Jewish holidays; the museum is also closed Sundays and other holidays. There's an admission charge (phone: 42-77-44-72). If hunger strikes, stop in at *Au Gamin de Paris* (51 Rue Vieille-du-Temple; see *Eating Out* in THE CITY), a popular late-night eatery.

Walk back up Rue Vieille-du-Temple to where it intersects Rue des Francs-Bourgeois. A block to the left, at No. 60 Rue des Francs-Bourgeois, is the *Hôtel de Soubise,* a palace with an illustrious history that today houses the *Archives Nationales* (National Archives), containing about 220 miles of information. In 1700, the house was acquired by François de Rohan, the Prince of Soubise, thanks to the generosity of Louis XIV. Over the next few years, extensive remodeling transformed the mansion into a palace; the best painters and artisans were brought in to enhance its classical architecture. On the ground floor were the apartments of the Prince of Rohan-Soubise (which now can be visited by groups by prior arrangement). The princess's apartment on the first floor is now the *Musée de l'Histoire de France,* with interesting historical documents, among them the wills of Louis XIV and Napoleon, the diary of Louis XVI, and the revolutionary Declaration of Human Rights. There is also a model of the *Bastille* carved from one of its original stones. *Hôtel de Soubise* is closed mornings and Tuesdays; admission charge (phone: 40-27-62-18).

Turn right on Rue des Archives and walk past the *Archives Nationales* complex to Rue des Quatre-Fils. At the corner is the *Hôtel Guénégaud* (60 Rue des Archives), built by Mansart in 1650 and regarded as one of the finest 17th-century mansions in the Marais. It has been remodeled only twice since the 18th century and has retained its simple lines. Visit the small formal garden behind the *hôtel* on Rue des Quatre-Fils. On the same property is the *Musée de la Chasse et de la Nature* (Museum of the Chase and of Nature), which features a collection of hunting souvenirs and the arms collection of a Monsieur Sommer, who restored the house during the 1960s. There is also a collection of tapestries, ceramics, and sculptures related to the hunt, plus a bookshop. The museum is closed during lunch hours, Tuesdays, and holidays; there's an admission charge (phone: 42-72-86-43).

Walk east along Rue des Quatre-Fils to Rue Vieille-du-Temple and turn right. At No. 87 is the *Hôtel de Rohan,* which became another annex to the *Archives Nationales* in 1927. It was at one time the residence of Cardinal de Rohan, the son of the Prince of Soubise, and became home to four other members of the Rohan family, who were also cardinals. It was later converted into the imperial printing house under Napoleon. Though the courtyard is not as elaborate as the one in the Soubise mansion, the former stables are quite interesting because of the splendor of the sculptured façade, which depicts the Horses of Apollo drinking at the trough.

If this inspires thirst, walk directly across the street to *Le Clos Follainville* (72 Rue Vieille-du-Temple; phone: 42-78-21-22), a casual and rustic tea salon/restaurant/wine bar, suitable for a light lunch and a selection of wine sold by the half glass, glass, or bottle. (Note that if there are many diners and you want only a glass of wine, you may have to stand at the bar.)

Return to the corner of Rue Vieille-du-Temple and Rue des Quatre-Fils and turn right onto Rue de la Perle. At No. 1 is the *Hôtel Libéral Bruant,* built in 1685 by the architect of *Les Invalides* as his own residence. This stately mansion now houses the *Musée Bricard* (Lock and Key Museum; phone: 42-77-79-62). Inside is an exhibit tracing the history of the lock from the time of the Roman Empire, as well as a collection of locks. It's closed mornings, weekends, and holidays. There's an admission charge.

Take a left on Rue de Thorigny, where stands the former *Hôtel Salé* (No. 5). This house was built in 1656–59 for a gentleman who made a fortune out of the salt tax, which is how it got its name (*salé* is French for "salty"). In the 17th century, the right to collect taxes was sold by the state to private enterprises working on a percentage basis. The three-story house has been restored over the years. Following the death of Pablo Picasso in 1973, when his heirs donated an outstanding collection of the artist's works in lieu of paying an inheritance tax, it became the *Musée Picasso.* The works are arranged in chronological order, providing a fascinating insight into Picasso's various periods. Especially interesting is his private collection of paintings by other artists (the Cézannes are best). The courtyard and the museum's garden are relaxing places to pause before or after touring the museum. It's closed Tuesdays; there's an admission charge (phone: 42-71-25-21). For additional information, see *Special Places* in THE CITY.

Glossary

Useful Words and Phrases

The French as a nation have a reputation for being snobbish and brusque to tourists, and, unfortunately, many Americans have allowed this stereotype to affect their appreciation of France. The more experienced traveler, however, knows that on an individual basis, the French people are usually cordial and helpful, especially if you speak a few words of their language. Don't be afraid of misplaced accents or misconjugated verbs—in most cases you will be understood.

The list below of commonly used words and phrases can help you get started.

Greetings and Everyday Expressions

Good morning/afternoon! (Hello!)	*Bonjour!*
Good evening!	*Bonsoir!*
How are you?	*Comment allez-vous?*
Pleased to meet you!	*Enchanté!*
Good-bye!	*Au revoir!*
See you soon!	*A bientôt!*
Good night!	*Bonne nuit!*
Yes!	*Oui!*
No!	*Non!*
Please!	*S'il vous plaît!*
Thank you!	*Merci!*
You're welcome!	*De rien!*
Excuse me!	*Excusez-moi* or *pardonnez-moi!*
It doesn't matter.	*Ça m'est égal.*
I don't speak French.	*Je ne parle pas français.*
Do you speak English?	*Parlez-vous anglais?*
Please repeat.	*Répétez, s'il vous plaît.*
I don't understand.	*Je ne comprends pas.*
Do you understand?	*Vous comprenez?*
My name is . . .	*Je m'appelle . . .*
What is your name?	*Comment vous appelez-vous?*
miss	*mademoiselle*
madame	*madame*
mister/sir	*monsieur*
open	*ouvert*
closed	*fermé*

entrance	*l'entrée*
exit	*la sortie*
push	*poussez*
pull	*tirez*
today	*aujourd'hui*
tomorrow	*demain*
yesterday	*hier*

Help!	*Au secours!*
ambulance	*l'ambulance*
Get a doctor!	*Appelez le médecin!*

Checking In

I have (don't have) a reservation.	*J'ai une (Je n'ai pas de) réservation.*
I would like . . .	*Je voudrais . . .*
a single room	*une chambre pour une personne*
a double room	*une chambre pour deux*
a quiet room	*une chambre tranquille*
with bath	*avec salle de bains*
with shower	*avec douche*
with a view of the Seine	*avec une vue sur la Seine*
with air conditioning	*avec une chambre climatisée*
with balcony	*avec balcon*
overnight only	*pour une nuit seulement*
a few days	*quelques jours*
a week (at least)	*une semaine (au moins)*
with full board	*avec pension complète*
with half board	*avec demi-pension*
Does that price include breakfast?	*Est-ce que le petit déjeuner est inclus?*
Are taxes included?	*Est-ce que les taxes sont comprises?*
Do you accept traveler's checks?	*Acceptez-vous les chèques de voyage?*
Do you accept credit cards?	*Acceptez-vous les cartes de crédit?*

Eating Out

ashtray	*un cendrier*
bottle	*une bouteille*
(extra) chair	*une chaise (en sus)*
cup	*une tasse*
fork	*une fourchette*
knife	*un couteau*
spoon	*une cuillère*

napkin	*une serviette*
plate	*une assiette*
table	*une table*
coffee	*café*
black coffee	*café noir*
coffee with milk	*café au lait*
cream	*crème*
fruit juice	*jus de fruit*
orange	*jus d'orange*
tomato	*jus de tomate*
juice	*jus*
lemonade	*citron pressé*
milk	*lait*
mineral water (non-carbonated)	*l'eau minérale non-gazeuse*
mineral water (carbonated)	*l'eau minérale gazeuse*
orangeade	*orange pressée*
tea	*thé*
water	*eau*
cold	*froid*
hot	*chaud*
bacon	*bacon*
bread	*pain*
butter	*beurre*
eggs	*oeufs*
soft boiled	*à la coque*
hard boiled	*durs*
fried	*sur le plats*
scrambled	*brouillés*
poached	*pochés*
ham	*jambon*
honey	*miel*
jam	*confiture*
omelette	*omelette*
pepper	*poivre*
salt	*sel*
sugar	*sucre*
beer	*bière*
port	*vin de Porto*
red wine	*vin rouge*
rosé	*rosé*
sherry	*vin de Xérès*
white wine	*vin blanc*

| sweet | doux |
| (very) dry | (très) sec |

Waiter!	Garçon!
Waitress!	Mademoiselle!
I would like	Je voudrais
a glass of	un verre de
a bottle of	une bouteille de
a half bottle of	une demi-bouteille
a liter of	un litre de
a carafe of	une carafe de

The check, please.	L'addition, s'il vous plaît.
Is the service charge included?	Le service, est-il compris?
I think there is a mistake in the bill.	Je crois qu'il y a une erreur avec l'addition.

Shopping

bakery	boulangerie
bookstore	librairie
butcher store	boucherie
camera shop	magasin de photographie
clothing store	magasin de vêtements
delicatessen	charcuterie
department store	grand magasin
drugstore (for medicine)	pharmacie
grocery	épicerie
jewelry store	bijouterie
newsstand	kiosque à journaux
notions (sewing supplies) shop	mercerie
pastry shop	pâtisserie
perfume (and cosmetics) store	parfumerie
pharmacy/drugstore	pharmacie
shoestore	magasin de chaussures
supermarket	supermarché
tobacconist	tabac

| inexpensive | bon marché |
| expensive | cher |

large	grand
larger	plus grand
too large	trop grand
small	petit

smaller	*plus petit*
too small	*trop petit*
long	*long*
short	*court*
old	*vieux*
new	*nouveau*
used	*d'occasion*
handmade	*fabriqué à la main* or *fait main*
Is it machine washable?	*Est-ce que c'est lavable à la machine?*
How much does this cost?	*Quel est le prix?/Combien?*
What is it made of?	*De quoi est-ce fait?*
camel's hair	*poil de chameau*
cotton	*coton*
corduroy	*velours côtelé*
filigree	*filigrane*
lace	*dentelle*
leather	*cuir*
linen	*lin*
silk	*soie*
suede	*suède*
synthetic	*synthétique*
wool	*laine*
brass	*cuivre jaune*
copper	*cuivre*
gold (plated)	*or (plaqué)*
silver (plated)	*argent (plaqué)*
wood	*bois*
May I have a sales tax rebate form?	*Puis-je avoir le formulaire pour la détaxe?*
May I pay with this credit card?	*Puis-je payer avec cette carte de crédit?*
May I pay with a traveler's check?	*Puis-je payer avec chèques de voyage?*

Colors

black	*noir*
blue	*bleu*

brown	*marron*
gray	*gris*
green	*vert*
orange	*orange*
pink	*rose*
purple	*violet*
red	*rouge*
yellow	*jaune*
white	*blanc*

Getting Around

north	*le nord*
south	*le sud*
east	*l'est*
west	*l'ouest*
right	*droite*
left	*gauche*
straight ahead	*tout droit*
far	*loin*
near	*proche*
airport	*l'aéroport*
bus stop	*l'arrêt de bus*
gas station	*station service*
train station	*la gare*
subway	*le métro*
map	*carte*
one-way ticket	*aller simple*
round-trip ticket	*un billet aller retour*
gate	*porte*
track	*voie*
in first class	*en première classe*
in second class	*en deuxième classe*
no smoking	*défense de fumer*
Does this subway/bus go to . . . ?	*Est-ce que ce métro/ bus va à . . . ?*
What time does it leave?	*A quelle heure part-il?*
gas	*essence*
regular (leaded)	*ordinaire*
super (leaded)	*super*

unleaded	sans plomb
diesel	gas-oil
Fill it up, please.	Le plein, s'il vous plaît.

the tires	pneus
the oil	huile

Danger	Danger
Caution	Attention
Detour	Déviation
Dead End	Cul-de-sac
Do Not Enter	Défense d'entrer
No Parking	Défense de stationner
No Passing	Défense de dépasser
No U-turn	Défense de faire demi-tour
One way	Sens unique
Pay toll	Péage
Pedestrian Zone	Zone piétonne
Reduce Speed	Ralentissez
Steep Incline	Côte à forte inclination
Stop	Stop; Arrêt
Use Headlights	Allumez les phares
Yield	Cédez le passage
Where is . . . ?	Où se trouve . . . ?
How many kilometers are we from . . . ?	A combien de kilomètres sommes-nous de . . . ?

Personal Items and Services

aspirin	aspirine
Band-Aids	pansement adhésif
barbershop	coiffeur pour hommes
bath	bain
bathroom	salle de bain
beauty shop	salon de coiffure
condom	préservatif
dentist	dentiste
disposable diapers	couches
dry cleaner	nettoyage à sec
hairdresser	coiffeur pour dames
laundromat	laundrette or blanchisserie automatique
post office	bureau de poste
postage stamps (airmail)	timbres (par avion)
razor	rasoir
sanitary napkins	serviettes hygiéniques

shampoo	*shampooing*
shaving cream	*crème à raser*
shower	*douche*
soap	*savon*
tampons	*tampons*
tissues	*mouchoirs en papier*
toilet	*toilettes* or *WC*
toilet paper	*papier hygiénique*
toothbrush	*brosse à dents*
toothpaste	*dentifrice*

Where is the men's/ladies' room?	*Où sont les toilettes?*

Days of the Week

Monday	*lundi*
Tuesday	*mardi*
Wednesday	*mercredi*
Thursday	*jeudi*
Friday	*vendredi*
Saturday	*samedi*
Sunday	*dimanche*

Months

January	*janvier*
February	*février*
March	*mars*
April	*avril*
May	*mai*
June	*juin*
July	*juillet*
August	*août*
September	*septembre*
October	*octobre*
November	*novembre*
December	*décembre*

Numbers

zero	*zéro*
one	*un*
two	*deux*
three	*trois*
four	*quatre*
five	*cinq*
six	*six*
seven	*sept*
eight	*huit*

nine	*neuf*
ten	*dix*
eleven	*onze*
twelve	*douze*
thirteen	*treize*
fourteen	*quatorze*
fifteen	*quinze*
sixteen	*seize*
seventeen	*dix-sept*
eighteen	*dix-huit*
nineteen	*dix-neuf*
twenty	*vingt*
twenty-one	*vingt-et-un*
thirty	*trente*
forty	*quarante*
fifty	*cinquante*
sixty	*soixante*
seventy	*soixante-dix*
eighty	*quatre-vingts*
ninety	*quatre-vingt-dix*
one hundred	*cent*
1995	*mille neuf cent quatre-vingt-cinq*

WRITING RESERVATIONS LETTERS

Restaurant/Hotel Name
Street Address
Postal Code, Paris
France

Dear Sir:

    I would like to reserve a
table for (number of) persons for lunch/dinner on
(day and month), 1995, at
(hour) o'clock.

or

    I would like to reserve a
room for (number of) peo-
ple for (number of) nights.

and

    Would you be so kind as
to confirm the reservation as
soon as possible?

    I am looking forward to
meeting you. (The French
usually include a pleasantry
such as this.)

    With my thanks,

(Signature)

Monsieur:

    *Je voudrais réserver une
table pour (number) person-
nes pour le déjeuner/dîner du
(day and month) 1995, à
(time using the 24-hour
clock) heures.*

or

    *Je voudrais réserver une
chambre à (number) per-
sonne(s) pour (number)
nuits.*

and

    *Auriez-vous la bonté de
bien vouloir me confirmer
cette réservation dès que possible?*
    *J'attends avec impatience
le plaisir de faire votre connaissance.*

    *Avec tous mes remer-
ciements,*

(Signature)

(Print or type your name and address below your signature.)

Weights and Measures

APPROXIMATE EQUIVALENTS

	Metric Unit	Abbreviation	US Equivalent
Length	1 millimeter	mm	.04 inch
	1 meter	m	39.37 inches
	1 kilometer	km	.62 mile
Capacity	1 liter	l	1.057 quarts
Weight	1 gram	g	.035 ounce
	1 kilogram	kg	2.2 pounds
	1 metric ton	MT	1.1 tons
Temperature	0° Celsius	C	32° Fahrenheit

CONVERSION TABLES

METRIC TO US MEASUREMENTS

	Multiply:	by:	to convert to:
Length	millimeters	.04	inches
	meters	3.3	feet
	meters	1.1	yards
	kilometers	.6	miles
Capacity (liquid)	liters	2.11	pints
	liters	1.06	quarts
	liters	.26	gallons
Weight	grams	.04	ounces
	kilograms	2.2	pounds

US TO METRIC MEASUREMENTS

	Multiply:	by:	to convert to:
Length	inches	25.0	millimeters
	feet	.3	meters
	yards	.9	meters
	miles	1.6	kilometers
Capacity	pints	.47	liters
	quarts	.95	liters
	gallons	3.8	liters
Weight	ounces	28.0	grams
	pounds	.45	kilograms

TEMPERATURE

Celsius to Fahrenheit $\qquad$ $(°C \times 9/5) + 32 = °F$

Fahrenheit to Celsius $\qquad$ $(°F - 32) \times 5/9 = °C$

Index

Index

"LE NOUTON A CINQ PATTES"

ON RUE VIEILLE DU TEMPLE

TAKE METRO 1 TO ST. PAUL